"Ryan Busse presents a fascinating, clear-eyed account of the gun industry's slide into extremism. *Gunfight* is an important book for anyone seeking to understand how our country's debate over the role of guns and gun laws in our society has become so bitter and fraught. I was left with a sense of hope that there is a path forward; one where the majority of Americans, including the majority of gun owners, stand up to the gun lobby's bullying and demand lasting change."

—GABBY GIFFORDS, former US congresswoman

"Ryan Busse is a gun enthusiast, conservationist, and defender of our Second Amendment. This is a must-read book for anyone who wants to understand how a wholesome part of America was twisted to radicalize wide swaths of our country, and it's all wrapped up in a wild-ride story that you can't put down."

—STEVE BULLOCK, two-term Montana governor

"*Gunfight* is a riveting account of how special interests have perverted the Second Amendment to create a culture of gun extremism that's radicalized a vocal minority. But gun owners like Ryan Busse are taking back the narrative from extremists who are trying to use guns to undermine our democracy."

—SHANNON WATTS, founder of Moms Demand Action

"Woven through this riveting personal story is a message for millions of reasonable Americans who are not happy with being branded and manipulated by the political extremes. *Gunfight* reveals the truth about the roots of our national division, and many people will see themselves in Busse's resistance to extremism. Ryan Busse is ready to lead that fight."

—JON TESTER, three-term Montana Democratic senator
and author of *Grounded: Lessons from Rural America*

"Busse's story is an incredible read, but it also shines a light on how guns have been used to divide this country. This is not a gun book, but rather it is the enthralling personal story detailing how our nation came to be divided."

—MARTIN HEINRICH, two-term New Mexico
Democratic senator and former US congressman

"Ryan Busse has ripped the curtain away from the firearms industry, revealing it to be the dark enabler of antigovernment conspiracies, racism, and the armed radicalization of the far right. Gun manufacturers supplied not only the guns, but the explosive ideological fuel that has led America to the brink of civil disorder. Busse has performed an inestimable service and, by the way, tells a riveting tale."

—ROBERT SPITZER, distinguished service professor of political science, the State University of New York, and author of more than 700 articles and four books on gun politics including eight editions of *The Politics of Gun Control*

"Gunfight is a wild ride you can't put down. More importantly, it is an illuminating, insider account of the 25-year radicalization of much of the Republican party with guns—and the myths the industry sells about them—at the center of the story. Anyone concerned about the rise of extremism that brought about the January 6th insurrection should read Ryan Busse's brave book."

—JENNIFER PALMIERI, former White House
communications director, author of the
#1 *New York Times* bestseller, *Dear Madam President*

"After two decades covering America's gun nightmare, what I've really come to crave is intel on our adversary. Enter Ryan Busse, a Big Gun executive with a harrowing personal story from deep inside the industry. A riveting account of what drives this belligerent force, and insights into how to temper it."

—DAVE CULLEN, author of *Columbine* and *Parkland*

"I'm a proud father, gun owner, and bird dog trainer. But I am also the feared outsider because I am an African American man. *Gunfight* is the essential truth of America's radicalized gun culture, and I could not put it down because people like me navigate these hard issues every day. We've been waiting for someone like Ryan Busse to come along beside us. Finally, we have an honest and gripping story that will be a catalyst for real change."

—DURRELL SMITH, educator, artist, author,
founder of Minority Outdoor Alliance, and
award-winning host of the *GunDog Notebook* podcast

GUNFIGHT

| My Battle Against the Industry
that Radicalized America |

RYAN BUSSE

PublicAffairs
NEW YORK

PublicAffairs
Hachette Book Group
1290 Avenue of the Americas, New York, NY 10104
www.publicaffairsbooks.com
@Public_Affairs

Printed in the United States of America
First Edition: October 2021

Published by PublicAffairs, an imprint of Perseus Books, LLC, a subsidiary of Hachette Book Group, Inc. The PublicAffairs name and logo is a trademark of the Hachette Book Group.

The Hachette Speakers Bureau provides a wide range of authors for speaking events. To find out more, go to www.hachettespeakersbureau.com or call (866) 376-6591.

The publisher is not responsible for websites (or their content) that are not owned by the publisher.

To protect their privacy, the names of some individuals have been changed.

Print book interior design by Linda Mark.

Library of Congress Cataloging-in-Publication Data
Names: Busse, Ryan, author.
Title: Gunfight : my battle against the industry that radicalized America / Ryan Busse.
Description: First edition. | New York : PublicAffairs, [2021] | Includes
  bibliographical references and index.
Identifiers: LCCN 2021012770 | ISBN 9781541768734 (hardcover) | ISBN
  9781541768727 (ebook)
Subjects: LCSH: Busse, Ryan. | Firearms industry and trade—Political aspects—
  United States. | Firearms industry and trade—Moral and ethical aspects—United
  States. | Firearms ownership—United States. | United States—Politics and
  government—1989– | United States—Social conditions—1980–
Classification: LCC HD9744.F553 U62355 2021 | DDC 338.4/762340973—dc23
LC record available at https://lccn.loc.gov/2021012770

ISBNs: 9781541768734 (hardcover), 9781541768727 (ebook)

LSC-C

Printing 1, 2021

For Sara
My earth person, my sky person

CONTENTS

AUTHOR'S NOTE

THIS BOOK IS BOTH A PERSONAL MEMOIR AND AN INSIDE story about the transformation of our country. The facts that relate to our nation are supported with official statistics, press releases, news accounts, and verified quotations, all documented in the notes section. The details that relate to my life are true to the best of my recollection. On the occasions where I rely upon secondhand information, I recount facts as they were presented to me at the time. Where possible, I cross-referenced decades of personal notes and written records. In many instances I spoke again to the people who experienced these things alongside me and then ensured that my written account represented the facts as those who were nearest remembered them.

The central portion of my story unfolded over twenty-five years, which means I have condensed timelines and selected important highlights.

Some names in this book have been changed. Conversations in this book are accurate, and some are reconstructed as I remember them. All of them happened.

This book is true, even the parts I wish were not.

PROLOGUE

"**Y**OU ARE AN EVIL LITTLE BASTARD!" SPIT FLIES AS THE middle-aged man screams at my younger son, Badge. "You know that?"

The man wears an American flag on his shirt and a pistol on his belt. He is enraged, the color in his face rising to match that of his Make America Great Again hat. Then the stranger pushes his finger into my son's chest.

Badge is a slightly built boy of twelve with blond hair and bright eyes, and he is terrified. But he straightens his back, looks at the man, and simply says, "I can't breathe," joining the protesting crowd chanting those three words in unison, over and over.

I snap into defensive mode and force myself between them.

"If you say another word to my son or even think about touching him one more time, it'll be months before you're able to stand again," I snarl at the man, yelling at him through the crowd noise. He looks up at me and eases off.

"You with this kid?" MAGA Man barks. All he can do now is shake his head before sneering at me. "Then you're an evil fucker too."

This man, and dozens like him, had showed up with their guns to frighten people like Badge and me. I knew that they called themselves "Second Amendment patriots," and as I glare at the angry man, he storms off, presumably to find someone else to intimidate.

I turn to Badge. "You OK?" He shakes, with tears in his eyes. But he brushes it off and keeps chanting with everyone else. Of course he's OK. He gets that kind of courage from my wife, Sara. Lost in the crowd, she hasn't even seen the brief confrontation.

"THERE WILL BE A LOT OF GUNS, AND PEOPLE COULD GET KILLED," Sara had warned our boys a few hours earlier, after reading the emailed alerts that had been issued by protest organizers. "We need to have an escape plan if shooting starts." Then she tightened her face and draped her long arms over their shoulders. She looked at both of them the way good moms do when they're trying to balance fear with courage. "If you hear shots, you run for safety any way you can. Just get to the grocery store, and we'll rendezvous there. Got it?"

I watched Sara as she reassured the boys about how important it was for us to be physically present as the tension of an entire nation spilled into the streets at Black Lives Matter rallies, even in Kalispell, Montana, where we live. Sara and I both knew how important it was to go, even despite the promise of armed counterprotesters wearing camo and waving flags and TRUMP 2020 signs. Sara then pulled Badge and Lander, our fifteen-year-old, in tight for a hug.

"I bet they'll have Confederate flags," Lander said on our drive to the protest. "What kind of idiots idolize losers?" After a moment, he asked, "Dad, are these the same people who keep coming after you at your job?"

"Yeah," I said, wishing my answer could have been different.

"Do you think they'll have any Kimbers?" Badge asked, referring to the major US gun company whose sales office is headquartered in Kalispell. "Cuz that'd be weird."

"I'm not sure what we'll see, buddy," I replied. "But they'll all have AR-15s and tactical gear. They're going to look scary and dangerous. That's because they want to frighten you—"

"Don't let them!" Sara finished my thought. "This isn't about them. It's not about us. It's about standing up with people of color." Then she shot a glance at me. "We're not going to let guns be a distraction."

That's when I realized I was probably the most frightened among the four of us. I was intimately familiar with the people and weapons that would confront us, and I knew what those guns were capable of. That's because I was, even then, an executive at one of the country's top gun manufacturers.

I am responsible for selling millions of guns.

ONE NATION UNDER GUNS

M Y INDUSTRY HAS PLAYED A LEADING ROLE IN FOMENTING the division of our nation, one aspect of which boiled over and into the streets of cities across America after the cruel murder of George Floyd in May 2020. In rural cities like ours these protests were met with angry White men who were encouraged and incited to exert the power of their privilege with intimidation and firepower.

In my job as Kimber's vice president of sales, I often reminded other gun executives that the worsening cultural divide had become a game of Russian roulette. I had watched as incidences of school shootings increased along with the national obsession over offensive weapons of war. As I became increasingly alarmed, I made the fateful decision to try to use my leadership position in the industry to convince those in power that someday soon a chambered bullet would tear America in half.

Those warnings all seemed strangely distant now, as if I had been observing the war in a planning room on impersonal maps with plastic soldiers to represent real people. Now the war was here, and my family was on the ground, alongside me. There were no more plastic figures, just us and the angry armed men my industry had empowered.

Kalispell, in the northwest corner of Montana, is home to a concerning number of White supremacists but also a growing number of people who feel called to stand up for higher principles. In many ways our town, like many other small cities across the country, is a microcosm of the nation's cultural identity crisis.

As I prepared to join Kalispell's Black Lives Matter rally in June 2020, I knew that my family and I would experience the culture war close-up, on a personal scale, and it troubled me. I felt guilty because I was still in the industry—although by that point I'd made a plan to get out. Nonetheless, I had built a successful career selling tools designed for a single, ultimate purpose: to take lives. But I believed that the guns I sold were different: they were used for self-defense and for hunting and target shooting, which were indelible parts of my childhood. I spent a career focusing on those other purposes. I believed I was different from those who actually *wanted to use* their guns for deliberate killing. And of course I was, but I was also tied to them whether I wished to be or not.

When I started in the industry, it wanted nothing to do with extremism. I stayed as long as I did because I believed in the ideals and values that I learned growing up as a ranch kid, as a hunter, and as someone who still appreciates the craftsmanship of well-built firearms. I thought I could keep the industry from changing, and then I spent years fighting to hold a battle line within it. By that day in 2020, I had begun the process of getting out of the gun business. But as I thought about the company I helped build, the countless guns we sold, and the question my son had just asked me, I kept telling myself, *I hope none of them are using a Kimber.*

I had worked hard during my career to help build a company that sold guns I would be proud to own. To me and many others, the lines between different types of firearms were clear. I was frustrated when cable news shows glossed over the differences between guns and the differences between gun owners because I knew it just played into the

National Rifle Association (NRA) plan. The powerful organization was just starting to reel from self-inflicted wounds and would eventually file for bankruptcy. Despite those setbacks, the country was living through chaos, which proved that our nation had already been transformed by the NRA and that there was no going back. The NRA had succeeded with a plan that required all gun owners to appear identical and march in lockstep. I wanted people to know that no matter what the NRA said, I was not like the men who would confront my family. I was one of the millions of gun owners who were disgusted at the thought of being lumped in with those who use offensive weapons to threaten and intimidate.

As we approached the rally, we joined up with a group of high school kids chanting, "No justice, no peace!" A few minutes later we stood with a local pastor. He and I actually had something in common. He also spent much of his time fighting against powerful societal forces unleashed by those who had appropriated something important to him. The look of anguish and guilt in his eyes felt familiar.

More than a thousand people had gathered downtown, and the protest grew tense. The dozens of armed men we knew would be there hovered behind us. They stood in a line, stiff, looking like out-of-shape military guards waiting to shoot an escaping prisoner. All of them were White. Most had beards and military boots. Some wore MAGA hats and Oath Keepers or "3 Percenter" patches, which signified membership in a growing radical militia organization founded around the concept that only 3 percent of American colonists were bold enough to fight the British. One man with a bright-red Marine Corps cap walked through the crowd, glaring at us with a baseball bat over his shoulder, his grip on it tight. He looped through the high school kids, then returned to stand with the armed men, who were all carrying loaded AR-15s with thirty-round magazines.

For decades my industry accepted and preached the rules of basic gun safety. Through a network of thousands of safety classes for hunters and gun owners across the country, the industry had long mandated avoidance of confrontation. Guns were to be used for defense and only as a last resort. The men at this protest dispensed with all those safety norms. Their loaded rifles hung from three-point tactical harnesses, muzzle down, on the front of their chests: each rifle a flashing neon sign of offensive intimidation. They had come here *looking* for a fight.

These men were, after all, amateurs, with one thing that unified them: assault rifles, which are anything but amateur. They had accessorized their guns with quad rails, electronic red dot sights, folding stocks, muzzle brakes, and a litany of other modifications—all designed to make the guns more lethal. These were the same specializations that elite military units use to increase efficiency in the heat of war. The soldiers in those units go through extensive training and use these weapons as unforgiving killing machines.

The amateurs at our protest were not from any trained unit. They had probably met one another through such booming social media sites as AR15.com, Funker Tactical, Demolition Ranch, and the Military Arms Channel. For years prior to this protest, advertising executives in the gun industry had been encouraging the "tactical lifestyle" by spending millions of dollars with these websites and influencers, who, in turn, cultivated millions of followers. The resulting feedback loop powered a culture that glorified weapons of war and encouraged followers to "own the libs." The more extreme the posts, the more followers they gained, and the more guns we sold. Eventually, those followers began showing up at the capitol buildings in Virginia, Michigan, and Kentucky with loaded rifles. Despite the fact that their aggressive actions violated all gun-safety norms once mandated by the gun business, I never heard a single gun-industry member criticize them or worry about the repercussions.

As I turned back to our group of protesters and toward the busy street, a large truck revved its engine to blow a cloud of black diesel exhaust into our faces. Men standing in the back of the truck began taunting us. One held up a large Confederate flag, and Lander shot me a look. Then the line of armed men behind us shook their fists and yelled back in approval over the top of us. They had just surrounded our group of protesters. I looked back at the armed men in disgust. Our country had arrived at the point where military guns were the symbols of an entire political movement.

The NRA and the firearms companies had long ago harnessed this fear and hate as fuel, then dropped a match into the middle of it. The sparks and the kindling for the blaze had been stacked since the beginning of my career in the gun business, and now it exploded into a national inferno from which emerged the angry MAGA Man who had pushed his fat finger into my boy's chest.

After I told the guy to keep walking, his buddies stepped in to challenge me. One carried an AR-15 loaded with a high-capacity magazine. Another held a tactical shotgun slung over his shoulder; this is a preferred weapon in close combat, designed to be quickly fired in tight spaces and to deliver a wide spray of deadly shot. Professional military officers and tactical law-enforcement units use these short-barreled weapons to clear entire buildings and to shoot multiple assailants in moving vehicles.

The tension diffused just enough to avoid disaster, but it all could have gone so wrong. People around me at our local protest were shocked by the amateur militia and the unhinged man who screamed at my twelve-year-old son. I wasn't shocked. I had seen this coming.

I studied these men now, disgusted but also curious. I saw a man I thought I knew as he passed by. Our eyes met, and he nodded at me as if to say, "Thank you." Then I looked at his hip. There it was: a holstered Kimber pistol. My stomach dropped. But I wasn't surprised.

Over the previous twenty-five years, I had worked hard to keep Kimber from jumping on the exploding AR-15 bandwagon. Despite immense pressures, I had succeeded, and Kimber stayed out of that market. I wanted a company that was more focused on what I believed to be a defensible and sustainable approach, not on the commoditized "black guns" that fed the tactical lifestyle. Our products were based on century-old designs and featured exquisite craftsmanship. The Kimber pistol I saw that day was proof that I could do only so much in the face of a wave of radicalization. The industry I once loved and helped build was now almost unrecognizable to me.

Had the men who just confronted me known about my day job, they might have done a double take. The day before this protest I sat in my comfortable office, directing the sales of guns and marveling at the effects of an unprecedented sales boom. We started the day with an impromptu sales meeting. Allen, our longtime manager of sales operations, arrived at work, bursting through the door with his usual intensity.

"Just about everything in California is still shut down," he said. "People can't buy a hamburger, but damn, have you seen the pictures from Turner's?" He showed me the photo of long lines of customers waiting to get inside the gun store. "It's like Black Friday times five!"

"I mean, what does it say about our country that we've been hoarding toilet paper and guns?" he added. "NICS is going to be off the chart again!"

A federal law named after President Reagan's press secretary, who had been wounded in an assassination attempt, created the National Instant Criminal Background Check System (NICS) in 1998. The Brady Act mandated that all gun sales by licensed dealers require one of these checks before finalizing a gun sale. The initial purpose of the system was preventing criminals from purchasing guns, but it also served as the closest thing to an official record of gun sales in America. After some data adjustments, the firearms industry generally accepted that one NICS check equals one gun sold.

Each month, the federal Bureau of Alcohol, Tobacco, Firearms and Explosives reported NICS numbers for the previous month, and the gun industry dutifully studied and mined these data for indications about market trends. The NICS report for March 2020, when the COVID-19 virus shut down the world, contained five of the ten highest days ever recorded. More guns were sold on March 20 than on any other day in the history of the United States. As most of the country came to grips with the uncertainty of a global pandemic, gun retailers made 201,308 sales that day. Allen was right about the monthly totals as well. In fact, March 2020 was the largest gun-sales month *ever*, with nearly 2.4 million guns sold, averaging nearly eighty thousand sales per day—almost double the previous March record. April and May also produced record NICS numbers. Many of those guns were Kimbers.

"Booze!" another salesman piped up. "It's flying off the shelves too. I went to buy vodka last night, and they were out! Guns, toilet paper, and booze."

As I thought about so many guns flooding into a market of scared, toilet-paper-less, heavy-drinking Americans, I remembered an often-repeated truism about the industry: "The gun business is just like the booze business; it's pretty good when times are good, and it's fucking great when times are bad."

Times were, in fact, great for gun companies: unlike many economic sectors, guns were deemed essential. During the COVID-19 outbreak, President Trump had tipped his hat to the core of his political base with the proclamation to keep gun stores and gun companies open. The gun-manufacturing industry's trade group, the National Shooting Sports Foundation (NSSF), quickly thanked Trump for the "essential business" designation in a press release. "We are deeply appreciative to the Trump Administration and Department of Homeland Security for recognizing the vital role our industry fulfills in our nation," said Larry Keane, senior vice president and general counsel of the NSSF.[1]

As we wrapped up our sales meeting the day before the protests in my town, I sensed a national disaster on the horizon. It was June, and gun sales were still smashing records. Manufacturers cranked out guns at full capacity, producing nearly one hundred thousand of them per day. They still could not keep up with demand.

For years, the gun manufacturers and the NRA had used fear and conspiracy whenever gun sales sagged. The logical outcome was frightening, but when I warned others about this, I was met with stares from people whose fortunes were tied to the monetary benefits of more fear, more conspiracy. *This is the road map the NRA created. We are now a country that profits from disaster. Fear and hate are the only new products our industry needs.*

Although many in the gun industry knew deep down that I was right, most executives did not want to believe it. Years earlier, just a few weeks before the 2016 election, I found myself at dinner with one of them. The gun industry revered Smith & Wesson's CEO, James Debney. Tall and handsome, with a closely cropped salt-and-pepper beard, Debney led an iconic company that boasted worldwide name recognition just a half step behind Coca-Cola. Despite being a wealthy Brit, he had mastered the part of a red-blooded regular American gun guy, and our industry embraced him with open arms.

Debney knew that part of his role required large, conspicuous contributions to the NRA, and his generous financial donations earned him the organization's coveted Golden Jacket (yes, it's an actual jacket).

Kimber's owner also had a Golden Jacket, which meant that he was part of the NRA's Golden Ring of Freedom. Like Debney, he had received the prize directly from the NRA's powerful leader, Wayne LaPierre, in a tightly orchestrated ceremony that stroked egos and encouraged more mega-donations. Kimber's own press release was blunt about it: "The NRA Golden Ring of Freedom is known for distinguishing the eminent leaders within the NRA who have donated in excess of one million dollars."[2]

As we swirled the last of our wine in crystal glasses, the conversation turned to politics. I asked Debney if it seemed contradictory that a CEO of a publicly held gun company was helping finance the presidential candidate whose victory would ensure a drop in business, resulting in a drastic loss in shareholder value. He paused. "You really think that if Trump is elected, gun sales will dive?" he asked in a crisp English accent.

I laughed as the wine kicked in. "James, people in this industry want to think all of this growth is due to business genius, but gun sales in this country are largely driven by irrational fear. For your entire tenure, you've operated under President Obama. Trust me, without a Black president or some new conspiracy theory to rely on, sales are going to tank. You're cheering for Trump, and if he wins, your stock price will fall like a rock. You know that, right?"

He just stared at me for several seconds as he processed what I said and then quietly laughed. "I don't think you're correct about Trump. If he wins, it won't have much impact. But I do think that if Hillary wins, we'll have a brilliant four years!"

This was Debney's way of both ignoring and admitting the truth about the undeniable impacts of politics on gun sales. I had heard the same sort of thing from others, and I knew that no industry professional wanted to believe that the main driver of our business was anything but genius. But Debney's comment also exposed the fact that our industry was just fine with the indisputable sales benefits from a new Democratic administration. Over the years and through the election cycles, the trends were clear: gun sales tended to rise during times of tragedy under, and in anticipation of, Democratic presidents, and they tended to slump during Republican administrations.

Not long after Trump's surprise win, Debney experienced this for himself. His company lost more than $1 billion in value as fear dissipated and sales slumped. By 2019, journalists also hounded him with questions about the Smith & Wesson M&P15 rifle that was used to murder innocent high school students in Parkland, Florida. Encouraged by the power of a new social movement, the nation responded differently to the Florida tragedy. Journalists were more dogged; they poked at Debney's wealth and noted that he profited from guns used in mass shootings.[3]

And before the year was out, he had lost one of the most prestigious jobs in the industry.

When I heard of Debney's departure, I wondered if he wished that instead of funding Donald Trump's victory with Golden Jackets, he had contributed to the certainty of continued fear and a "brilliant four years" under Hillary Clinton.

Debney did not survive at Smith & Wesson long enough to experience what ended up being a delayed payoff from the NRA's hardwon Trump victory. By the middle of 2020, Donald Trump bucked the normal Republican gun downturn by using fear, riots, racial division, hate, protests, Twitter lies, politicization of science, a raging pandemic, intimidation, and guns to generate incredible sales that brought our industry roaring back to profitability. The ridiculous fear of a Black Democratic president had been replaced by the fear of radical leftists, marauding gangs, and even *neighbors* whose politics might be suspiciously progressive.

I detested everything about the Trump-driven boom, which meant that my entire livelihood was a contradiction. I had to make certain my company was successful. I knew if I was good at my job, I'd earn credibility and respect. This meant that I had a seat at the table in the places where decisions were made. I got to make whispered deals at cocktail parties. I had the rare opportunity to make sure that top industry leaders heard me, and they did. I got to speak truth to power, and I did. I had more clout than most when it came to speaking up for reason and common sense at a time when it was desperately needed. That also made me a royal pain in the ass. I expected to be fired on more than one occasion, but I made it hard for them because I always put big numbers on the bottom line. As long as I helped make Kimber profitable, I had a get-out-of-jail-free card in my pocket.

My family had watched me confront the industry's growing addiction to fear. They supported me as I found ways to challenge it. My activism angered the increasingly vocal crowd of tactical enthusiasts, many of whom were now using military weaponry to intimidate ordinary citizens and lawmakers across our country. These were the same men who formed the base of a growing market and who functioned as an army of industry enforcers.

On many evenings, Sara and I sat with our boys around the dinner table to explain the new calls from that growing army for me to be fired. On the difficult days after unspeakably horrible events such as Las Vegas,

Parkland, and El Paso, Sara dared to publicly speak up as a concerned mother and citizen; she offered empathy and shared frustration over social media with the victims of the mass shootings. When this happened, trolls who defined themselves by the power of their military weaponry stalked her online. They used our marriage to threaten our family and my job.

Other times I confided in my family as I saw overt racism and growing acceptance of conspiracy theories in the industry. Like me, our boys were frustrated by this because we knew dozens of gun owners like us who did not tolerate racism or believe in crazy conspiracies. Like them, we owned and used plenty of guns. But guns did not define us, nor did we embrace them as symbols of intimidation. I wanted my family to know I was different, that we weren't alone in holding this position when it came to guns, and that I was working to lead Kimber in a way that never lost sight of the principles the industry once insisted upon.

Our boys rightly sensed that mine was a tightwire act. For their sake, I tried not to seem too concerned, but they were worried. They had heard the after-dinner whispers between Sara and me as I bemoaned eventual and unavoidable impacts to our country and my livelihood.

As guns combined with heated national politics and then boiled over, most firearms executives I knew were celebrating. This upheaval was very, very good for gun sales. All of it—the fear, the racism, the hate, the militarism—sold guns. After years of trying to stay above it all, now I just wanted out.

The products of my industry, especially the AR-15, had become the most important political symbol for President Trump's base, maybe even a religious one. Many of the men at our protest wore the outline of the assault rifle on their hats and T-shirts, and those images sent a message of common faith. More powerful than even their flags, this symbol also let everyone else know that its bearers were armed with an efficient military killing machine, easily deployed when under threat, whether real or perceived.

In a nod to the overriding need for higher sales, I watched as the industry turned its back on safety instructors and hunters. They were marginalized and even given the pejorative nickname "Fudds" in a reference to the simpleton cartoon character Elmer Fudd.[4] The lessons and warnings that Fudds believed in were now just impediments to higher sales. Millions of people who recoiled from seeing Americans terrorized with the offensive use of guns, or people who still believed in safety, background checks, and decency, were forced into the shadows.

I am not one to live in shadows. I have never been that kind of person. While in the industry, I helped develop new sales models and create new markets. It was my job, my career. I was good at it. Pitching in to build the tools of political extremism was once part of my job too. But slowly, then far too quickly, those political requirements meant that the firearms industry was not just another slice of the US economy. It and I were part of something much larger: a powerful political machine radicalizing our nation.

In 1995 I was a young man, and I rushed into the industry, believing that it embodied wholesome parts of a country that valued and relied on guns but did so responsibly. Those were still the days of magazine covers featuring the warmth of father-son hunting trips. For years, my early assumptions seemed correct, but by 2000, things were changing, and the industry was being molded into a powerful political machine. By 2004, I came to terms with the disastrous potential of that machine, and I spent the remaining sixteen years of my career fighting it.

I fought for people like my father, who taught me to shoot on the ranch where I grew up. I stayed for the gun owners across the country who also embraced safety and reason. I refused to cede ground, and I still believe that the millions like me have the right to insist on our own reasonable approach.

I realize that many reading this book might disagree with the line I chose to walk for so long. I can appreciate how many Americans believe we'd be better off without *any* guns—not just with a system of reasonable regulations. Many of these people have lived and suffered in ways I have not. I am a proud gun owner who hunts and shoots with his boys whenever I can, yet I share a common concern with these people who oppose guns because, like them, I'm worried about extremism and radicalization. I realize that a gun industry which mocks responsibility while celebrating armed extremism only strengthens the argument to end gun ownership. Millions like me know that the future of firearms ownership depends on responsibility, decency, and reason for the simple reason that the future of the democracy that grants us the right of gun ownership depends on the same things.

My story, like the story of our nation, is complex. To understand it all, we need to know the truth about how our country's fascination with guns and power forms the framework of our modern existence.

This is the inside story of an industry that changed America and of a gunrunner turned gunfighter who lived through it all.

TWO

HOLE IN THE WALL

"I N THE TOP CORNER OF KANSAS, TWENTY MILES FROM Colorado, twenty miles from Nebraska." That was always my answer when someone asked where I was from. There was no town large enough to provide any other reference, so the square corners of surrounding states offered the only orientation. We lived in a ranch house a hundred yards off a dirt road. The empty flatness of the high plains meant that on most nights we could see the flickering lights of towns nearly sixty miles away. That's where you'd find the nearest movie theater or fast-food restaurant.

I was fourteen in 1984. I worked hard on our ranch, spending countless hours on tractors or in the hot sun, building barbed-wire fences to keep the cattle from roaming. There was always a job to do, and that meant even at the age of ten, my younger brother, Cory, was often hard at work too.

Although the work never ended, during the summer we got some time to enjoy baseball. On special days we could convince Mom to take us to town to spend a few hours at the small local swimming pool.

On other days we would have friends over to build forts, fly kites, or swim in a muddy pond if a thunderstorm had passed by and dropped some rain. Many of the kids in my class at our small school could do nothing but dream of escaping to a big city, but I loved growing up on the ranch. I remember many of the best days as if they were depicted in a Norman Rockwell painting.

Cory and I also spent countless hours roaming the ranch with our rifles, seeking out rabbits or setting up old tin cans to shoot. A few months earlier our grandpa had given Cory a Marlin Model 60 rifle. The smooth wood stock bore a strong resemblance to many of the guns that had been used in World War II, and the elongated square receiver hinted at the design of modern military guns. The fact that Cory's rifle looked like a weapon of war meant that it conveyed a lethal seriousness. I noticed Cory swaggered a bit when he carried it.

Like most modern military designs, Cory's Marlin was built on a semiautomatic fire-control system. Once the rifle was loaded and cocked, he could fire it as fast as his finger could pull the trigger. The energy from the explosion in each round cycled the rifle for the next shot, over and over until the gun was empty. Shooting rapid-fire at a line of cans was pretty fun, and Cory got good enough to rip off seventeen accurate shots in just a couple of seconds.

I had a Browning BL22, a lever-action rifle just like the guns of the Old West. My gun required cocking the lever with the back of my hand between each shot. I was pretty quick with my gun, but Cory's rifle was much faster and more fun to shoot. Occasionally, I would borrow his gun so I could fire almost as fast as the guys on our favorite shows.

We didn't get to watch much TV growing up, and we had only three channels. But like a lot of other American kids in the 1980s, Cory and I never missed *The A-Team*. It featured a group of former Special Forces commandos who used military rifles in almost every episode. And like many shows of its era, even though they fired thousands of rounds, the characters on the show rarely killed anyone, sparing its young viewers the true consequences of solving problems with firepower. Mr. T played B. A. Baracus, the witty muscle of the gang. There was also Face, the gregarious salesman, and the team leader, John "Hannibal" Smith, played by George Peppard. One of our favorites was H. M. "Howling Mad" Murdock, who escaped from psychiatric hospitals and spoke to his imaginary dog, Billy. Murdock was central to every mission, but luckily for the A-Team, he was never subjected to a modern background check.

There was no mistaking the takeaway for us: guns, an unlimited supply of ammunition, a pinch of bravery, and a healthy dose of testosterone gave the A-Team all they needed to make the world right. For a couple of boys on a ranch twenty miles from Colorado and twenty miles from Nebraska, the fact that they often rescued beautiful women did not hurt.

Those *A-Team* episodes stuck with us, and a few days after watching one of those shows, when Mom and Dad were away, Cory grabbed his Marlin and decided to play Mr. T out behind the house. He jammed in cartridges as fast as he could, then held the gun at his hip and started firing real bullets at imaginary targets.

I watched it all as a volley of shots rang out in just a second or two. He yelled at foes, just like those on the show. Then he reloaded again, this time picking out an old tree stump to stand in for the bad guys. Again, he fired off a full magazine in quick succession. He reloaded a third time and began spraying his celebratory shots into the air, but this time, something didn't sound right. I yelled to stop him and then pointed up at the house. One of Cory's shots had pierced the corner of our home, just above our parents' bedroom window.

"Don't tell Mom and Dad!" Cory begged, with a mix of embarrassment and fear. But we both knew they'd find out anyway. So I agreed to bear the bad news, but I also agreed to leave out the part about how fictional vigilantes had inspired Cory's crazed reenactment. I just made up something about me daring Cory to take a risky shot at a distant bird.

"Thank goodness neither of you are hurt," Mom said as she glanced at Dad with a look that suggested she didn't buy our story. Mom had not grown up immersed in guns, but she accepted them as an ordinary part of our lives. She wanted her kids to be well-rounded and well-behaved. Having fun with our guns was fine as long as we also got good grades, practiced piano, and never missed church. She made sure that accomplishment and responsibility were part of our lives too.

When it came to guns, irresponsible behavior did not sit well with Dad either. He wanted to believe that his sons had not done anything stupid. He watched us with a raised eyebrow for a while, then gave us a stern safety lecture, reminding us of all the nonnegotiable rules that he had recited to us hundreds of times. Fingers were never to approach the trigger until the target was safe and certain. Gun muzzles were always to be pointed in a safe direction and never toward a place where there might be people. Our rifles were not even to be loaded until we were positive it was safe to fire. Obviously, Cory's *A-Team* scene had violated almost all those tenets. As Dad patched up the hole in the house, he noted that things could have been worse. "Good thing you didn't shoot through the window, boys." Then he lowered his head to look directly at us, and he slowed his voice: "Good thing no one was in there."

Dad's sternness shook me. Things had gotten out of control so quickly. Cory was usually the careful one, the younger kid who didn't do stupid stuff. He was usually giving me the warnings. If a show like *The A-Team* could make a boy like him put a hole in the wall, then what else could happen?

That night was a rare exception to almost all of the shooting that Cory and I did together. For the most part we were safe and had fun: two brothers plinking with their rifles. We could have been in a magazine advertisement for an ammunition company or one of those calendars sold in sporting-goods stores.

Most days of my childhood reminded me of the fun and romance of guns. Rifles and shotguns played a central role in so many of the best days of our youth. Those days of the early 1980s seem so innocent now.

We had never heard of assault weapons or school shootings back then. Thankfully, a hole in the wall of our home was about the worst thing we could imagine.

Like many gun owners, my dad belonged to the National Rifle Association because he believed the organization to be the keeper of the same firearms-safety lessons that he recited to his sons. Dad liked old guns, so he also appreciated the idea of camaraderie with others who collected guns and took pride in firearms ownership.

As part of his NRA membership we received the *American Rifleman* magazine each month. Cory and I often leafed through the pages, reading the articles about interesting guns that we yearned to shoot. Through all my childhood years, the NRA magazines never featured angry politics or dramatic assertions about the impending demise of the republic. Instead, they devoted entire issues to celebrating the results of shooting competitions. The most famous was the NRA's annual Camp Perry national shooting championship in Port Clinton, Ohio, an event that had been held every year since 1907. The NRA's flagship magazine also featured lengthy articles on the history of firearms and helpful tips on shooting and gun cleaning. Most of the articles were about rifles or shotguns, but by the time I was fourteen, a few of those NRA magazines featured handguns too.

We had a few handguns in our family. Dad carried a little Ruger Bearcat revolver in his truck and used it occasionally for rattlesnakes that surprised him. The same gun would one day be highly sought after by Dad's six grandsons, all of whom badgered him to give them the little revolver. Back then, I loved the thing too and begged him to teach me how to shoot it. One day he took a few minutes to show me. "It's hard to hold steady," he said. "You'll need to practice keeping that front sight on your target as you squeeze the trigger." I practiced with that Ruger for weeks.

I grew to love the smell of the burning gunpowder as it wafted from the spent cartridges. Sometimes I blew gun smoke away from the muzzle just like the guys in the movies. Weeks later, after much practice and when I thought I was good enough, I waved at Dad to stop working long enough to watch me shoot. "You're getting pretty good with that thing!" he said after I knocked several old beer cans off the fence. Dad's affirmation of my ability was a small compliment, but it stuck with me forever.

That moment with the little Ruger represented a short break from ranch life, which mostly consisted of attacking one job after another. Some days I watched my dad sweat as he dug miles of irrigation ditches with a small shovel. By the time I was twelve, I was helping stack hay in the hot sun. Cory learned how to drive the truck through the field so that Dad and I could load the bales. The cattle were always escaping, which meant that we were always fixing fences. There were sick cows, dry water tanks, vaccinations—the work of the ranch never stopped. Because there was so much to do, we rarely took family vacations.

So my rifle became my personal respite from the work. That little Browning was my ticket to escapism. Whenever I got the chance, I wandered alone over the hills, the air sweet with sunflowers and kosha. I could hunt prairie dogs or fend off coiled rattlesnakes. I could bring home dinner or imagine I was a hero or a villain. My rifle was the conduit for it all.

Pheasant season started each November, and that's when I borrowed an old Model 42 Winchester pump shotgun from Dad. Even before I could legally drive, I'd load the little pump .410 and my bird dog, Daisy, in an orange 1974 Chevy farm pickup and drive to a place on the ranch where pheasants were plentiful. I loved supplying my family with food that I harvested myself. Only later did I realize it was also wild and organic: the kind of wholesome, sustainable food people in big cities now pay top dollar for.

Through my teen years, I followed Daisy through hundreds of miles of Conservation Reserve Program land. Dad was a pioneer and advocate of this visionary federal program that pays farmers and ranchers to plant native grasses on marginal stretches of land in an effort to conserve soil and cultivate the natural habitat for wild animals. Dad loved the wildlife, and even if he did not get to enjoy it as much as he wanted, it was enough for him just to know that he was doing his part to put things back like they once were.

He read books that other ranchers did not: titles by Theodore Roosevelt, Aldo Leopold, and other influential thinkers of the modern conservation movement. Dad felt a need to help bandage up the country's great national prairie wound.

On our frequent pickup rides together it was not uncommon to get a short speech from Dad on the importance of conserving wild things. He might say, "We don't want the whole countryside to be a big industrial zone. Life's not really worth living if we don't have a place for the wild animals." Dad took great pride in the fact that he converted thousands of acres back to native grass. I was happy that he did it too, because not long after the grass sprouted, pheasant and deer populations exploded, and Daisy and I reaped the benefits.

One year for Christmas, when I was about fifteen, Cory and I noticed shotgun-long boxes under the tree. Mom and Dad had scraped up money to buy two guns that they probably couldn't afford. The Winchester double-barrels were beautiful. Mine was a side-by-side Model 23, and Cory's was an over-under Model 101. The satin stainless receivers were engraved with simple but elegant game birds. The walnut stocks were long and sleek, shaped in the style of classic English straight grips.

"These are guns you boys can use for the rest of your life," Dad announced proudly as we admired them. "These are very nice guns, and they'll always be ready for you to take them hunting." Even then I had a sense that these guns were more than just the tools for hunting that he described.

Many times throughout the coming years, when I did not have time to hunt, I would pull out my Winchester Model 23 and just stare at it or shoulder it, and I'd aim at an imaginary fast-flying pheasant in the distance. I came to understand that for my dad and me, like many gun owners, guns like this were more than tools. They were the symbols of our hopes and of our relationship to each other. They represented things that we wanted to be true. Unlike a hammer or a shovel, we had a deep emotional connection to these tools.

Dad also never missed an opportunity to remind us of the responsibility that came along with using guns. Even before we removed those Christmas shotguns from the box, he grabbed our shoulders so he knew we were listening.

"These are not toys," he added intensely, looking at each of us in the eye. "They are serious things. They can end a life in an instant." We nodded. "Promise me you'll always be safe and you'll never do anything foolish when you're shooting." He kept looking us in the eyes until we made the promise aloud. This lecture was commonplace in our lives, whether when Dad was handing over a gun for us to admire or calling after us as we jumped a fence to find a few pheasants after the day's chores.

Dad gave his warnings with an exaggerated seriousness that belied the darkness of his own past. When he was growing up, one of his best friends, Larry Khelbeck, lived on a farm just a few miles away. Larry's father, Fritz, owned land bordering the farm of an angry hermit named Tolly Bolyard. During the spring and summer of 1962, Bolyard became convinced that Fritz and Larry were scheming to steal his land, and he began digging a deep, impassable ditch in their field as his defensive boundary. Even as the hot summer sun bore down on Tolly, he labored with fear, sweating while piling old steel bars and jagged concrete blocks into the ditch as insurance against any invaders.

On July 14, 1962, when Larry was sixteen, he and his father drove their tractor to fill in the ditch just enough so they could access their land. Tolly confronted them and then accused the pair of scheming to invade his property before pulling his loaded gun and shooting Fritz twice in the stomach and once in the forehead.

Larry watched his father's murder and ran for his life, struggling to escape for nearly a half mile across a sandy field. Bolyard chased Larry down with his old truck, knocked the teenager to the ground with the bumper, then shot him in the head.[1]

In the blink of an eye on a sweltering Kansas afternoon, my dad's best friend was murdered by a troubled man with a tool designed to do exactly that: end a life in an instant.

I got only small hints about the kind of impact the murders had on my dad. Recounting the tale was understandably painful for him, and he rarely spoke of it. I was left to collect bits and pieces of the macabre story from others.

"That's where I waited in the grass with the KBI," my grandpa once recalled, referring to the Kansas Bureau of Investigation, as we drove past a high point on the dirt road. "We lay there and watched Old Tolly through rifle scopes for hours."

News reports from the event confirmed Grandpa's memory of the double murder and the long standoff with the KBI, culminating in Tolly Bolyard's arrest and eventual sentencing to consecutive life terms with hard labor. The reports also mentioned several surrounding residents, including my grandfather, who had been enlisted by the KBI to surveil Bolyard until it was safe enough to apprehend him.

I could tell I was expected to consider this story carefully. Grandpa and I leaned out of our open windows dodging grasshoppers and saying nothing as he drove past the high spot and then on down the bumpy road to what was left of Bolyard's broken-down homestead.

Grandpa slowed to a stop, turned the engine off, and then let the dust settle around the truck before he spoke. He had something important to tell me, something he didn't confide to many people. "After they caught him, we found his gun over there. It was a .45, a 1911. Old Tolly shoved it into a barrel of grease thinking no one would find it, but we figured out where it was."

My grandpa Clarence was a product of the Dust Bowl, the Great Depression, and World War II. He was impervious to hardship and accustomed to pain. I almost never saw him show emotion, but Fritz had been one of my grandfather's best friends, which meant that Tolly Bolyard annihilated two father/son friendships in an instant. Grandpa looked away, choking up as he remembered the last details.

"Everyone knew Tolly was crazy," he said. "He threatened to kill Fritz. He shouldn't have been allowed to own that gun." Grandpa paused and collected himself again. I had seen him cry only one other time, from the pain of a heart attack years earlier. Like that night, when I saw him collapse and grab at his chest, I knew this story was important and that he was struggling to let me know something was wrong. For him it was literally as painful as a heart attack.

Like many of his generation, Grandpa was a New Deal Democrat who revered Franklin Delano Roosevelt and believed that the personal sacrifice of all Americans had saved democracy. He was also a proud gun owner who reserved his favorite black-and-gold NRA ball cap for social gatherings or community events. For Grandpa, that NRA membership fit perfectly with his personal politics. His treasured NRA cap signified self-reliance and the understood need for shared responsibility: Principles. Safety. Camaraderie. Pride.

All these experiences in my childhood combined to form my outlook on firearms, but as I prepared to enter the job market after college, I mostly remembered how guns had played a positive and important role in my life. Harkening back to the best parts of my youth served as a sort of professional guidance. For years, after I became a successful firearms executive, I often joked, "I'm just trying to figure out a way to get paid to hunt and fish, and this industry is as close as I can get." There's a lot of truth in that.

I got to relive parts of those magical childhood memories. Just like millions of other Americans, I found that firearms represented times I wanted to remember, people I wanted to be with, and things I wished to be true. I believed that being part of a gun company brought me closer to this vision, allowing me to work and play at the same time.

But I assumed that my career in the gun industry would also be balanced with the other things I knew to be true: the values Dad taught me. Safety and reason had to be at the forefront of any gun experience. "Pay attention and be responsible," Dad would say during our precious time together. "None of this is worth losing a life."

Before long I'd combine my farm-boy work ethic with my affinity for guns. I'd win awards and find myself in the upper echelon of the gun industry. But even in those early days, my success felt complicated. My achievements won awards largely because of my work in successfully rebranding and selling a century-old gun design for Kimber. Serious aficionados considered the gun to be iconic, and dozens of companies followed our lead and marketed their own versions. I then developed an innovative team to sell them across the world.

In fact, I'm responsible for selling more of those pistols through the gun stores of America than any other single person in the history of the industry. But I did it all while performing a balancing act of my own. After all, the gun design I helped improve and revive in the modern market was the same model my grandfather had found in a barrel of grease. I helped build a company around the 1911 .45ACP: the same pistol that had killed my father's and grandfather's best friends.

THREE

GROUND FLOOR

I F I SPED THROUGH DOWNTOWN GREELEY AND RAN A COUPLE
of red lights, I could make it to my second job at the MCI call center only fifteen minutes late. My day job ended at 5:00 each evening, and my second job as a telemarketer started at exactly the same time. I should have been fired for being late, but I told my supervisor that if he wanted me to sell for him, that's the way it would have to be.

"OK, Busse," he grumbled. "*You* can show up a few minutes late. But don't tell anyone else." And so for several hours every night I put on a headset and tried to sell long-distance service to people across the country who were just sitting down to dinner.

I had taken this second job to make some extra cash. It was 1994, and a few years earlier federal antitrust litigation had forced the breakup of AT&T. In the mid-1990s companies such as Sprint and MCI fought to gain a foothold in the emerging long-distance-telephone market. Federal law required that consumers had to be aware of the changes, which meant that skilled salespeople had a lot of explaining to do.

Most MCI telemarketers did not make it through their first week. Even after months on the job, I still relished the challenge.

One day, as I tried to sell long distance to a man, he became so enraged that he hyperventilated on the phone while screaming curses about me and MCI at the same time. He was one of many people who didn't want to be disturbed during dinner and who weren't eager to switch from their familiar, century-old company. Many had stock in AT&T. Some had relatives who worked there. I knew that sales was all about relating to people, so I sought out these details as I looked for any point of leverage.

Once, in the middle of a profanity-laced tirade, a man from Ohio asked, "How'd you like it if I called *you* at home, you son of a bitch?"

"I'd love you to call me at home," I replied, in violation of MCI's strict corporate protocol. "Go for it!" And then I gave him my home number. The man from Ohio called me up at 1:30 a.m. that night, and to his surprise, I answered.

He got the first words: "How do you like it now, you asshole?" He thought that would be the end of it, but I refused to hang up; after all, I had a long-distance plan to sell. I talked to him for twenty minutes, and we ended up laughing about the whole thing. The next day I sold him an MCI plan.

The job I left every day at 5:00 sharp was supposed to be my first step toward a dream career in the shooting-sports industry. Burris Optics produced rifle scopes in the meatpacking town of Greeley, Colorado. The scope factory was only about a mile from a huge industrial meatpacking plant. On Thursdays in Greeley that plant processed the blood of countless cows slaughtered that week. The plant cooked their blood into products such as fish-food pellets, resulting in a stench that settled over the entire town. It permeated everything at Burris.

Before I got the job at Burris, I had imagined what a career in the industry might look like. This was a time before the proliferation of AR-15s, before the militarization that would one day dominate almost all related companies, even optics companies such as Burris. Maybe I'd get to go hunting every third day. I'd have thoughtful meetings about developing top-notch new scopes. I'd win awards for innovations. However, Burris did not come close to any of that.

My title at Burris, customer service manager, sounded far better than it actually was. The Burris office included a small portion of a dingy machine shop. Unless it was Fish Pellet Thursday, the smell of burning machine oil filled the air as it wafted in from the swinging double doors of the shop floor.

For the first year I was the only employee in my department, which meant that I managed only myself. I earned six bucks an hour, which was at least a little better than minimum wage, and I would have a chance at a raise in a year.

Customers returned defective scopes, and we piled them in the office with little documentation and no process to shepherd them through our repair facility. Angry customers called every day for technical help or status updates. I had been handed a mess, and the extent of my training or instruction was "Fix it."

Most days, my other job—bothering people at dinnertime—was actually a pleasant diversion. And it wasn't long before I began looking for other options. And that's when I found Kimber.

"Greg is a fucking genius," Dwight told me one day. "And they are damn nice rifles. It's a tiny company, but we can make this thing into a gun-industry powerhouse!" Dwight Van Brunt was Burris's director of marketing, and he was talking about a company I had just barely heard of. At that time Kimber was an almost unknown manufacturer outside Portland, Oregon. Dwight spoke to me with the same wide-eyed intensity that scared the shit out of almost everyone else he met.

When excited, he sometimes forced a toothy smile that bore an eerie similarity to Jack Nicholson's "Here's Johnny" scene in *The Shining*. Dwight was driven and intense, and he always seemed to be on the verge of an outburst. In his midthirties, he was smart and dedicated to making something of himself while also being miserly and proud of it, often bragging about owning the same suit that he had bought in college.

Two years earlier, on my first day on the job, I had toured Burris with Dennis, the company's director of engineering, who pulled me aside with a warning: "Look, kid. Dwight can be a little crazy and has an ego the size of Dallas."

I laughed nervously. "Thanks, Dennis. I'll take that under advisement. He *is* my boss, you know." But even with Dwight's frightening intensity—and even despite warnings from other employees—I became friends with him. Like me, Dwight was headstrong and determined. I liked his passion, and I had a hunch that one day we might accomplish something big together.

Dwight loved guns even more than I did, and he grew up reading every gun book he could find. He knew the names of every industry executive. He knew gun-company histories and the biographies of people who wrote about guns. He could quote nuanced technical details about obscure guns that most people had never heard of, and then he'd tell you about the time he bought or sold one of them. He believed he was born to work in the gun business. And he believed Kimber was his ticket out of Fish Pellet Town.

In 1995 Kimber was a tiny rifle company that was headquartered in one of a dozen sterile warehouses on the edge of Portland. The company's president and owner, an Australian named Greg Warne, had immigrated to the United States as a young man and took a forgettable job as an accounting consultant at Price Waterhouse. He spent his spare time on Kimber, which he and his father, Jack, had started in 1979. By 1988, Greg had given up his accounting career to work at Kimber full-time.

Greg's Australian roots and his accent had combined to form the name of the company. Before they moved to America, Jack took his boys shooting and hunting around his favorite Australian outback town. Jack was born in Kimba, South Australia, and the place had remained the favorite getaway for the Warne family. When Jack and Greg debated what to name their new company, Jack wanted to call it Kimba. Greg didn't think that was just right, and because he rolled the "ahs" at the end of words, *Kimba* became *Kimber*, and the company got its name.

I knew only that Kimber had limped and bounced along since its founding. It had experienced some critical acclaim and more financial ruin. Kimber had twice filed for bankruptcy, and each time Greg used his magnetic personality to revive it from the ashes. Greg was also an artist who knew how to style and build fine bolt-action rifles. These were traditional hunting and target guns, uncluttered by the sharp an-gled technical advancements that would one day improve the lethality of AR-15s. These were the kind of guns that people collected and that grandfathers passed down as heirlooms. This meant that Kimber rifles elicited strong, emotional connections for their consumers, and Greg knew how to use that passion to pull money from investors.

Dwight and I often debated the attributes of various designs or wood types. Like Dwight, I wanted to be deeper in the industry. And so over the nearly three years we worked together in Colorado, Dwight and I schemed about a next move that might get us closer to at least the middle of the gun business. It was in one of these weekend scheming conversations when Kimber first came up.

"You mean the little company that makes rimfire rifles?" I asked, referring to the small cartridges, like the .22, that fired from a charge on the outer rim instead of the more powerful central primers of larger and deadlier chamberings. "Shit, man, haven't they gone bank-o a time or two? I love those rifles. I mean, they're beautiful, but I don't know about working for a company that can't stay afloat. I wouldn't mind getting paid once in a while."

"Yeah. It's been a shit show, and it's not a very big company," Dwight replied. "But they are damn sexy little guns."

Dwight was almost exactly ten years older than me, and Burris was his third job since graduating from college. He was not born into money and had not struck it rich in his first couple of jobs. People at Burris joked that Dwight still had the first nickel he ever made. I knew he had actually lost that nickel to Greg Warne. "I took a chance on him," Dwight admitted. "Well, actually we lost a big chunk of our life savings."

"That sounds like a red flag, Dwight."

"Well, I still love him. He's a gun genius and a hell of a guy. You'll love him too. He just had some bad luck with the company. Ryan, I'm telling you: we can make this company into something huge. You can run sales. I'll run marketing."

"But Portland? I don't want to live in Portland. It rains all the time, and it's a city. I don't want to live in a damn city."

Nonetheless, Dwight settled on the idea that we would work at Kimber together. And once Dwight Van Brunt decided to sell an idea, he would succeed or die trying. The Portland question was a softball for him. "Mr. Busse, that's the best fucking part." Dwight's intense eyes grew to the size of saucers. He leaned over the table, cutting the distance between us, his crazy smile shining across his face. He paused and held his gaze on me. He was either going to murder me right there at his kitchen table or deliver the most important line of the night: "I told Greg we would *never* live in Portland, but we *can* live in goddamn Montana, man! *Montana!*"

I had always wanted to live in Montana, whose nickname, "the Last Best Place," had called to me. For a kid who loved to hunt and fish, no place in the lower forty-eight held a more iconic status. I waited only a few seconds. "OK. Fuck it. I'm in. Let's run some guns!" I gave Dwight a high five. That's all it took. I reasoned that I had nothing to lose and everything to gain. Kimber may have been a little company built on shaky ground, but it produced very-high-quality guns that I loved. If I could make it work, no one would be able to tell me I had lucked out. I could help build a company that I could be proud of. That was my professional rationale, but it was mostly an excuse to move to Kalispell, Montana: the new worldwide sales and marketing headquarters for Kimber.

A few months later, I packed everything I had into a Chevy pickup and drove northwest from Colorado to a new life as a rookie gun salesman. I'd soon refer to myself as a "gunrunner," the casual term we all used for the small gang of firearms-industry salespeople.

As I drove north, I wondered why Greg Warne would hire us. Dwight and I both believed in our abilities, but it seemed like another big risk for Kimber. Two guys running the front of the company from a remote office in Montana was not exactly conventional, but Greg was a gambler, and he loved to sell his company to investors. In our final interviews, he sold me. "Look, Ryan, no one makes guns that look like Kimbers," he told me over the phone. "This is the ground floor, but come aboard and we can build it up." To this day I don't know if Greg believed it or just loved the challenge of convincing me, but I joined up for a whopping annual salary of $32,000. At least I could stop smelling fish pellets and making people hyperventilate during dinner.

I rented a small house and settled into the beautiful Flathead Valley. As I stood on my front porch, I could see three different mountain ranges. The vastness of it all was intimidating. I wanted to explore, but I hardly knew where to begin. My enormous professional challenge was intimidating too, and for the first few months it dominated most of my time.

We began selling guns out of Dwight's new home east of Kalispell. His house was tucked up against the Swan Mountains at the head of a clear lake, just fifty miles south of the Canadian border. Dwight carved our office out of one of the bedrooms in his home. Deer and an occasional bear wandered through the yard outside our window. We sat back-to-back and worked eighteen-hour days. We regularly shared meals with Dwight's young family and learned to speak more quietly after the kids went to bed.

That year, 1996, the gun industry was in the middle of a massive hangover after the sales spike generated by the 1994 Clinton assault weapons ban. Gun companies produced only about 5.5 million units that year, a fraction of the total achieved in the coming boom years.[1] Kimber was also tiny compared to what it is today. On many days, our little company struggled to produce between ten and fifteen rifles, and our annual production totaled only a few thousand guns. However, by the time I was being nominated for national awards and trying to influence the NRA from the inside, Kimber was approaching production rates of nearly two thousand guns per day.

Back then, our job was to market to consumers and develop a dealer network to sell our high-end rifles. I found dealer lists and cold-called buyers across the country, begging them to buy some of our guns, trying anything I could to generate some cash for our struggling company. I visited key customers in person and slowly began to make relationships, building up my network of Kimber master dealers. I'd eventually grow that network to become the largest the industry had ever seen.

Selling guns was hard, but not any worse than selling long distance to contented AT&T customers during dinnertime. And hard work didn't bother me either. Back on the ranch in Kansas I had built four-wire fence in steep cattle pastures. I cleaned toxic, rotten corn out of grain bins in hundred-degree heat. I spent half of my childhood on a tractor or in a grain harvester despite the fact that my father's hay fever had found its way into an obscure curl of my DNA. The grain dust made me sneeze so violently that I would duct-tape myself into the cab for an entire day to prevent contamination from the outside. It didn't work; I still sneezed so bad I soaked my shirt sopping wet. With a childhood résumé like that, even the most challenging white-collar job like selling guns wasn't difficult.

My work at Kimber required a bit of personal skill; luckily, I had inherited just enough of that too. I brought to Kalispell all of the work ethic my parents taught me, plus my hard-knock experience from MCI and Burris. Importantly, I also brought my limited view of politics. I was busy chasing success and didn't give politics much consideration other than to know I was a hardworking, red-blooded, gunrunning American. In other words, I thought of myself as a Republican. Most of the people in my world told me that's what I needed to be, anyway, and I complied.

I also found that my "flyover-state" conservatism was a selling point for gun dealers. A right-wing joke here or there, and an occasional complaint about Bill Clinton or Portland liberals, made it easier for me to break the ice. I'd use any advantage I could get.

Just after I moved to Kalispell, I pulled up beside a big truck at a stoplight to see a sticker on the back bumper that read "Liberals: Limit 1 a day, 3 in possession." The message was a play on a state regulation limiting how many ducks a hunter could shoot and keep. I laughed and gave the guy a thumbs-up. Political philosophies that could fit on bumper stickers seemed like the way to go.

I started at Kimber never having actually met Greg Warne. My early impressions of the man had mostly been formed by Dwight's glowing reports. A few months into my new job I picked up the phone to hear Greg's thick Australian accent. "Ryan, I need you to get over here to Portland to help me manage the company. I need some help hiring and firing."

"Um, OK," I replied. "I don't have much experience—" But he had already hung up. I had my orders. I spun around to tell Dwight, reminding him I had almost no management experience. Kimber needed sales. That's what I was good at, and I knew I should stay to focus on my work.

"He knows what he's doing," Dwight said without even looking up. "Better get packed."

I loaded up my Chevy again and drove nine hours west to Clackamas, Oregon, just southeast of Portland. I checked into a Super 8 and settled into what became my home for the next thirty-six days.

I showed up early the next Monday morning to the long white warehouse that was Kimber. It was 7:00, and a few people were already in the office. I knocked, and they let me in. Immediately, I sensed something was off. "Are you here to help?" they asked. "It's so good to meet you." "We need you here!" "I hope you can fix this . . ."

I worked in the office for a couple of hours, waiting for Greg to arrive, then decided to check out the production floor. I walked back through the heavy doors to where two dozen men hovered over whir-ring industrial machines. Some were cutting metal parts, and some were drilling holes or grinding on long, steel rifle barrels. They all wore blue Kimber aprons stained with the same machine oil I remembered from Burris. Like the front-office employees, they immediately began con-fiding in me.

The manager, Dave Fitzgerald, broke away to speak with me in the corner, away from the noise of his machine. "Glad you're here, Ryan," he said. "Heard a lot about you." *That's weird*, I thought. *Someone has taken a lot of time to build me up to these people. Or maybe they're just really desperate?*

Back in the office I staked out a workspace. At about 10:00, Greg's BMW screeched to a halt, and he stomped in. Greg stood about five feet eight and had a thin ring of blond hair around his bald head. He wore wire-rim glasses and had a slightly hunched back. He bore a strong resemblance to Elton John and constantly flashed a suspicious, boyish grin. He knew exactly who I was without a formal introduction. "Ryan, good to see you. Damn, I'm hungry. Let's go get some breakfast."

I followed him to his BMW and jumped in. Ten minutes later we parked in front of a building with a suggestive silhouette of a stripper on the sign. "They serve breakfast at the Acropolis?"

"Oh, yes, it's the best breakfast in town," he winked. Inside, at least a dozen dancers, many of them topless, made their way to greet Greg by his first name. Several hugged him.

"You've got some glitter on you," I said as I brushed his shoulder.

"That's stripper funk. Can't say you've been working if you don't have a little stripper funk on you!"

We sat down in front of the grimy stage at the Acropolis, and Greg ordered breakfast for both of us as a young woman danced in front of him. As we waited for the food, he yelled over the booming music. "Good to have you out here! We're going to make money at Kimber and have a lot of fun doing it! I need your help with the Model 84 Varmint rifle. We have to get that stock right, and I know you love to shoot." He slapped me on the back and then pointed at a dancer spinning around the pole onstage. "She's a good one," he said, then looked at me over his glasses and added: "Her real name is Stephanie."

A Tina Turner song started, and another stripper Greg knew began to dance as he finished up his breakfast. As she got closer to him, she shed the last of her lace and crouched in front of his plate. He slipped her some money and then looked at me as he wiped the last bit of egg yolk from his upper lip. "Ryan, if that's not worth a dollar, then I don't know what is!"

"Don't we need to get back to the plant?" I yelled over the music. Greg looked around and then down at his watch, a Rolex Submariner. It was almost 11:00.

"Yeah, I guess. Let's go build some guns!"

FOUR

ROOKIE OF THE YEAR

O VER THE NEXT FEW DAYS AND WEEKS I SPENT A LOT OF
time with Greg and the office staff. We held meetings with
the two production supervisors. I struggled to finalize price sheets.
I encouraged Greg to decide on specifications and told him that I
needed production plans, shipping dates, and final designs before I
could sell guns the way I needed to. Company employees who attended the meetings thanked me for saying obvious things. In one
meeting I became frustrated by the lack of progress. "Greg, we can't
keep changing prices or stock shapes and stay in business. We have
to get our shit in order."

After the meeting, Kimber's accountant, an unassuming woman
named Celeste, cornered me to thank me for speaking up. "Greg is,
um, awesome," she said nervously. "But we really need someone like
you to help *lead*."

Early one afternoon Greg called me into his office. He held a
hand-carved rifle stock, almost caressing it. "Isn't she beautiful?" he
asked. It *was* beautiful, crafted from fine walnut with perfect shape

and intricate checkering. I knew how to appreciate a fine gun, and I knew Greg had an eye for what made a rifle exceptional. "We'll put this on our 84M Varmint, and it'll be the nicest little rifle on the planet," he proclaimed, carefully setting the woodwork on his desk. This was *passion*. It is why I joined Kimber.

Just as we congratulated each other on the execution of that final sample, Celeste slipped into the office and whispered in Greg's ear. His mood instantly changed. He looked at me and gritted his teeth. "The goddamn bank is choking us again," he sneered. "We're short of money in the payroll accounts, and we have to cut checks tomorrow." He then yelled at Celeste as she tried to run out of the office. "Tell those fuckers to fix it! We're a good customer!"

She looked at me and said nothing, but her face told me that Kimber had not, in fact, been a good customer.

"Enough of this depressing bullshit!" In an instant Greg flashed his boyish grin again. "Ryan, it's Dave Fitzgerald's birthday today. You go back to the plant and tell everyone they can quit at four. Then go to the liquor store and get us a bunch of booze. Find some girls and tell them to come to my house. Celeste will give you some money. Probably need about five grand."

I pushed back and suggested to Greg that this was not a good use of company time or money.

"Goddamnit, Ryan," he replied. "You have a lot to learn about management. This is how you motivate people. They need to have fun and know that you'll take care of them. Consider this a graduate-level management lesson." Greg's charming enthusiasm and Australian accent had a strange power over people, even when they knew his ideas were crazy. I was no exception.

Celeste was mortified when I asked her for $5,000, but she went to her desk and cut me a check anyway. As she handed it to me, she whispered, "Help!" Then, as Greg asked, I went in the back to tell the two dozen men that they could quit early and come to Dave's birthday party at Greg's place.

I then went to the liquor store and stopped by the Riverside Corral on the way. It was Greg's favorite strip club. It didn't take me long to line up some entertainment for the evening. I paid the dancers, who gave me only their stage names. To make sure they showed up, I told them Greg would give them a tip after the party; they all knew that Greg tipped well. I dropped the booze off at Greg's house and then went back to the office. Once everyone left for the party, I found Celeste nearly in tears. "We're going to bounce payroll checks tomorrow," she sobbed. "We don't have enough in the account, and the bank isn't going to help." Before Greg's mandated birthday party, Kimber was about $20,000 short. Now we needed about $25,000, and we had to get it before noon in order to pay our employees.

"I'll figure out a way," I sighed, knowing how much easier it was to say than do.

Celeste hugged me and dabbed her eyes. "Thank you. You're the only one who understands."

—◆—

"Yes, I'm fucking serious," I said into my phone a few minutes later. "This is the only way the deal works. You'll get the guns, and I get a certified check. You'll have to get it to the Northwest Airlines counter now. Tell them it is an urgent freight package. If I don't get the money in the morning, the deal is off."

"You have to be yanking my chain, Ryan! What kind of Mob bullshit is this? I warn you, I have friends back in Chicago that will take care of this problem if Greg fucks me on this deal. You need to tell him that these people *do not* fuck around."

"Listen, Ed, you just have to trust me." I remained calm and firm, but I clearly needed to convey urgency. "Kimber is going to bounce payroll checks to everyone in the company if I don't get the cash. Half of the production staff will quit if that happens. I'll take care of you with the guns. Check has to be certified, and it's got to be on the first flight out. Just let me worry about Greg."

Ed West was a kind, grandfatherly man. In his late sixties, he had a full head of thick, wavy gray hair and an impressive mustache to match. He wore cardigan sweaters and spoke with the soothing deep voice of a late-night radio announcer. But Ed was a hardened former Chicago beat cop you couldn't fool twice. He had retired from the police force and moved to Albuquerque to escape the weather and crime of Chicago. Retirement had not suited him well, so he founded Olde West Guns, a gun-sales operation based out of his tidy suburban stucco home, where he kept his inventory of a few hundred guns stacked neatly in his garage.

Olde West Guns had an official business address, but transactions never happened in Ed's house. Rather, he worked the southwestern gun-show circuit from Oklahoma to Arizona. Each week he packed up his Ford pickup with a hundred or so guns and drove to a show. Once there, he would unfold his tables and display his wares. After each show he settled back into his home and took inventory. Then he called me to let me know how many guns he sold. Over the months since I first signed Ed as a Kimber dealer, we had become friends, often chatting for an hour after we finalized the week's restocking order.

Technically, he violated the rules of the Kimber dealer program, which required that he must have a traditional retail store. But I let him skate, which meant that he owed me. And I liked Uncle Ed, a nickname he seemed to be OK with. He was my chance to interact with a hard-nosed character plucked from a crime novel, and he sold a lot of guns for us.

Uncle Ed did not have deep financial resources, but he could afford to invest in guns because they were a safe business bet. In those days, before the sales spikes and massive production increases, guns always held their value. By the end of my career, gun factories would multiply their capacities by as much as 500 percent, which would result in wild price fluctuations, but back then gun companies were small, and supply was limited. This meant that prices went up every year. Uncle Ed could invest in guns with little fear of losing money. They were even better than cash.

As Dave Fitzgerald began celebrating his birthday across town, I proposed a simple transaction that meant risk for Uncle Ed. In exchange for a $25,000 prepayment in the form of a certified check, I would provide Ed with guns worth at least $35,000 on his next order. In other words, I'd pay him $10,000 to bail us out. Ed knew Kimber's delivery system was sporadic in those days. His business depended on getting the right guns in time, and Kimber often missed shipments to him. I told him that Greg was the reason.

"OK, Busse," Ed said, after thinking about my plan. "I'll do it because you asked me to do it. But I swear—"

"Thanks, Uncle Ed! I owe you. Now go get the check. You don't have much time."

I grabbed my jacket and drove to Greg's house for the party. I could hear the thumping music even as I parked. As I opened the front door, I saw a stripper lying naked in the middle of Greg's living-room floor. She had shaving cream smeared from her neck to her knees with a tic-tac-toe grid drawn through the Barbasol. She looked up to see me as I opened the door.

"Hey, Ryan! Remember me? I'm *Unique*." I knew Unique, or whatever her real name was, from the many impromptu business meetings that Greg had conducted at the Riverside Corral. I smiled at her as I continued walking.

I found Greg leaning in the corner of his kitchen, laughing with Dave and a few other machinists. Between jokes he chugged white wine from a bottle. He looked up to see me, and then yelled over the loud music. "Ryan! Great fucking job on this party. See, this is how you motivate a workforce!"

I leaned toward him so that I could yell into his ear. I explained that I had found a way to get the money for payroll and that one of our dealers would send us the money in the morning. He was ecstatic and handed me the bottle. "That's fucking awesome, Ryan. I knew I could count on you. Now let's get fucked up and have a good time."

Just as I took a drink, I heard an excited cheer from the living room: "Tic-tac-fucking-toe!"

The next day I drove to the airport to get the check from Uncle Ed. I then sped back to Celeste so that she could deposit the money just in time to keep everyone's checks from bouncing. When I found her at the office, she was waiting for news. I just nodded and handed her the check, and she hugged me again.

Greg arrived at the office late that afternoon. He stomped into the building but not as fast as he usually did. When he saw me, he asked me to stay into the evening to discuss strategy. He had recently launched a woodworking operation in San José, Costa Rica, that employed about a dozen women. His stated reason for the operation was that labor costs were low and Kimber could save money by outsourcing the woodworking to Central America.

He called me into his office again after dark. When I found him, he was in the middle of the room leaning back in his office chair, looking over the top of his glasses at the checkering on another hand-carved gun stock. He tossed the stock on his desk and rolled his chair in front of his large file drawer. He yanked it open, and a dozen warm cans of Miller Genuine Draft banged around. He grabbed one and began chugging it as it foamed over his chin and onto the floor. He then tossed me a beer and motioned for me to drink. "Ryan, this Costa Rica deal is going really good. You would not believe how they treat a guy with a few American dollars down there. Like a god, I tell you! I'll let you in on a little secret. Some people go to Costa Rica for the sport fishing, but most never get past the sport fucking!" I just nodded as he opened another beer. "That reminds me. Have I shown you my interpreters?"

"Nope, I don't think so."

He then opened his top drawer and grabbed a handful of photos of beautiful Costa Rican women, shuffling through them like a deck of cards. "You should come down with me, Ryan." He smiled. "I could teach you more management lessons."

"Greg, I think someone better stay here and focus on making some American dollars."

He slammed his beer on the desk, then slid a piece of paper out from under the can, wiping the beer from it as he read. "Let me help. Celeste gave me this report today. We have some past-due accounts. There are some dealers on here who owe us a bunch of money. Like this one." He pointed to the top line on the list:

Account 347
Vern's General Store
Salmon, Idaho
$15,755
PAST DUE: 90 Days

"When you get back to Montana, I need you to start taking care of these receivables," Greg said, "and especially this Vern asshole." For some reason when Greg said things like this, his accent just made them all sound like fun.

"Sure, Greg. I'll look into it next week."

That night I called Dwight to inform him of the situation. I was pretty worked up, and I told him about the strippers and the parties and the booze. I gave him my candid assessment of Greg: "It's a complete disaster, man. We're gonna crumble at any time. Shit, your paycheck would have bounced if I had not cashed in a favor to get money from Uncle Ed."

Dwight didn't want to hear that our risky experiment with Kimber might just fail. He believed that I was a naive ranch kid and probably just exaggerating. "I trust Greg. He knows what he's doing, and it's all going to be fine."

"If you say so," I sighed.

The next day Greg flew to Costa Rica, and I left my room at the Super 8 to drive back to Kalispell. Kimber once again teetered on bankruptcy. I worried that Dwight and I would add our names to the list of people that Greg had suckered into his Kimber game. He was hardly the genius that Dwight had made him out to be. Many, including Dwight, had invested personal money, and now we had both invested our careers.

On the six-hundred-mile drive back to Montana I had a lot of time to think. *This is not how I imagined my rookie season might go.* I remembered back to Burris and how it had not lived up to my expectations either. I remembered the excitement I felt as Dwight and I discussed our shared dream of working in the gun business. None of these dreams included stripper breakfasts, shaving cream, or overnight checks arriving via Northwest Airlines. And they certainly did not include cargoes of illegal gun confiscations and late-night border runs, but I'd soon figure out a way to jam those into my rookie season too.

A dozen years later I'd play for big industry trophies and fight important political battles. But for now I was just trying to be the rookie of the year and keep this little company afloat for another day.

FIVE

MOVING IRON

*D*ING! DWIGHT EXCITEDLY SLAPPED THE ORANGE BELL ON the table between us. It was the same sort of bell you would tap to call a sleepy motel manager from the back room. Dwight had bought the thing and then demanded that we use it to celebrate our wins as we spent long hours together.

"Jim Carmichael loves our guns! He's gonna do a story on them!" Carmichael, the longtime shooting editor of *Outdoor Life* magazine and an industry icon, could sway sales with a single positive article. Dwight paused, expecting me to respond with excitement or a high five. I just sat there in silence as a thought came to me. He rang it again and looked at me for feedback.

"Moving iron!" I finally said. Dwight cocked his head in curiosity. "'Moving iron,' that's what we're going to call it when we sell guns. You know, like a bartender at a college bar. They don't just serve drinks; they sling beer! We need our own term like that—for gunrunning."

"Um, OK, yeah," Dwight replied as he started to see the fun of developing our own slang.

"Hit the bell again," I said. He slapped it, and I followed with another snappy bark: "Moving iron!" Dwight smiled, and a few minutes later I finished a sales call with a large dealer in Texas, then swung around to smack the orange bell. Dwight beat me to it. "Moved some iron!"

If we had needed to come up with our own term twenty-five years later, it would have been a trending social media hashtag. Over time, at bars and trade shows and on phone calls, we started to spread the term to dealers and other gun companies. They did not have a motel bell like ours, but before long, gun salesmen across the country were moving iron.

Although Dwight and I had made a dent in sales, I was still concerned by what I had learned in Portland. I repeatedly tried to explain to Dwight that Kimber was on the verge of collapse and that Greg was little more than an oversexed frat boy with a bald head and an accent. Dwight had none of it. "All we can do is sell guns," he snapped. "Even if you're right, the only way to get out of this is to be really good at what we do, right? Whether this company lives or dies is probably up to us."

Dwight promoted and made connections with writers from important gun magazines, hoping to create more consumer demand. I built the dealer network and sold guns. The orange motel bell got a lot of use because we would not tolerate failure. Dwight and I moved a lot of iron.

After Greg returned from Costa Rica and whatever fun he had with his "interpreters," he settled back into running the company and throwing parties in Portland. We held a few meetings to talk about customers and new rifles, but eventually Greg got around to making a call about our last conversation in Portland. I could hear the thumping music of a strip club in the background. He must have seen that past-due report again over breakfast.

"Ryan, goddamnit, I told you. That Vern's General Store place. Account 347. They owe us a bunch of money. It's not that far from you. I want you to get your ass down there and collect the debt. It's about bloody time we get that money!"

"I'm not a debt collector," I told him. "And it's farther than you think. I need to be here selling, not playing collection agent."

That's when Greg pulled rank. "Ryan, time for another management lesson," he said, seriously. "You need to do whatever it takes in a small company. *Everything is your job.* Today, you are a professional salesman. Tomorrow, you are a professional debt-collection specialist. Got that?"

"What if they have no Kimbers left on the shelves? Or what if they won't pay?"

"Ryan, goddamnit, just get over there and figure out a way to get the money. Just dream up something! I hate assholes who don't pay their bills!"

I paused for a moment, hoping Greg would realize the irony of what he just said. But he didn't. He was too comfortable spending his life shuffling money around and stiffing vendors in order to keep his company and his lifestyle afloat. The urgency in his voice probably meant that we were about to bounce payroll again or that he needed to fund a few more parties.

VERNON AND DARLA SEYMOUR HAD BUILT VERN'S GENERAL Store, a small all-purpose retail store, on the banks of the Salmon River on the west side of Salmon, Idaho. They spent a lifetime selling groceries, fishing licenses, ice, and guns. Vern and Darla were hardworking entrepreneurs who dedicated their lives to their small business. Vern took pride in his store and in paying his bills, but about the time I started at Kimber, he started transferring the store to new owners, who quickly got in over their heads. It was months before Kimber realized that we were shipping them guns without collecting money for them. The new owner of Vern's owed Kimber more than $15,000.

"Shit, I have to go to Idaho tomorrow and try to get the money out of Vern's," I told Dwight as I spun my chair around to explain the instructions from Greg.

Dwight laughed. "Guess you won't be moving any iron tomorrow. Does Greg know it's a five-hour drive?" Then he lowered his voice. "And I bet they don't have any Kimbers left or any money to pay. They've been dodging calls from Celeste for weeks! You'll have to shock them to get anything."

Early the next morning, before 4:00, I pulled on a pair of freshly pressed khaki pants and a starched shirt. I threw a tie and a navy-blue coat on the passenger's seat and set off for Idaho. I pulled into the parking lot of Vern's before it even opened.

There were two other trucks waiting in the parking lot. One belonged to a family logging operation. It was dirty and dented with a big diesel tank in the back and winch cables on the front bumper. A man in pitch-stained logging pants jumped out of the truck. He was unshaven, with big, calloused hands. The man held a gun case in his right hand, and I guessed that he needed to sell it for some quick cash before he went to work.

Parked a few spaces from him was a flatbed ranch truck. An Australian shepherd looked at me curiously from its perch on a hay bale in the back. This was the sort of truck I grew up with, and I knew the man inside would emerge with worn cowboy boots and a sweaty felt cowboy hat. As he stepped out and pulled the hat on, he shoved a few bills into the back pocket of his Wranglers.

I finished with my tie in the rearview mirror, pulled on my sport coat, and climbed out of my truck to join the other two in the parking lot. The logger and the rancher both stopped in their tracks and looked at me as if I came from another planet. They made it to the door before me, and I stood in the back as the store's new owner, Aaron, completed the first transactions of the day. Aaron kept one eye on me through it all. Indeed, the logger traded in his rifle for some cash, and the rancher made a layaway payment on a handgun, and then they both left.

Now I was the only person in the cramped store, stuffed with dusty knickknacks, elk and deer mounts on the walls, and shelves of fishing and hunting gear—including a few dozen rifles and shotguns I recognized. I made my way through the PowerBait and life jackets to Aaron, who stood behind the gun counter.

"I am Ryan Busse," I said, trying to command the situation, just like Mr. T would. "From, um, Kimber. And you owe us $15,000." Aaron narrowed his eyes and stuck his chin up. "And I'm here to collect the money you owe our company."

"I figured as much. Nice tie," he scoffed. "Well, I don't have any of your guns. We sold them all." I let the pause in conversation become uncomfortable. "But let me talk to my wife."

Aaron disappeared into his back room as another customer came inside and browsed. I heard Aaron make a phone call, but I couldn't hear what he was saying. When he returned to the counter, he raised his voice. "Why don't you just get the hell out of here," he snarled. "I don't want you stressing out my customers." The browsing customer in the corner looked surprised. "I just talked to Bruce, and he said I don't have to let you in here."

"You don't have to let me in, but since I'm already here, I'm telling you you're past due. And who's Bruce?"

"Bruce is my attorney. If you don't get the hell out of here, I'll make another call that won't be to Bruce. And you'll be shown outta here the quick way."

"Why don't I call Bruce, then?"

"Get the hell out of my store!"

I didn't say another word and headed back to my truck. Frustrated and famished, I drove back down the road and stopped at a diner to have breakfast and consider my options.

"Clearly you ain't from here," the waitress said, pouring my coffee. Self-conscious, I loosened my tie. "Where ya from?"

"Montana. Not too far."

"Business?"

"Hopefully. Say, you don't know an attorney named Bruce, do you?"

WILS

PET

xxxxxx3788

Exp: 10/2/2022

Item: 0010104445811
338.47623 B967B

"How many attorneys do you think we got around here? Of course I know Bruce, honey. Want me to get the phone book for you? You can use our phone to call him."

I found the attorney's number and slipped behind the counter to use the phone in the diner. "Bruce, I know you just talked to Aaron, and apparently you told him he doesn't need to pay me."

"I don't have a lot of time for the likes of you," Bruce told me.

"Well, let me tell you about my company. My boss is Greg Warne. He is wealthy and mean, and he has an army of lawyers. He will spend a hundred grand just to get the $15,000 your client owes us because he considers it a wise investment to spend $85,000 sending a message to everyone else. I'm guessing Aaron doesn't want to be our test case, and I'm guessing he's not exactly making you rich. So unless you want to get bogged down in court for a year with a client who won't pay you, you might want to tell Aaron to do whatever needs to be done to settle this with me today." Bruce didn't say anything. "I'll be finishing my coffee at the diner for a few more minutes, and I advise that you call me back while I'm still here."

I hung up knowing that I had gone for broke with a long-shot story mostly consisting of bullshit, but I reasoned it was my only chance. I gave the waitress a five-dollar bill as she walked by. "If he calls me back, can you grab me?"

Moments later the waitress came back to my table with a pot of coffee and said, "Well, Bruce just called. Didn't want to talk to you. But he asked me to tell you that you can go back and take care of it. Don't know what that means, but sounds like you need some more coffee."

A few minutes later I returned to Vern's. As I walked in, Aaron and his wife were standing angry and square-armed behind the gun counter in the back of the store. "We don't have any of your guns, and we don't have any cash!" Aaron yelled.

I stopped and looked around. "Look, I know that your lawyer gave you what I'm sure is good advice. You have a lot of good guns in here. How about I pick out $15,000 worth of guns and we call it even?"

Aaron didn't say a word. He slowly looked at his wife, who shrugged. Then he looked back at me and nodded. I started on the north wall and picked out a nice Winchester Model 70 chambered in .270, and then I saw two Thompson Contenders. "I'll take those two Remingtons and that Beretta too." Before long, I had about twenty guns stacked up on the counter. "That should be about $15K worth. Let's load 'em up."

As Aaron threw the last of the guns in the back seat of my truck, he glared at me. "We are square, right?"

"Yup, we are square," I answered. "You're debt-free, as far as Kimber's concerned."

"I hope I never see your ass again," he muttered as he ignored the offer of my handshake and stormed back into his store.

I jumped in my truck full of guns and drove out of town as fast as I could go. I realized that I might be mistaken for a criminal in a movie. I had no receipt and had done no background check. For all anyone knew, I was transporting a load of stolen guns.

An hour down the road, I nervously yanked off my tie and wriggled out of my jacket behind the wheel. As I approached the Montana state line, I started to worry. Aaron was angry, and I knew I had stretched the rules of engagement with my creative debt-collection tactics. Surely he would also realize that I didn't even have any paperwork to verify my story. I thought he might call the logger or rancher to chase me down. Or maybe he would just call the Bureau of Alcohol, Tobacco and Firearms to report stolen guns. I wouldn't have blamed him, and either scenario would mean an end to my budding career.

I made it home late that night, and the next morning I peered outside to make sure there were no angry loggers or federal agents at my doorstep. But then another sinking realization started to overcome me. On one hand, I had "figured something out" as Greg instructed. But I knew he really expected a cash payment and that he likely needed that cash immediately. As this sank in, I worried that Greg's reaction to my acquisition of confiscated guns might mean the end of my job.

"Bet that was a long day," Dwight said as we sat down in front of our computers. "How'd it go?" Before I could answer, Greg called. He never called this early. I put him on speaker, and Dwight listened to the whole story along with Greg. I prepared for an angry tirade about funds for another house party or threats about paychecks bouncing, but Greg just erupted with congratulatory laughter.

"That's fucking great, Ryan! Holy shit, there are some good guns in there. I knew I could count on you! I've always wanted a good Model 70. You and Dwight pick out two or three others for yourselves, then send me the rest. We will call the debt erased!" Technically, I had not recovered a single dime on Account 347, but Greg was ecstatic. "Ryan, when you get back to Portland, I'll treat you to a great breakfast, and Stephanie will be working!" And then he hung up before I could respond.

This sort of stunt would never fly today. Most gun stores are now filled with tactical guns, many of which were illegal then. Today, gun stores are staffed by armed employees who would never allow a stranger to take valuable merchandise without a literal firefight. Back then, all it took was bravado and a tie. I pulled the whole thing off by the seat of my khaki pants. For a moment I wondered how I had ended up running guns in this industry for a crazy Australian, but as far as I knew, this is how all gun companies worked. I grinned at my success and at the craziness of it all. *I have some talent for this*, I realized.

Dwight sat in his chair, stunned and silent, slowly shaking his head and doubting what he just heard. I looked at him and slowly reached over and quietly tapped the orange bell.

"Moving iron!"

SIX

KILLERS, CLINGERS, AND CLINTONS

F OR MORE THAN TWO HUNDRED YEARS THE UNITED STATES operated under unspoken rules that governed our politics and the firearms industry. Since the ink dried on the parchment of our founding documents, gun manufacturers have simply evolved with the growth of our country. Yes, the Second Amendment protected basic gun ownership, but as firearms became more lethal, cheaper, and accessible, the laws that governed them changed to keep up too—at least for the most part.

Our nation came to expect the legal evolution. When the military developed powerful weapons of war, Congress passed laws to protect average citizens and prohibit civilian ownership. When gangster murders ravaged the country in the 1930s, the public spoke up to demand laws limiting access to fully automatic weapons. When John Kennedy was murdered with a gun that was advertised on the back page of the NRA's *American Rifleman* magazine and then ordered through the mail, Congress passed laws to require in-store retail licensing and gun transfers. During testimony on that 1968 law, the NRA's own vice president offered reasoned and sober congressional testimony: "We do not think that any sane American, who calls himself an American, can object to placing into this bill the instrument which killed the president of the United States."[1]

This was how it was supposed to work. The gradual application of laws applied to guns and gunmakers just as they did to all other facets of life. Imperfect as it was, this basic structure meant that for more than two centuries people like me, who worked for gun companies, paid close attention to news and political events. Everyone knew that the laws governing the manufacture and sale of firearms were directly related to both.

Throughout the early part of my career we carried on the tradition of watching the news. We were consumed by current events and politics because we all assumed that most of what we observed was part of that two-hundred-year-old system. But something new was rumbling below the surface. The evidence of tectonic shifts came in headlines about domestic, anti-government insurrections such as the standoffs at Waco and Ruby Ridge, and the bombing of the Alfred P. Murrah Federal Building in Oklahoma City. The 1980s and 1990s also saw the rise of a terrifying and inexplicable new kind of domestic terrorism: mass shootings.

All Americans would eventually live within a new kind of politics where these horrific events only increased pressure in a political world that blocked all solutions, a system in which gun executives like me no longer had to watch the news because no report, no matter how shocking, could produce legislative actions that threatened to remake our business.

By the time I sped back from Vern's General Store with that truckload of confiscated guns, five men were already triggering the change. John Hinckley Jr., Patrick Purdy, George Hennard, Gian Luigi Ferri, and William Jefferson Clinton were the catalysts, and the industry I had just entered was poised to play the leading role in this massive remaking of US politics.

It all started in March 1981, fifteen years before my trip to Salmon, Idaho. On a blustery day in DC, John Hinckley Jr. fidgeted outside the Washington Hilton as he waited for President Reagan to finish speaking at an AFL-CIO luncheon. As President Reagan smiled, waved, and then walked across the sidewalk to his waiting limousine, Hinckley pushed through security and began shooting at the president with a small .22-caliber revolver, a gun that functioned just like the Ruger Bearcat I had learned to shoot as a boy.

Hinckley only wounded the president, likely because the caliber of the gun and the size of the bullet were so small. But all firearms are lethal weapons, and even small bullets caused horrible injury to the president and two other men, one of whom was the president's beloved press secretary, James Brady.

One of Hinckley's bullets struck Brady in the head and caused life-threatening brain injuries, then serious speech and motor issues for the rest of his life. For years after the shooting, Brady appeared in interviews and on news shows with slurred words and physical difficulty that constantly reminded the public of the horrible impacts of gun violence.

Sarah, Brady's wife, formed the Brady Center to Prevent Gun Violence, and she became an outspoken advocate for gun-control measures. James and Sarah Brady's signature cause was to ensure that gun sales require background checks in an effort to prohibit people like John Hinckley Jr. from owning a gun. Sarah Brady made progress. Because of her savvy lobbying and dogged determination, Congress considered the so-called Brady Bill a few times, but never with enough political pressure to vault it over the final hurdle.

In the meantime, the gun industry kept moving iron, and lead as well. Eight years later, a troubled man entered a store in Oregon and purchased a Chinese knockoff of the Russian Kalashnikov assault rifle. On January 17, 1989, Patrick Edward Purdy shoved that rifle into his Chevrolet station wagon and drove to Cleveland Elementary School in Stockton, California. As he parked near the school, the twenty-five-year-old lit his car on fire with a Molotov cocktail, loaded his AK-47 rifle, and walked into the crowded schoolyard playground, where he began shooting randomly at young children. He fired 106 rounds in less than two minutes. When he stopped, five children were dead, and thirty-two more were injured.

This event became known as the Stockton schoolyard shooting. Purdy finished his bloody spree by taking his own life with a Taurus pistol.

Police had arrested Purdy multiple times and knew that he supported White supremacy organizations. As news of his background leaked, there was a growing call for action. Days later, *Time* magazine summed up the mood of the nation: "The easy availability of weapons like this, which have no purpose other than killing human beings, can all too readily turn the delusions of sick gunmen into tragic nightmares."[2] In words that echoed the pleas of Sarah and James Brady, *Time* also addressed the background-check issue: "Why could Purdy, an alcoholic who had been arrested for such offenses as selling weapons and attempted robbery, walk into a gun shop in Sandy, Oregon, and leave with an AK-47 under his arm?" Politicians took notice. A copy of the magazine almost certainly made it into the governor's residence in Little Rock, Arkansas.

And then in October 1991, barely a year before the 1992 presidential election, George Hennard, an unemployed thirty-five-year-old former Merchant Marine, drove his truck through the window of a crowded Luby's restaurant in Killeen, Texas. After the crash, Hennard waded into the diner with a Glock 17, a gun that came standard with seventeen-round high-capacity magazines. Hennard screamed his misogynistic screed as he targeted and shot mostly women. By the time his massacre was over, he had killed twenty-three people and injured twenty-seven. Like Purdy, Hennard used the last of his ammunition to kill himself.

Unlike today, when many politicians offer little more than "thoughts and prayers" without an actual legislative response, the calls for tighter gun control began the day after Hennard's mass shooting during a scheduled vote on a crime bill in the US House of Representatives. Proposed language in that bill would have banned high-capacity pistols like Hennard's Glock. Even then, the NRA succeeded in narrowly defeating the measure, but the pressure in our old system crept ever upward. Legislative relief was on the way.

As political pressure built up, an aspiring Texas politician watched the fallout with a keen eye. By the time George W. Bush became Texas governor a few years later, in 1995, he was already on the "less control" side of the gun issue.

Four years after the Luby's shooting, during the debate over guns in Texas, the young governor listened earnestly and sided with a lobbyist named Suzanna Hupp. Hupp had survived the 1991 Luby's attack as she watched Hennard murder both her parents. Rather than fight against guns, she became an outspoken advocate for *greater availability* of guns. Hupp was an early adopter of what would come to be known as "the good guy with a gun" theory, which argues that if more people have guns, there is a higher likelihood that a bad guy will be shot by the good guys. Hupp ultimately convinced Governor Bush to expand the right of all Texas citizens to carry concealed guns.

Bush's role in the larger national gun debate would come, but back then the moment belonged to another young governor, Bill Clinton. The mass shootings wrought on America by Hinckley, Purdy, and Hennard had frightened the country and provided Clinton a political opportunity. Clinton was a talented student of American politics, and he ran his 1992 race against Bush's father by leaning into the controversial Brady Bill. In fact, the young governor even made it a central promise of his campaign.

This bold embrace of gun control was new for the Democratic Party. Governor Clinton used it artfully against the incumbent president. During their hard-fought 1992 campaign, Clinton reminded voters that George H. W. Bush had vetoed the Brady Bill and that he had repeatedly caved to pressure from the NRA. Clinton painted President Bush as soft on crime and beholden to special interests. The same public that created this pressure bought Clinton's message, and he won in a rare defeat of an incumbent president.

In the White House, Clinton kept his promise. After lengthy debate, he and a carefully crafted coalition of thought leaders and lawmakers beat back intense lobbying by the NRA, and the Brady Bill passed. Just one year after becoming president, Clinton had rallied the nation's elected leaders, including several Republicans, to create a new gun policy in defiance of the NRA. With James Brady in a wheelchair by his side, Clinton signed the bill on November 30, 1993.

To most citizens this simple signature and its complex ramifications seemed as natural as gravity or the change in seasons. This was how America's democracy was supposed to work: our gun laws evolved with the will of a majority of our nation. This was a law that would keep thousands of people like Tolly Bolyard from buying a gun. It was a good thing for our country, yet inside the NRA and the gun industry some were already starting to envision a new reality that would force unimagined stress tests onto our political system.

The nation started on its final steps toward that new reality on July 1, 1993, when Gian Luigi Ferri walked off an elevator inside a California law firm wielding two Tec-9 assault pistols. The menacing Tec-9 pistols were known to be the choice of street gangs and criminals. Ferri equipped his guns with controversial "Hellfire" triggers and high-capacity magazines, legal features that greatly increased the speed and lethality of the guns. In the hands of this troubled man, who left hateful, incoherent notes in his wake, the impacts of these guns were disastrous. In a matter of seconds, Ferri killed eight innocent people and wounded six others.

President Clinton knew how to read the mood of a frightened public, and he knew it was time to act. The Brady Bill had been a start, but it was not enough. Across the country, troubled men had taken innocent lives at random, with warlike speed and godlike power. Ferri's massacre, known as the 101 California Street shooting, provided the last nudge that the Clinton administration needed to pass the 1994 crime bill. It seemed clear to most reasonable political observers that the massive bill should include the Public Safety and Recreational Firearms Use Protection Act, more commonly known as the assault weapons ban. Senator Joe Biden of Delaware agreed. He sponsored the legislation and promised to play a central role in shepherding it through Congress.

As the bill made its way through the Senate and House, lawmakers had to first agree on the definition of *assault weapon*. This quickly became a hot debate because many popular hunting rifles and shotguns shared the same semiautomatic fire-control system as AR-15s, AK-47s, and Tec-9s. Knowing that most Americans thought of hunting as relatively safe, wholesome, and harmless, organizations like the NRA used this social acceptability to frighten voters by claiming that Clinton was trying to ban hunting guns, adding that people inside his administration were so out of touch they couldn't tell one gun from another. Their arguments gained some traction because gun-control advocates often confused such terms as *semiautomatic* and *fully automatic*.

Fully automatic firearms, including any military rifle that can be converted to shoot in a continuous mode of fire, had been strictly regulated since the days of Al Capone's tommy guns. Just like the political pressures of the 1990s, an outcry over gun violence in 1934 produced the National Firearms Act (NFA). In proof of the NFA's efficacy, none of the guns used in the shootings of the 1980s and 1990s were *fully* automatic. Indeed, no mass shooting over the past twenty-five years has involved a fully automatic gun.

From a distance, there is no easy way to distinguish fully automatic guns from semiautomatic guns. In fact, many assault-style guns such as the AR-15 can be either semiautomatic (for civilian use) or fully automatic (for military use). Semiauto guns, like my brother Cory's Model 60 Marlin, must be loaded and manually cocked for the first shot. Then the gun uses the gases and energy created by the explosion of a cartridge to cycle the next shot.

But unlike fully automatic guns, the shooter of a semiauto gun must pull the trigger to fire a single bullet. The rapid, "zipper-spray" sound of weapons common in movies or *A-Team* episodes comes from fully automatic guns. A semiauto can be fired quickly, but only as fast as the shooter can pull its trigger.

Because fully auto guns were already strictly regulated, the assault weapons ban focused on the semiauto fire-control system. So what exactly was an assault weapon? Some guns, such as the Tec-9, needed no debate, and Congress specifically banned them by name. The broader definition was more complicated. It started with semiauto weapons but included add-on features such as folding stocks, detachable magazines, pistol grips, flash suppressors, and grenade launchers. The parameters in Congress's final version of the law meant that a gun would be considered an assault weapon if it had two or more of these features. Congress also banned any magazine with more than ten rounds, therefore setting the definition of *high capacity* at eleven rounds or more.

The NRA and firearms enthusiasts fought like hell to weaken the bill. They made the case that the technical definition was so broad and would include so many guns that no reasonable person could define them. Those writing the legislation ultimately agreed, and more than 650 specific guns, including hundreds commonly used for hunting, were exempted from the final regulation. Under the new law, Cory's rifle, a gun that held seventeen rounds in a tubular magazine, remained legal. In a final nod to the powerful gun lobbyists, lawmakers also added a grandfather clause to the bill that exempted any guns or magazines sold before the law's enactment.

During the whole debate, as I cut my teeth in this industry, manufacturers, dealers, and consumers went into a frenzy. All the uncertainty and attention, plus a strong fear and distrust of Bill and Hillary Clinton, meant that consumers rushed to buy any guns that might be banned, and gun sales *exploded*.

In 1991, prior to the shootings in Texas and California and before Clinton's election victory, the people of America purchased about eleven thousand guns per day. By 1993, when Dwight and I were just starting to discuss Kimber, gun enthusiasts began to fear the outcome of Clinton's legislation, and the nation's appetite for guns doubled to nearly twenty-one thousand per day. The sales increased when the NRA and the industry simply switched their name for the legislation to the simpler—and scarier—"Clinton gun ban."

Gun-rights organizations succeeded in helping to temper the bill's language, but at the end of the day the NRA could not stave off a bipartisan surge in support of the law. In a final snub to the NRA, former presidents Carter, Ford, and even conservative icon Ronald Reagan sent a letter to all members of Congress urging them to "listen to the American public and to the law enforcement community":

> This is a matter of vital importance to the public safety. Although assault weapons account for less than 1% of the guns in circulation, they account for nearly 10% of the guns traced to crime. . . . While we recognize that assault weapon legislation will not stop all assault weapon crime, statistics prove that we can dry up the supply of these guns, making them less accessible to criminals.[3]

The letter worked. On September 13, 1994, the bill passed with a slim 52–48 majority in the Senate. Clinton wasted no time. His team rushed a ceremony at the White House, where he signed the bill into law that afternoon.

From that day forward, guns and magazines that were legal under the bill were termed "post-ban." Grandfathered guns that were now illegal to manufacture were called "pre-ban." The grandfather clause dictated that the pre-ban weapons could be owned and sold, just not manufactured. So for years, these pre-ban guns and high-capacity magazines commanded high prices at gun shows and in private sales.

That autumn day in the White House Rose Garden marked the turning point for our national politics. The NRA learned important and unforgettable lessons in this narrow defeat, reactions to which were so loud that a sleeping giant in US politics stirred awake. The organization had fought hard, but not hard enough. It had chipped away at defectors, but it failed to demand 100 percent loyalty. It had used fear of loss, but not enough to convince elected officials that they would lose their seats to pissed-off and terrified single-issue voters. The NRA had criticized leaders who voted for the bill but did not *demonize* them. The organization linked the gun issue to other hot-button right-wing social issues, but not enough to sway the last few senators they needed. The NRA allowed debate on the merits of the law instead of using all-or-nothing arguments and wild conspiracy theories. It even allowed a beloved Republican former president to lobby against its cause. These were all important lessons for the organization to quickly correct. They were not errors the NRA would make again.

In the aftermath of its stinging loss, the NRA also found three reasons for celebration. The first was the elevation of Bill and Hillary Clinton, who turned out to be fundraising megastars for the NRA. From that day forward, any mention of the Clintons and their easily understood threat to freedom and guns resulted in ready cash and new memberships. The NRA would go back to that well time and again, eventually elevating Hillary Rodham Clinton to her own special fundraising category.

The second reason was a realization that fear of impending elections or legislation could be used to *explode* gun sales and NRA memberships. The NRA knew it could deploy this tactic at the slightest whisper of any anti-gun legislation or even a candidate who had been a community organizer in, say, Chicago.

The third reason for celebration was language slipped into the legislation in an attempt to garner enough Republican votes for passage. At the insistence of the NRA, negotiators added a sunset provision to the text, mandating the expiration of all components of the ban if a future president did not reenact the bill with a simple signature. Including that provision seemed safe. Back then, most Americans broadly accepted it. Even a New York real estate developer named Donald Trump weighed in with support. As he said in 2000, "I generally oppose gun control, but I support the ban on assault weapons and I support a slightly longer waiting period to purchase a gun."[4]

At the time, statements like Trump's illustrated why no one could conceive of a political situation where a president would be foolish enough to publicly allow assault weapons back into everyday life. But no one could conceive of the political changes on the horizon or that George H. W. Bush's son, the same Texas governor who responded to the Luby's shooting by expanding gun rights in his own state, would be president on September 13, 2004, the date of the long-awaited sunset.

Reaction to the new legislation consumed every waking moment for members of the shooting industry. By the time I was taking orders from Greg Warne, the 1994 sales boom was long over. Many of the stores that cashed in during the run-up to the ban had gone out of business. I had not picked the best time to become a gunrunner. Keeping a company afloat was hard. Building a new one? Almost impossible.

There was no fear, no impending crisis, no legislation, and nothing to scare people into buying more guns. By the time I was working to be rookie of the year, gun sales in the country had been cut in half, dropping down to fewer than four million units per year.

The NRA used the difficulty in the gun business to convince gun companies and gun owners that Bill Clinton and his political party were starving and marginalizing them. This was the first effort by the NRA to create anger and a perception of aggrievement, and it worked. Exceptionally well.

This is when the NRA realized that it had to play a long game. Immediately after Clinton's 1994 legislative win, it began forming a strategic coalition with the religious Right. From that day forward, guns would be intertwined with other divisive political issues such as abortion, which resulted in religiously loyal single-issue voters. Twenty years later, America's first Black president would say that these aggrieved voters "clinged to their religion and guns," without necessarily realizing that his words only made the situation worse.

In November 1994, before either the NRA or Newt Gingrich had any idea that these voters would come to be labeled as "clingers," the confrontational House leader connected the social issues together and harnessed the firepower of the NRA to give Clinton a stinging defeat in the midterm elections. Just two months after Clinton signed the assault weapons ban, Republicans gained eight seats in the Senate and fifty-four in the House, retaking control of both chambers of Congress. This was the first visible sign that guns and the NRA were to be central in the nation's unfolding political upheaval.

As the feelings of aggrievement took hold, most people in the gun business believed that we were fighting a war being waged by Democrats who were directly targeting our industry. Like many young men itching to fight, I instinctively wanted to help win the battle. Without thinking too much about it, I found myself casually bad-mouthing President Clinton and often taking part in industry banter that labeled all gun-control legislation as evil. Politicians who supported it were even worse.

This was the same feeling of marginalization I remembered from my days growing up in flyover country. By the time I got to college, I had been ready to take on the liberals directly. I suppose that I was a gifted student, but I considered myself wise to the ploys of educators whom I had been warned about on the conservative talk radio that flowed freely in ranch trucks and tractors. I spoke up in classes and regularly played the role of devil's advocate. When given the opportunity, I expressed conservative opinions and stood up for kids like me who felt put upon and disrespected, completely oblivious to the fact that I had grown up with more opportunity and privilege than most.

My background and antipathy meant that I fit into the firearms industry perfectly. Just like ranch kids, gun people were disrespected and flown over, dismissed by faraway, pompous elitists who thought they knew better, and that created a lot of simmering anger. People like me were grappling for a unifying point of resistance, and guns fit the bill perfectly. Magnifying guns as symbols became the central project for the NRA, and that symbolic resistance would grow into the hinge pin of our new national political system.

As I found my footing professionally, the NRA was using the anger in the gun business to make up its own definition of good and evil. Soon it succeeded and bound up the industry with the Republican Party: one huge, reliable block of moral activists. The immediate message was clear: Bill Clinton and the Democrats were *evil*. I was supposed to fight them. It was *right* to fight them. After all, my industry had given me plenty of fear and hatred to work with.

Sure, the blind anger seemed justified, but we should have all seen the warning signs telling us how dangerous it would all become. Just months before I started at Kimber, Timothy McVeigh, a man who sealed his letters with "I Am the NRA" stickers, was so motivated by this fear and hatred that he blew up the federal building in Oklahoma City. Other early extremist events should have urged caution against taking this rhetoric too far. David Koresh and the Branch Davidians, the Freeman in Montana, and the Unabomber—they were all motivated by guns and irrational fears.

But back in 1996, I just wanted to slap that orange bell. I wanted to live the life I wished to be true—just like those days with my dad. Many of my assumptions seemed fixed. Guns were central to the best parts of an American life, the NRA was just a club for enthusiasts and responsible gun owners, and success was worth fighting for.

Today the power of the NRA and the pervasive growth of guns in our society seem clear, but to those of us inside the industry back then, the path was not at all certain. We believed that we had to fight for survival. I was by nature an optimistic person, and that meant I focused on what I thought was good about my job and my industry. Besides, we all assumed that warning flags such as McVeigh were just aberrations. After all, almost everyone I knew owned plenty of guns, but we did not think of ourselves as potential mass murderers. Focusing on personal experience was a way for us to explain away other contradictory truths.

As my career advanced, there would be more and more red flags, but once I decided to rationalize a few, it was easy to ignore the next ones as well. I guess you could say I was a frog who had jumped into the gun-industry pot when the water was tolerable, and now the temperature was creeping up.

Many of the things I would encounter personally at Kimber should also have been warnings, but I found ways to explain them away too. I wanted to be successful and build a company. So did everyone else I knew in the business. Encouraged by the NRA, our entire industry seemed willing to accept the ideology and rhetoric just as long as these abstractions sold guns and built careers. After all, how bad could it really get?

SEVEN

BEATING A HANGOVER

IN THOSE EARLY DAYS AT KIMBER I FOUND WAYS TO FORGET OR rationalize the fact that guns were what connected all the stories of these extremists in the news. During those first couple of years I focused on my work, and this meant that I had almost daily conversations with Greg Warne. My time in Portland had shown me the hard truth about Greg's inability to manage a growing company, but he was the boss—or at least I thought he was—and that meant Dwight and I answered to him. Dwight believed there was genius in Greg, and I tried my best to see it. And I did learn a few valuable lessons from him that made me realize that our little company had a lot of promise.

Greg wanted to build and sell only guns that were beautiful and functional. As he used to say, "I don't ever want Kimber to be a company that sells cheap crap that ends up at crime scenes." On this point we agreed with each other entirely. But Greg was never a strong and principled leader or a dogged salesman. He had a passion for building beautiful, expensive guns with craft and care, leaving the hard part of selling them to me.

So I traveled the country visiting large gun dealers, and when not traveling I spent long days on the phone trying to knock down orders. We enjoyed some successes, but back then, sales did not come easy. The boom that had occurred before the assault weapons ban had sucked almost every available dollar out of every gun buyer's pocket, leaving me with a difficult job.

"It's like a massive hangover," Greg complained. "All these guys went out and bought all this military crap like they were drunk at a bar and were never going to be allowed to buy another shot. Now they're all sleeping it off, and we can't wake them the hell up."

Greg is right, I thought. *And this guy knows more than anyone about hangovers.*

Even years after that 1994 sales spike, firearms sales across the country remained at historic lows. Without the fear of another big election or more impending legislation, sales between 1995 and 1998 stagnated at barely half of what the industry experienced during the boom. I did not know it then, but the difficult market, along with Greg's lack of cash-management skills, had forced him to look for creative alternatives to keep Kimber afloat. He let one of them slip in an afternoon strategy conversation.

"Sorry, Ryan, but we're going to have to sell those old Mauser rifles that Nationwide has, and Leslie might even force us to sell that Daewoo shit. I hate it, but it's going to be part of Kimber for a while."

"Whoa, Greg," I replied. "A lot to unpack there. What Mausers? *Daewoo?*"

Nationwide was our distributor. And I was just beginning to understand that although Greg presented himself as founder, owner, and president of Kimber, the behind-the-scenes financial responsibilities belonged to Leslie Edelman, who was slowly and steadily purchasing percentages of Kimber. By then, Leslie was probably already Kimber's majority owner.

Leslie was in his midforties, but he seemed older. He shuffled when he walked, mumbled when he talked, and was notoriously moody. The first time I met Leslie, Dwight warned me about another of his traits just in time to save me from having an embarrassing reaction: "Be ready. It's like a cold *dish towel*." Dwight's warning didn't quite prepare me for how strange Leslie's cold and limp handshake really was.

Leslie had grown up under the wing of his entrepreneurial father, Harris Edelman. Harris started selling sporting goods and shooting accessories from his car, and he eventually founded Edelman's, a small sporting-goods chain based in eastern Pennsylvania. Leslie spent his youth in and around those stores, learning the retail business and dealing with traveling salesmen.

Then as now, most of the guns and ammunition in America were sold first to distributors, which held the inventory and then resold it to dealers across the nation. Before long, Harris grew tired of buying products from middlemen. As he calculated the markups on guns, he saw the promise of big profits if the volumes were large enough. So he founded Nationwide Distributors. Harris's new business became one of the country's top firearms wholesale distributors and eventually spread to several locations, including warehouses in Pennsylvania and Reno, Nevada.

By the time Leslie and Greg were cooking up deals, the Edelman's retail stores were fading away. But Nationwide saw plenty of success, and Harris handed the reins to Leslie, his eldest son. Somehow, even in a wholesale business known for being cutthroat and unforgiving, and probably partially because of Leslie's unfortunate wet-towel handshake, Nationwide managed to stand out with business strategies that maximized short-term profit but jeopardized long-term relationships. Greg and I both found this troubling, and he often expressed his concerns to me in exasperated phone calls. "I don't like it any more than you. Edelman cares about Kimber making him money. Period. That means we'll sell the cheap crap, then figure out how to make Kimber into something we can be proud of." By "crap," Greg was referring to the cheap guns manufactured by Daewoo, the same South Korean conglomerate also known for making VCRs, oil tankers, and cheap cars.

At Kimber, a small group of us lived and worked by an unspoken company vision based on shared love of high-quality guns. But to me, it never felt like Leslie willingly shared this vision. He seemed just fine with selling Daewoo and other lower-quality guns as long as they were profitable. True, Nationwide carried guns from respected factories such as Browning, Winchester, and Smith & Wesson, but it also sold low-quality imported assault rifles and inexpensive pistols, the kind of stuff that could only tarnish a respectable brand. I believed that profit was the only vision at Nationwide, and the company found success in the profit department.

Leslie took control of his father's company just before the time that murmurs about Bill Clinton's first election victory began boosting gun sales. He anticipated increasing demand and scrambled to stock up on more inventory. When he heard about giant containers of old military Mauser rifles in Australia, he bought them. Leslie formalized an exclusive relationship with Daewoo, whose cheap guns were even worse than its cheap cars. But the Koreans had the capacity to produce their guns, and in a hot market every company was scrambling for inventory, so Leslie bought thousands of them.

By the September 13 enactment date of the assault weapons ban in 1994, everyone with a gun to sell was making money. This also opened the door to widespread unscrupulous business practices. Every distributor tightened policies to increase profit—that was to be expected. Even in this environment, where most distributors did something to anger dealers, Nationwide managed to develop an exceptionally poor reputation. The resulting stories of Nationwide's price gouging and poor service persisted in the firearms industry for years.

The day that Clinton put his signature on the assault weapons ban, things got much tougher for Leslie and Nationwide. The boom-time practices that angered dealers caught up with him. In a declining market, dealers wanted to do business with distributors they liked and trusted. That meant Leslie's inventories stacked up. Suddenly, the easy money was gone.

With the hangover in place, dozens of distributors and hundreds of dealers went bankrupt or just closed up shop. Between 1994 and 2000, licensed firearms dealers in the United States dropped by almost two-thirds, from a high of more than 215,000 to fewer than 78,000.[1] Nationwide barely stayed in business, and Leslie began searching for any creative way to keep his distributor afloat.

Ever the entrepreneur, Leslie warmed to a new idea: if he got an exclusive relationship with a high-end manufacturer—a company with a little cachet and sex appeal—maybe he could get the upper hand he was looking for. He could use the appeal of a boutique company like Kimber to help him sell all other inventory gathering dust in the warehouses. Before long, Leslie Edelman, a distributor who needed an exclusive product, and Greg Warne, a manufacturer who always needed cash, struck a deal.

Kimber already did business with Nationwide when Dwight and I started. Greg downplayed the relationship as "just another customer." As Greg would tell me, "Ryan, you just worry about selling to the big dealers. This distributor will be the only wholesaler we sell to. I've got a relationship with Leslie, and I'll manage the account. Don't worry about it."

Greg wasn't being generous. He needed to manage the Nationwide account himself because he was already engaged in a scheme to pre-bill Nationwide for future orders. Greg kept Dwight and me at a distance because he knew we'd ask questions. As long as Greg could control the system, he could generate just enough cash to stay afloat: it was a house of cards.

But Greg felt the weight of his failing plan and was beginning to let me in on the truth. He and Leslie came up with what they hoped would be a solution. In what is still a common firearms-industry practice, US distributors and manufacturers sought out cheap foreign gun manufacturers to supply firearms for an additional income stream. Because US domestic consumers represented such a large part of the world market, gun-selling entities in America could just use their existing sales and marketing infrastructure to push the additional imported guns into the market for extra easy profit. It worked fine when the market was hot, but when the market cooled, importing big quantities of unproven, low-quality guns did not seem so smart. Nationwide had started when the market was hot, but by 1996 and 1997, the market was stone-cold. "Leslie has some excess inventory that he's stuck with," Greg told us with a sigh. "It's all shit, but we need to help sell it."

For me, this might as well have been a public merger. Nationwide, the wholesaler of imported assault weapons with a poor reputation, and Kimber, the company I was trying to build into a respected supplier of high-end heirlooms, were going to be joined. This was far from what I dreamed about when I took a chance on Kimber, so I pushed back at every opportunity. "Greg, this is not what I signed up for," I told him once, frustrated by everything Greg was doing. "This is not the company I want to build, and these are not the guns I want to sell."

Greg was surprisingly understanding. "I know they're awful, but it's just what we have to do to get through this."

I hated the direction Greg was taking the company in, but I still needed a job. I needed to cover rent and my truck payment. There wasn't much I could do. So I reluctantly agreed to sell the Mauser rifles, at least for a few months.

Later that afternoon, Greg called back. "Can you hold your paycheck for a couple weeks? We're short again." I should have known then that Greg's days as the company's leader were numbered.

———

THE MAUSERS HAD BEEN STORED IN CONTAINERS SINCE BEING retired from military service in the 1950s. They were old, rough, and cheap, but I reasoned that at least they were sturdy bolt-action guns that could be modified or "sporterized" into hunting rifles. That same afternoon I called in a favor with a large dealer in Houston, and it bought five hundred of the old Mausers to use in a promotion. After the sale I called Greg to give him the news. "I can sell those Mausers to help with cash flow, but I hate that Daewoo shit."

"Thanks, Ryan. I get it," Greg said. I could hear the heavy beat of the Riverside Corral in the background. "Look, taking dollars for old Mausers is not exactly as sexy as giving dollars to Stephanie or Unique, but remember, *everything* is your job. We are going to be big, Ryan. Big. Just you wait."

With my career at stake, I poked at Greg for more information. As I pried small bits of intel and gossip from him, I came to understand that a financial arrangement between Leslie and Greg had actually been slowly transferring ownership of the company for more than a year. Every time Greg pre-billed orders without fully delivering them, another chunk of Kimber went to Leslie. As I began adding it all up, I slowly came to terms with the fact that Kimber had a new owner who seemed to have no problem doing whatever it took to make a buck and who had struck deals to import cheap guns from South Korea and dusty clunkers from Australia. Leslie Edelman was about ready to become my new boss.

I did my best to ensure that my own paychecks would cash. I sold those Mauser rifles and took orders for the Daewoo, but I never lost sight of what I wanted Kimber to be either. I worked even harder to sell our quality Kimber products. That's where my heart was.

I was privately thrilled when the difficult market continued to take its toll on Nationwide. Soon Leslie faced reality, and Nationwide filed for bankruptcy. Like so many other companies left in the wake of the ongoing industry downturn, the distributor founded by Leslie's father just went away. I quietly cheered because I knew this meant that I'd be done selling cheap imports.

Relieved to be finally rid of Daewoo, I dug in and worked even harder to make Kimber take off. Each day I held my breath, hoping Leslie wouldn't call with some new importation idea. To my relief, when he did call to inform me about a new product, it was to tell me that a project was coming together but that this one was for high-quality guns.

"I've bought the old Jericho Precision Factory in Yonkers, and we're going to make 1911 pistols," Leslie explained. Jericho was a failing defense contractor on the financial ropes. Just as he had done with Greg, Leslie saw Jericho's weak position and swooped in to purchase the factory. "We're turning this place into the Kimber handgun factory," Leslie told me with his voice lighting up. For once, he had an idea that I agreed would be good for the kind of company I wanted to help build.

The 1911 pistol was named for the year in which legendary gun designer John Moses Browning designed this handgun for the US military. Browning chambered the gun in the high-caliber .45ACP ("automatic Colt pistol") cartridge, so named for the gun manufacturer Colt. Founded by Samuel Colt, it was the first and most famous builder of the gun that Browning designed. Still today, many refer to the gun as a "Colt .45." The military supposedly wanted defensive pistols with a .45 cartridge because its large, 230-grain bullet packed enough force to stop a two-hundred-pound man running at full speed in battle. Soon after John Browning presented his 1911 to the military, the armed forces quickly adopted the weapon. Hundreds of factories built and supplied them to millions of US soldiers across the world for decades.

Unlike many military guns, the 1911 was meant for self-defense. In fact, even when carried by the soldiers, the old pistol was considered to be the defensive gun of last resort. It had a standard capacity of only eight rounds and a basic design unchanged for nearly a century, so no one considered the gun to be of the same sort as the modern high-capacity rifles that would one day dominate the market. Customers for the 1911 understood fine craftsmanship; they usually collected guns as investments and heirlooms, and they valued the century-old design as the pinnacle of self-defense guns.

The truth is that almost all handguns are primarily designed to be used for self-defense. Nearly all are chambered in cartridges with very limited ranges compared to any rifle. This is why people like Greg, who had a visceral dislike of cheap or military guns, did not have a problem with high-quality pistols. Yes, there were certainly people who used handguns offensively, but back then we all believed in effective laws to limit those sort of gun crimes. Greg and I understood that there was a balance, and we both believed, as I do today, that the basic right to defense is an important component of our rights as Americans.

At the time, most of America agreed with us, and by directing Kimber's move to build handguns, Leslie found himself on the front of a growing wave that focused on supplying the gear for effective self-defense. Prior to the 1990s, US gun consumers usually purchased rifles and shotguns. But our country's appetite for handguns had grown over the previous decade. Handgun sales were even beginning to eclipse rifle and shotgun sales. This trend accelerated in the coming decade as the act of carrying concealed firearms became legal in almost every state.

The promise of expanding Kimber with a high-quality defensive pistol was my way of threading the needle. Pistols had never excited me, but if there was any pistol that I wanted to own, it was the high-quality, venerable 1911.

Placing a bet on the old pistol was a contrarian move because by the 1990s, more-modern guns had displaced the 1911. Military units across the world had also adopted the newer guns. But by then, the 1911 had found its place in gun lore; it was officially a classic. Because the newer designs were simple to operate and were cheaper, they became more popular with criminals too. I told myself that only the last generation's criminals, relics like Tolly Bolyard, would use a 1911 in a crime. It was a rationalization, but official government statistics mostly confirmed my assertions.

The important thing for me was that we saw fresh business opportunities swirling around the old 1911. A vibrant refurbishment and customization industry had emerged to upgrade the millions of 1911s already in circulation. Enthusiasts wanted the classic grip angle and slim build of the old gun.

We often called guns like Glocks "guns for dummies" because they had no safety and could be operated easily by people who knew nothing about guns. Numerous safety tests confirmed the "dummy" label. In those tests people who knew nothing about guns usually figured out on their own how to fire pistols like Glocks in just a few seconds, whereas figuring out a gun like the 1911, which has two external safeties, might take them a minute or two.

Conversely, we took pride in those who believed the 1911 was the "expert's pistol." Many serious shooters agreed, as evidenced by the fact that select SWAT teams and military Special Forces units still carried their old 1911s. For the most part, those highly trained users understood that a defensive gun did not need more than a few rounds.

The 1911 found a cult following, and people paid hundreds to add new, modern features to their existing old guns, much like upgrading a classic car. I could see that if we just based our pistol on the bones of the old design but added shiny new features as a matter of standard, we would have a hot-selling winner.

And there was another huge, lingering opportunity—this one *created* by the assault weapons ban—the same law that companies like Glock loved to hate. As I considered the future of Kimber, I began to appreciate the law that made all those newer, high-capacity guns obsolete. Just like the Glock 17 used in the Luby's shooting, most of the newer guns were chambered in the smaller 9mm, which meant their main selling point was the fact that they held more ammunition—in other words, they were high-capacity handguns.

The assault weapons ban still allowed for the sale of those models, but only with ten-round magazines. The rationalization for limiting capacity in handguns was that there is a point at which a defensive gun becomes an offensive weapon. Limiting handguns to only ten rounds removed the limited offensive nature of those guns and removed their advantage in the gun market. This opened up the possibilities for old, lower-capacity designs such as the 1911.

With a lot of help from Dwight's growing marketing effort, consumers soon decided that if they were limited to guns with only a few rounds, they might as well have a classic 1911 in a powerful caliber. The law that had gutted sales of most other guns had given our particular model a big advantage, and Kimber was about ready to make the most of it.

In short order, our new Yonkers factory began building new Kimber 1911 pistols. Federal law required every gun manufacturer to hold a valid FFL (Federal Firearms License). Kimber's FFL was still headquartered in Oregon, and that meant we had to ship every gun built in Yonkers all the way to our place in Clackamas. That's where we logged each gun before shipping them to dealers. When the first production samples were ready, I traveled back to Oregon and sat in Greg's office as we unboxed the very first Kimber 1911s.

The guns in that box incorporated all the expensive customizations popularized by the best gunsmiths across the country. They fit our marketing plan perfectly. Kimber would make those fancy gunsmith upgrades standard, and we could offer them at big discounts because our factory could scale up the work.

As we held the first gun, a pistol with a low serial number that I still own today, I knew we had knocked it out of the park. "This is the gun that's going to make Kimber into a real gun company," I told Greg, looking up from the sleek new Kimber. "I don't think we'll need to hold back any paychecks."

Greg, though not a pistol aficionado, knew I was right. That meant he faced a disturbing reality. "Shit, they *are* nice," he grumbled, knowing that the gun had not been made in his part of Kimber. Then he sighed. "I guess it's what we have to do to stay in business." He then added a truth about the state of the changing American gun market: "People love to talk about nice rifles, but I think they are growing to love *buying* pistols."

Inside that first box of Kimber 1911s, Greg Warne could see the future. That future did not involve exclusive focus on handcrafted, artisan rifles with custom-carved stocks. *Those* were his passion—at least one of his passions, anyway.

I knew that Leslie wanted me to call him with my honest assessment, and I picked up the phone to give it to him. "Leslie, Greg and I are standing here with the first Kimber pistols." I paused for dramatic effect as Greg sat back.

"What do you boys think?"

"Goddamn, they look great. Give me a little time, but I am going to sell *thousands* of these!"

I believed what I just promised my boss, but I also realized I had no other choice. If I didn't find success in selling Kimber's 1911s, I knew Leslie would probably find some other import deal like Daewoo. So I went to work on making my sales promise a reality, and Leslie had already begun expanding the capacity of his Yonkers factory.

It wasn't easy at first. Kimber had no reputation for making pistols, which meant that it took time for us to gain the trust of dealers and consumers, and of course I had to deal with all the dealers who already hated anything to do with Nationwide, including Kimber. But within a few months it became clear that I would indeed sell thousands upon thousands of 1911s. By late 1997, Dwight was starting to drum up press too. Before long, we had the hottest new gun on the market. And within months I was putting big sales numbers on the board. Our little company, which until recently struggled to pay its own employees on time, finally started taking off with new dealers all across the country.

One of my best sales ideas hinged on supplying a new fundraising system that the NRA had developed. The NRA Foundation hosted more than a thousand "Friends of the NRA" banquets across the country as fundraisers. By law, that wing of the NRA could fund only educational field programs such as gun-safety classes and shooting competitions. This was the same organization that I remembered from those magazines back on our Kansas ranch. The NRA's political wing would soon prove to be very controversial, but working with the NRA Foundation at the time aligned with my mission of promoting safety and selling collectible, attractive guns.

It was around that time that I developed a friendship with Kyle Weaver. Kyle started at the NRA at about the same time I started at Kimber, and he eventually oversaw the planning and purchasing for all those NRA Foundation banquets. I knew Kyle needed a lot of guns to raffle and auction as the main draw of the banquets. The NRA could be, in effect, one of Kimber's largest dealers, and it would eventually host nearly twelve hundred banquets across the country each year. Every one of those banquets needed dozens of guns for fundraising.

Both Kyle and I knew that Kimber products would fetch a lot of money. Over the next twenty years, Kimber developed and sold tens of thousands of our new 1911s through those banquets, making the NRA one of Kimber's most reliable sales outlets. It also cultivated a bond between us and would provide me with inside access not afforded to most firearms executives.

I also used Kimber's new guns to build up our growing commercial dealer network. After the downfall of Nationwide, I had enough of distributors and decided to focus on selling directly to dealers. My approach was new for the industry and would result in the largest dealer-direct sales model the industry had ever seen, a fact that would eventually earn me recognition as one of the most respected members of our industry.

With my sales model and our new take on a century-old pistol, Kimber suddenly became a serious player. Our competitors noticed. We perfected the customization theme, selling well more than two hundred different variations of the 1911, many of which retailed for more than $2,000 apiece. I had an eye for what consumers wanted and often helped design different colors and shapes, grip materials, and sight options. After decades of fighting to stay afloat, Kimber had finally found its niche. We'd brought our own pistol to the gunfight.

EIGHT

COFFIN FACTORIES AND HORROR MOVIES

L ESLIE'S HUNCH ABOUT THE SUCCESS OF KIMBER'S 1911 AND my initial enthusiasm for the pistol's sales potential proved to be spot-on. Modernizing the old design put Kimber on the map as one of America's premier gun companies. Sales exploded. Dwight even secured exclusive cover features in magazines such as *American Handgunner, Handguns, Shooting Times,* and the NRA's *American Rifleman.* After every new article, we saw a spike in sales. Soon the monthly demand for our 1911s surpassed the annual sales for our high-end rifles.

Leslie originally estimated that we might be able to sell five thousand pistols per year. After all, our small, grungy factory in Yonkers could handle that sort of volume. But soon I was selling as many as five thousand of them in a single month.

Only a stone's throw off the Saw Mill River Parkway, Kimber's factory looked old and worn, sandwiched between more old buildings, crumbling houses, and a few flailing restaurants. The whole neighborhood, in a tired, gray, and greasy part of New York City, hadn't changed much since the 1950s. A rusty chain-link fence surrounded the property, topped with foreboding concertina wire that spiraled over the top. In the southwest corner of the parking lot stood a dilapidated house with scraggly shrubs growing up through the walls. That old home was inside the Kimber security fence and was the only nonindustrial structure on the property.

On a factory visit, I watched an old man quietly slither out the back door of the house. He nodded a thanks at the Kimber guards, and they opened the creaky gate just enough for the guy to squeeze out.

"That's our squatter," a security guard reassured me when he saw the confusion on my face. "The law says he's got a right to that old shack, but—"

"But he lives in our parking lot?"

"I mean, we gotta park cars next to him cuz there ain't more room," the guard chuckled. "Maybe we can drive him out?"

Although the Kimber factory looked old and sleepy on the outside, it bustled on the inside. Every few hours a break bell sounded, allowing dozens of workers to pour into the parking lot to smoke cigarettes, eat sandwiches, and chitchat until another bell signaled that it was time to get back to work. As I walked through the crowd, I admired the diversity of them all. Young Central American women dusted themselves off from their work as woodworkers. A gregarious older man with an Eastern European accent joked with a Black man who spoke with the melodic cadence of the Bahamas. The pistol assemblers were all first-generation Russians. Most of the machinists were from Ireland; many of the managers were Israelis. Most everyone else belonged to other countries, and almost all of them were first-generation immigrants.

"Know Spanish?" one of the assemblers asked me through his Russian accent. He nipped at a small bottle of vodka he had just pulled from his pocket. "It's how most of us talk here. It's our common language." It was all a far fetch from Kalispell, Montana, where it was difficult to find someone who looked or spoke any differently from me.

The man laughed with his coworkers and then passed his bottle around, unaware that I was a senior manager from faraway Montana. It wasn't even noon.

Before long, it became clear that Kimber needed even more manufacturing room to keep up with demand. So Leslie set his sights on an old gray building across the street. I reminded Dwight of our last trip to Yonkers, when we looked through the fence at that old building. A few people came and went through its small door, as if working on a clandestine military project.

"That place gives me the fuckin' creeps, man," Dwight said. "It's dark as hell, even for Yonkers."

A security guard next to us lit a cigarette. "Know why that place is creepy?" he asked, flashing a smile short of a few teeth. Then he lowered his voice. "That's a damn coffin factory. And looks like we're gonna move in."

"That's kind of ironic, isn't it?" Dwight said with a chuckle. "A gun company buying a coffin factory?"

"What's gonna happen to all the coffins?" I asked the security guard. He shrugged.

"I dunno, but people still dyin', that's for sure."

I returned to Montana but kept up with the news about our new building with reports from friends in the New York office who were giving me the play-by-play. They let me know that Leslie Edelman drove a hard bargain on that discount-coffin factory. After making an offer and settling on a deal, he realized the seller was desperate. So at the last minute, Leslie dropped his offer significantly. The owner was livid, and some of the people at Kimber wondered if there might be a coffin with Leslie's name on it. The guy was pissed off, but he had no choice, and the deal squeaked through.

Over the next couple of years, Kimber converted the coffin factory into a modern firearms-production plant. But Greg would not be around to see it happen. In fact, not long after Greg and I opened that first 1911 box in his office, his questionable judgment and haphazard lifestyle caught up with him.

Greg's pre-billing scheme had made Leslie Edelman the de facto president and owner of Kimber, but Greg still controlled the finances of the Oregon operation. Then things got real when Leslie hired a chief financial officer to oversee the entire operation between Oregon and New York.

That CFO, Denis Schusterman, was a fast-talking New Jersey accountant with a thin red beard and oversized eyes. We wondered why Leslie hired him. Despite its sudden growth spurt, Kimber was probably not large enough to need a big-time CFO. Leslie reasoned that with the complexities of the Nationwide bankruptcy and two Kimber locations, he needed help.

In meetings, Denis fidgeted nervously, and he often made awkward statements. "I'm going to get a new BMW 740," he once announced, prompting the rest of us to shoot glances at one another. "It fits me. It's what they call an executive car." Most of us drove modest vehicles. I had a ten-year-old Chevy truck barely big enough to haul guns from Idaho.

Denis tried hard to fit in, but people did not naturally warm to him. He compensated for the distrust by driving a fancy car and smoking expensive cigars, which he forced on everyone after company lunches or in bars following strategy meetings.

Most of Kimber's hundred or so employees seemed to understand the need to make personal sacrifices until there was enough success to allow a little bit of luxury. Denis flaunted his affection for luxury, skipping right over the sacrifice part, which irked most everyone else. After one of our first meetings with Denis, Greg put words to the distaste and doubt that many of us felt. "I just don't like that greasy fucker," he said. "There's just something not right about that guy. Who the hell bounces around like a kangaroo and carries a box of thirty-dollar cigars with him all the time?"

Denis was awkward and ostentatious, but he did have a talent for forensic accounting, and—unsurprisingly—this too would end up rubbing Greg the wrong way. As Denis plowed through the records of Kimber's Oregon operation, he noticed a recurring irregularity: Greg listed himself on the IRS filing, which meant that he was personally liable for ensuring that payroll taxes were deducted from employee checks and sent to the IRS per federal law. Denis discovered that Greg was indeed deducting the payments but that for more than a year the IRS had not received its share. Denis had just uncovered a stream of cash that Greg was using to fund birthday parties and company breakfasts at the Acropolis.

So Denis informed Leslie, and Leslie must have realized that this was his chance to seize whatever Greg could still claim of Kimber. Leslie tasked Denis with finishing the job. Denis's first order of business was to go to Clackamas. None of us knew that he also rented a fleet of big moving trucks.

Fearful that federal agents would discover the malfeasance and then show up to seize the company, Denis quietly called the IRS and alerted them to Greg's fraud. As Denis apologized profusely to the government agents, he also promised quick payment to settle the outstanding balance. He knew the plan would buy at least a couple more days.

In Oregon, Denis invited Greg to a dinner at Jake's, Greg's favorite restaurant that wasn't inside a strip club. In an overt play to build drama, Denis waited for the right moment at dinner, then announced his discovery of tax evasion and presented Greg with his very limited options.

Greg could have avoided the worst of his fate if he had the money to repay the IRS, but Denis rightfully suspected that Greg's problems had left a messy money trail between Portland and Costa Rica. The money might have been spent on a few company assets or raw materials. Maybe employees like me had been paid, but Denis knew that most of the money had been tucked into G-strings, used to fund lap dances, spent on shaving cream, and paid to the finest Costa Rican "interpreters."

Greg at first denied everything. Then he angrily called Denis every name in the book. But within a few minutes, reality hit him. Greg sank into his chair and realized that his best option was to jet to some foreign country with limited extradition practices. Denis pointed out that a second and less desirable option involved facing federal prosecution and prison time. After dinner, Denis picked up the check and left Greg to mull over both options, without insisting on a thirty-dollar cigar.

Soon after that dinner, Denis directed the moving trucks to meet him at the Clackamas factory. And by morning, everything Greg had built was jammed into those trucks: machines, office files, gun parts, ammunition, even a few cans of warm Miller Genuine Draft.

Denis next padlocked the doors and sent the moving trucks three thousand miles east to the Yonkers factory. Only then did Denis call the IRS with the truth: "About those payroll taxes? Yeah, on second thought, Kimber of Oregon will just file bankruptcy. For further questions, please call Greg Warne. You'll find his contact information on your corporate paperwork."

Before the IRS could track down Greg, he had exercised "option No. 1" and flown to San José, Costa Rica. Just like that, the guy who I had spoken to almost every day and the man who Kimber advertised as its visionary founder and president was gone. We didn't hear from Greg for more than a year.

A few weeks later, after the trucks unloaded everything from Kimber of Oregon into Kimber at Yonkers, Denis finished the paperwork to create an entirely new company, the more expansive "Kimber of America." That's the name that still pops up on the company website today.

Denis had proved quite useful for Leslie in the formation of this new American Kimber, but Schusterman was not finished putting his mark on our company. Denis had a knack for sniffing out opportunity, and the scent of Kimber's growing cash flow commanded his attention.

Whereas most business in the firearms industry was done by extending credit to dealers and allowing them to pay for their products in sixty to ninety days, Denis required Kimber to expect cash on delivery (COD) for our shipments to many of our dealers. This safer accounting made my job more difficult, but in keeping with my willingness to sacrifice, I went along because when Leslie muttered things like "I don't trust any of them," it made sense. Gun dealers, after all, were still struggling to make ends meet because of the ongoing post-Clinton hangover; not many were great credit risks, and more than a few harbored simmering anger over the treatment that they had received from Nationwide.

Kimber was still relatively small, and we needed the money fast. We had a small accounting staff, and COD required no credit check or receivables team. The UPS driver just collected the money; then it was wired to Kimber the next day.

Kimber of America also had a small leadership team, and we often discussed the need for conservative finance keeping. But we all bemoaned the tight financial reality of our company. Most of us could see that we were running more and more guns, but Denis's financial updates remained bleak. "We're making progress, but there is not much profit to spare," he'd report. "It might be a couple years before we really make any money."

"I'm no CPA," I pushed back in discussion with him. "But damn, it seems like we should be in better shape than we are. Are our expenses really that high?"

Denis responded quickly in an attempt to cut off any more of my questions. "Just keep up the hard work, and we'll get there, I promise."

After my pushback seemed to unnerve Denis, he soon called me up with an offer. "I want to make sure things are fair for you, Ryan. I think we owe you a favor. Just send me an expense report for $10,000."

"I don't have any expenses," I replied, stunned. "I mean, I heard your reports. Aren't things tight?"

"Don't worry about it," he said. "Just send me the report: $10,000. I'll make sure it's paid, OK? We don't want to give raises, but you deserve it. Just don't forget your buddy Denis. Now go sell something!" I knew that this was not how bonuses were really supposed to work, but everything at Kimber had the feel of "just doing what it took to get through one more day." I assumed that all growing companies had to cut a few corners. I also knew that this was Denis's way of letting me know that he was really in charge of the finances and that he knew I was playing a big role at Kimber. It felt good to get some appreciation for my hard work, and I needed the money. That kind of cash went a long way for a ranch kid with a truck payment.

Denis encouraged me to view this money as a bonus for hard work and for future results. He wanted to make sure that I was motivated enough to grow our list of COD customers. He'd happily pay a few thousand bucks to make sure that it happened.

Denis also tried to build rapport by giving me odd personal updates at strange hours. On one Saturday, when he knew I was in the office, he called with manic enthusiasm. "Hey, man! I'm about ready to fly back from LA. I'm producing a movie, and it's going to be fucking great. A horror flick. We even got Corbin Bernsen to star in it. It's called *Killer Instinct*. It's about all of this scary shit that happens in a small town. You're from a small town. You'd love it. I'm also working on one called *A Demon Within*." Then, invoking Greg, Denis added, "There are all kinds of hot actresses out here. You wouldn't believe what they'll do for a part. Maybe you should come out here and visit. You could help with the casting, if you know what I mean!"

"That's OK, Denis. But I bet the movies will be great." *Surely no actress is desperate enough to give Denis the time of day*, I thought.

Not long after our discussion about movies I heard Denis bragging about his second large home. He showed me a couple of pictures of the place in San Diego. It looked like something out of a movie: a real movie. All of Denis's ostentatious spending raised my antennae. Even someone like me, who had not been raised around growing companies and financial maneuvering, suspected that although Denis's financial skills might have been well suited for finding corruption, he might also be using them to perpetuate it.

When the FBI knocked on the Kimber doors, they screwed up Denis's ill-conceived script. The investigators interrupted our bustling Yonkers gun factory with news about interesting financial irregularities. Federal investigators had uncovered deposits moving in and out of accounts controlled by Denis's mother, who was being investigated for embezzling money from the Temple Sinai synagogue in Dresher, Pennsylvania.

The FBI let us know that there was a good reason for Kimber's ongoing financial stress. Denis, with the help of his mother, had been diverting COD funds through the synagogue and then to various personal accounts.

That first call from the FBI led to a full-blown investigation. Within months, Denis was found guilty of embezzling more than $10 million from Kimber, and his mother was sentenced for embezzling nearly $2 million from her own synagogue. Among other things, the investigation uncovered fund transfers to three pathetic movies, to the $2.2 million house in San Diego, and to five mistresses. "Schusterman is one of the most specially talented liars that I have ever met in my life," the presiding judge said during the sentencing hearing.[1] When his gavel went down, the judge awarded Denis with a third residence to brag about: a 168-month stay in a federal penitentiary.

WHILE DENIS'S AND GREG'S LIVES AND FUTURES GOT BLEAK, MY life was undergoing an immensely positive shift. Even through the chaos of bankruptcies, cheap horror movies, converted coffin factories, and century-old pistols, I found the time to ask my girlfriend, Sara, to marry me.

I had met Sara at the wedding of my brother, Cory, three years earlier. At six feet tall, she strode across the room in long wool pants and a bright red sweater. Athletic and strikingly beautiful, she was a force of nature. She was witty and deeply devoted to making the world a better place. She also challenged me in my thinking almost every time we had a conversation.

When I started to talk about work, Sara tried to switch my focus to parts of our life that were less stressful. Good thing, because Kimber with all of its craziness was putting me through the ringer. Long days and the stress of running the office, hiring new staff, and dealing with

Greg, Denis, and Leslie often pushed me to the edge. I tried never to show it, but it pushed me far enough that I developed a painful case of shingles months before we were married.

"You are perfectly healthy," the doctor told me. "You must be under extreme stress. That's how shingles happens to someone like you."

I needed some balance, and Sara provided that positive detour. She made me think of more than just a professional life that was so insane that it weakened my immune system.

We were both strong personalities who held an innate desire to challenge and to be challenged. Like me, Sara loved Montana and was ready for an adventure far away from home. Even though we did not yet understand the strength of the team we would form, we both had the quiet confidence of two people who just knew they belonged together.

We were married on a beautiful Montana afternoon in 1999. With our partnership cemented, Sara almost immediately started pushing me to expand my life beyond Kimber and the simple, thoughtless politics of the gun business.

Sara grew up in a hunting family with a father who was a wildlife biologist. We both had an affinity for nature. I had always been passionate about the environment and, for a long time, naively believed Republican rhetoric about sharing a love of and respect for the natural world.

It did not take long for Sara to sense that that rhetoric didn't amount to much, and she regularly questioned me on the topic. Were the Republicans really representing me on the things that I said were so important? Had I carefully chosen these politics? Or had I just adopted them like most everyone else in the industry? Then I realized I couldn't really answer her questions as elegantly as she asked them. I just assumed that people in the shooting industry were hunters and that Republicans supported guns and hunters; therefore, Republicans had to be for the environment. Sara started pulling on this thread, a thread that eventually unraveled my entire ill-fitting political ideology.

She asked me other questions too, like why I drank from that awful fountain of talk radio and why I never questioned simple bumper-sticker slogans. Years before I realized the truth or wanted to recognize the real story about the gun industry, she also questioned me about who was really running the gun business and what it might mean for our national politics.

Sara seemed to understand that together we could be a great team. She wanted me to live up to my true potential, and according to her, that meant I needed to be engaged in thorough self-reflection. I had never done much of that. But with her help, I was about ready to start.

NINE

WAS IT A KIMBER?

"**I**T'S THE PLACE WITH THE BIG HAYFIELD OUT FRONT," Dwight explained to me with excitement. "Hell, I think we could shoot off the back porch!"

The growth resulting from Kimber's jump into the pistol market meant that I suddenly needed a lot more people in Montana and more office space to house them. The building, at 2590 Montana Highway 35, seemed perfect to us. Built just a few years earlier by a timber-frame home builder, our new office resembled a rugged hunting lodge. Miles from town, the rural setting meant that we could watch geese flying over the back deck in the mornings and whitetail deer browsing on the shrubs in the evenings.

Kimber Montana quickly became our version of gun-company Grand Central Station, bustling with salespeople arriving to and departing from meetings, attending strategy sessions on upcoming trade shows or new products, and throbbing with the constant energy of hundreds of daily calls and outgoing mail bins full of glossy promotional materials.

On the morning of April 20, 1999, I held a staff meeting in my office. "It's going to be a big show this year," I said, eyeing some of my newer employees, who had never attended an NRA convention. We were getting ready to showcase more than a hundred new Kimber pistols and about forty rifles. "I would expect our booth to be packed, and you'll need to be on your game. It will be nonstop, all day, for three days in a row."

The annual NRA convention was set to begin in about ten days in Denver. Our entire staff would need to work long days with potential gun buyers who would come to our booth to admire our guns. Many of them would walk away with a glossy Kimber catalog. The tough job of producing our annual catalog was Dwight's baby, and we all took pride in knowing that copies of each edition became collector's items among gun aficionados across the country. Up to fifty thousand people would attend the NRA show, and that meant we would hand out thousands of our coffee-table-quality catalogs.

We also planned to attend plenty of cocktail parties and important events at the show. I reminded my staff that the most important extracurricular event was the annual awards dinner for the gun-manufacturing industry, hosted by the trade magazine *Shooting Industry*. "Kimber may not be up for any awards this year," I said with some prophetic motivation that Tuesday morning. "But one day we will be, and that day we will be important enough for all of us to be in the front row."

The NRA show, and all the scheduling around it, was an enormous undertaking. Just as I began to discuss the logistics for our hotel rooms and airline reservations, our office secretary stuck her head in the meeting. "You guys need to watch the news," she said before a big swallow. "There is some shit going down in Denver."

Maybe my face conveyed annoyance over the interruption, but she shot me a look that indicated she was serious. So I fumbled with a radio and then clicked through slow and clunky news websites to see what was happening in the Denver suburb of Columbine.

The early reports of the shooting at Columbine High School indicated that two students had used a variety of guns and explosives to kill thirteen and wound twenty-four more. My usually loud and gregarious sales staff sat quiet and motionless as we waited for each new bit of information.

Photos that slowly flashed across my screen began to answer our questions. We saw screaming kids, distraught parents, and teachers comforting students. People raced across the parking lot to escape the carnage. For those of us sitting there in the sales office, a single question we hadn't voiced but was on all our minds remained unanswered: *What guns did they use?* One of the sales guys let it slip: *"Was it a Kimber?"*

Not long after the entire nation began learning about the massacre in Columbine, my phone rang. "You watching this?" Sara said, her voice trembling. "Those poor kids! The gun industry is OK with this shit?" I must have stammered for a few awkward moments before she added, "Are *you* OK with this, Ryan?"

"No, I am not OK with it," I whispered into my phone, careful not to let anyone in the office know how upset Sara was. "Look, I'm pretty sure that they did not use any Kimbers."

"That's what you have to say for yourself?" she retorted. "That they didn't use *your* guns?"

"Sorry, Sara. I gotta go," I answered. "I'll talk to you tonight."

Everyone in the building wanted to believe that we were immune to the guilt that would follow if the world learned that Eric Harris and Dylan Klebold used Kimbers as they murdered their teachers and classmates in cold blood. Somehow, it still seemed reasonable to all of us to believe that the terror in Colorado was beneath Kimber. After all, we had not been making handguns that long. And they were expensive, classic, and not high capacity.

Of course, we also knew that nothing was certain. Deep down, everyone understood there would always be the possibility that our product could end up in a scene like Columbine.

As we processed the horror and pondered that possibility, my screen flashed with the disturbing scene of a bloodied boy dangling out of a high window in the school. Three shots from the killers had struck seventeen-year-old Patrick Ireland, two of them in the head. Despite profuse bleeding, he somehow managed to crawl across the floor to the broken window, then lobbed himself over the edge of the opening.

A primal fear of dying and a more primal instinct of flight pushed Patrick to escape the rampage inside. Two SWAT officers caught his fall from the window, and despite his terrible injuries, he survived. It took months for Patrick to walk and talk again, but he eventually recounted the harrowing day: "I rolled over on my back and began to push myself with my left leg that still worked and just wound my way between tables and chairs and backpacks. Eventually, I made my way over to the windowsill."[1]

For a nation dealing with its first high-profile mass shooting in a school, Patrick's dramatic escape came to represent an almost unspeakable fear. It was and still is horrific to watch. But like those at the other gun companies, we were conditioned to convert news of events like the Columbine massacre into calculations about how they would affect our work of selling guns.

Within a couple of hours the staff slowly trickled back to their offices and began returning calls and speaking to dealers. It was easier than it should have been to just go back to work. We claimed to be above it all, and that was my doing.

It began with Greg Warne's admonition from years earlier: "We don't want Kimber to be a company that makes guns found in crime scenes." For all his other irresponsible behavior, I deeply respected Greg's principles on this topic. Greg and I both knew that there was an unspoken line of bifurcation in the gun business. We all knew that higher-quality, more-expensive, lower-capacity guns were far less likely to be used in crimes. Lower-quality, less-expensive, high-capacity "assault"-style guns were far more likely.

The industry wrestled with this reality too, but it also understood the basic laws of economics. In order for a company to grow, it needed new business. Less-expensive products would appeal to a higher number of customers. Edgy or "dangerous" products also had an upside because they could garner press attention, or maybe they'd have a chance at selling at higher numbers. The trick, as I saw it, was to try to find just the right balance to have cake and eat it too. I'd build a growing company that focused on high-quality products. And this meant that I'd have to find a way to buck the basic laws of economics. To pull it off, we'd need a trained eye for style and more than a little bit of luck.

I managed to stay successful in demanding the quality side of our product line. "Don't worry. You don't have to be embarrassed about selling a Kimber," I'd say while recruiting salespeople. "Ours are not guns that will end up in BATF criminal traces. . . . We don't make that kind of stuff and never will as long as I'm here." That was a promise I made to my staff. I made a promise to myself to keep it.

But, of course, it wasn't long before the events in Denver affected us too. It started late in the day when dealers, especially stores around the Denver area, began calling to adjust their orders. In only a few hours, Columbine had produced a sick business-success story for the entire industry.

"These dealers think there might be a sales spike," one of my salesmen told me after I stuck my head into his office. Dealers were parroting three years of NRA talking points: "The Democrats are going to use this to jam more gun-control shit down our throats. So they're doubling and tripling their orders!"

This quick and fearful reaction was a relatively new development. The passage of the Brady Bill and the assault weapons ban had simmered over time. The finishing touches, like pinches of salt, took another year of nuanced political debate. The American public waited, but it was eventually served. That slow process of building to a political solution was officially a thing of the past.

Despite Bill Clinton's reelection in 1996, the NRA and Republicans kept their majorities in Congress, which meant that gun sales dropped and membership drives for gun ownership and gun-rights organizations became more challenging. But 1994 had exposed the fear-driven boom, and fear was still an obvious and powerful source of revenue. To gain maximum advantage, the NRA realized it needed to keep the ingredients ready, to keep stirring the pot. So it set out to supercharge the nation's political landscape. The NRA developed a system that could capture the sales upside of gun-control politics without having to wait on the long legislative process. To make it work, the entire country would have to be constantly held barely below the boiling point as the NRA waited for the next triggering event. When it came, just a few assertions and accusations could make the situation boil over.

For that to happen, the NRA needed constant heat. In fact, it had started priming the reaction to the Columbine massacre three years earlier at its 1996 national convention, an event conspicuously held on the first anniversary of the Oklahoma City bombing. When industry members like us asked about holding the convention on this solemn anniversary, we were told that consideration had been given to changing it but that no one in the NRA wanted to show any sign of weakness.

I attended that 1996 convention in Dallas. It was a presidential election year, and I could feel the fear pulsing through the attendees as they stumbled out of dim ballrooms following speeches meant to drive down reason and to drive up sales.

While working Kimber's booth and talking to customers, I heard a lot of chatter about the NRA's new president. Marion Hammer stood under five feet tall, and she wore a simple bowl haircut and dressed as if trapped in the 1950s. But Hammer possessed a religious certainty when it came to her conservative politics, and she had the fiery southern grit necessary to shape those politics around an industry dominated by men. Just a week before the convention she reinforced the organization's "never give an inch" tone in a *New York Times* interview in which she smiled and suggested that America "just get rid of all liberals" instead of considering any form of gun control.[2]

Hammer became a legendary national political figure who, among other accomplishments, would be almost single-handedly responsible for passage of Florida's controversial "stand your ground law," which allows any person "the right to stand his or her ground and use or threaten to use . . . deadly force if he or she reasonably believes that using or threatening to use such forces is necessary."[3] This law eventually served as the legal justification for the acquittal of George Zimmerman, the Florida man who shot and killed seventeen-year-old Trayvon Martin. Hammer was also influential in the passage of many laws across the country that allowed Americans to carry concealed firearms.

In her speech at the Dallas NRA convention in 1996, Hammer seemed to tap into a new, long-lasting source of fear and hatred that could keep the pressure cooker of a divided America just one tick below maximum. Apparently, she also knew that it was important to divert attention from reality. For that, she needed boogeymen who looked different from the NRA members, and the Clinton administration's much-touted outreach to troubled inner-city youths in the 1994 crime bill provided the perfect target. "Too many [youngsters] have no wholesome recreational activities and as a result, they've been left hanging," she said with a voice deepened by years of cigarette smoke. "Hanging out in the malls, hanging around crack houses, and hanging out in limbo without a moral compass. . . . That is wrong and it has to be fixed, and midnight basketball is not the answer."[4]

Hammer's racist dog whistle echoed through the halls of the NRA for the next twenty-five years. And it was a frontal attack on President Clinton's plan aimed at helping inner-city kids in the most disenfranchised parts of our country. To Hammer and the applauding NRA members, all the problems in society were caused by those wayward Black kids and a few grubby Democratic politicians such as Bill Clinton. She made no mention of the White mass murderers Hinckley, Purdy, Ferri, and Hennard. She made no mention of the White supremacy and misogynist hate that motivated them—even back in 1996. She made no mention of the racist gun shows and militia meetings where Timothy

McVeigh had been "hanging out" as he drew up plans to blow up 168 innocent people in Oklahoma City.

After Hammer unscrewed the lid on the racial undertones, a speech by the NRA's chief lobbyist poured the contents on the floor, drawing a line in the sand between "them" and "us." As the organization's official statements proclaimed in Dallas: "The Second Amendment is facing the greatest political challenge of this century. Our opponents—the anti-prison movement, the anti-hunting movement, the anti-self-defense movement—are pouring tens of millions of dollars into this election year. Right now, Bill Clinton has pulled out all the stops to separate your Second Amendment from the rest of your Bill of Rights."[5]

The NRA was not successful in defeating Clinton later that year, but it had certainly frightened millions of gun owners over minorities and the plans of a nefarious Democratic administration that they believed was bent on confiscating guns and using disaster as a convenient excuse. So by the time that disaster struck at Columbine High School, millions of American gun owners and the entire industry were already poised for action.

The pressure only increased as news about the young shooters and their powerful guns spread across the country. Harris and Klebold had used multiple weapons, including the same model that had spurred the passage of the assault weapons ban: an Intratec Tec-9 assault pistol. The seventeen-year-old boys also equipped themselves with several high-capacity magazines for the assault gun, and those magazines held as many as fifty-two rounds.

The 1994 law specifically banned "hi-cap" mags and the Tec-9, and the killers weren't even old enough to legally purchase guns, but the grandfather clause in the ban allowed the sale of any guns made before 1994. A loophole in the Brady Bill also allowed individuals to buy or sell guns at gun shows without having to undergo background checks. All these two Columbine students needed to do was to enlist three older friends to purchase their weapons at gun shows for them. The boys had exploited cracks in the Brady Bill and the assault weapons ban to build their arsenal. And as with so many other mass shooters, racism was a fueling factor. The boys had deployed that arsenal to wipe out as many people as they could on April 20, the birthday of Adolf Hitler.

Columbine prompted reactions that forced the country one step closer to upending the 224-year-old political system that generally regulated firearms. Just as the NRA planned, there would be calls for action from society but legislative relief would be defeated. This meant that the heat and pressure in the American system just inched further toward the danger zone. But in our Kimber office that day, we had more immediate concerns. "Hey, Busse, we still gonna have the NRA show?" our sales manager, Allen, said as he stuck his head inside my office door.

"They canceled," I replied. "Just got off the phone with Kyle Weaver. Said they're still going to have the business meetings, but none of the manufacturers are going to display. And there's probably going to be a lot of protesting, so they're just going to send all of our guns and booths back."

Indeed, the NRA's business meetings went forward, and as Weaver had predicted, they did result in huge anti-gun-violence protests in downtown Denver. Most of us at Kimber watched from home as Coloradans showed up in force to protest the organization that had become the face of national gun ownership. More than eight thousand people packed the streets with signs that read "Shame on the NRA" and "NRA: Pusher of Child Killer Machines." As the NRA held its meetings inside the Adam's Mark Hotel, the protesters stood outside and chanted into the cameras: "Hey, hey, NRA, how many kids did you kill today?"

Hammer was there too, but no longer as the organization's volunteer leader. In a deft public relations move, she had stepped aside for a new president. She and her friend Wayne LaPierre realized the power of Charlton Heston's celebrity, especially among gunnies. They knew that his popularity would come in handy for times like this. The NRA's members loved Heston, and in the lead-up to 1999 the most popular convention hats and shirts mocked President Clinton with the slogan "Charlton Heston Is My President."

Almost immediately after the shooting at Columbine, the Clinton administration, along with many gun-control advocates, called for legislation to close the "gun-show loophole," just as the NRA had warned. Despite the horror of the shooting, the NRA dismissed the calls to enact legislation that would have prevented killers from exploiting the loophole, determined not to repeat the mistakes of humiliating defeats a few years earlier. The organization dug in. In Denver, where many were still mourning the loss of thirteen innocent people in a senseless massacre, the rhetoric fueled by the NRA was only heating up.

Heston was perfect for the role of NRA president. He spoke with a slow, prophetic gravity, which made sense given his nickname, "Moses," after his portrayal in *The Ten Commandments*. His faithful disciples needed no reminder that Heston's Hollywood role involved protecting aggrieved prisoners from an evil, authoritarian government. As if the whole thing was a movie sequel, both Heston and the NRA acted as if God was on their side.

After accusing the Clinton administration of using tragedy to push new gun-control measures, Moses issued a proclamation from Sinai: "We will not be silent or be told, 'do not come here; you are not welcome in your own land.' We're often cast as the villain. That's not our role in American society, and we will not be forced to play it. We cannot—we must not—let tragedy lay waste to the most rare, hard-won right in history."[6]

Tom Mauser, a Colorado man who had lost his son in the shooting and who took a leading role in the nation's gun-control battle for the next twenty years, spoke outside for the protesters who disagreed with Moses. As the crowd formed a human chain and quietly sang "We Shall Overcome," Mauser spoke, trembling, with tears in his eyes. "Don't let my son's death be in vain," he implored. "I am here today because my son would want me to be here. If my son was alive, he would be here too."[7]

Something in that moment struck me. In Mauser's grief I could imagine what my own father might feel and say if one of his children had been killed by a gun. "Promise me you'll be safe," my dad always said. "No gun is worth losing a life over."

The gun industry did its best to avoid letting its members have personal epiphanies like that. People like me were supposed to put self-reflection aside and wait this out. I struggled with my own thoughts. On one hand, I heard the industry voices saying this was just a one-off incident. No one could have seen it coming. There would always be evil in the world, and good people should not have to sacrifice their rights because of an occasional and unpredictable unhinged few who commit heinous acts. The loudest and most frequent argument revolved around the slippery slope: "If we give them this win, then pretty soon it will be all gun sales that are outlawed." I must have heard that a thousand times, even back in 1999.

On the other hand, I knew that the simple act of closing the gun-show loophole might have saved the kids in Columbine. It seemed like a sensible legislative action, one that might impose minor inconvenience on a few but that might also save lives of innocent people such as Tom Mauser's son. I also knew that the slippery-slope argument was foolish, and that is why, even back then, I started to advocate for supporting legislation that would close that loophole. I did it quietly, but I just did not understand why allowing sales without background checks made any sense or why passing laws to close a loophole that might lead to more murders was "anti-gun." In fact, I thought it was a pro-gun stance because I believed the potential public relations damage to gun ownership was dangerous from a business risk perspective.

Even though I was dubious about unchecked sales at gun shows, I had no powerful connections, and I was certainly not a lobbyist. Besides, I had my own more immediate concerns. So over time I also put Columbine on my own mental back burner and allowed myself to settle back into my daily responsibilities at Kimber.

In the weeks after Columbine, Kimber enjoyed a short sales spike, but this subsided after it became clear that no one seemed to be moving on gun control—something that would become a pattern over the next two decades. Were lawmakers wheeling and dealing over new legislation behind the scenes? Was the NRA finally drawing a line that no one dared cross? Whatever was happening, it was not driving sales. The pump had been primed for a big boom, but the NRA did not yet have enough power.

As soon as orders slowed down, I knew Leslie would call. Since he had taken over for Greg as the public leader of our company, I used our conversations as opportunities to try and decipher him on a personal level, hoping to tap into a hobby we shared or personal passion that might explain him better.

Leslie was smart but socially awkward, and I could tell that he struggled with acceptance. I could see why, but he was the boss. He seemed to sense that people like me at Kimber were trapped. Most of his employees, including me, swapped stories about Leslie blurting inappropriate jokes and then staring awkwardly at us, waiting for a reaction. Occasionally, his jokes were actually funny, but most of the time we felt obliged to provide a courtesy laugh just for the sake of our jobs. Many of us also had stories about his insensitive statements, but he was the boss. We had no one to complain to above him. I tried to view these instances as opportunities to understand Leslie, and when he called after Columbine, I got another chance.

After a brief, difficult-to-understand discussion about which dealers were buying and the obligatory off-color comments on politics, Leslie changed the tone. "So you say sales are a little tough since Columbine, huh?" he said, softly. Was he teeing up a terrible joke for me? Or was he serious? "I was thinking, Ryan, maybe we should just have a really good *back-to-school* sale."

He was amused at his own joke, but I was horrified. I saw Tom Mauser, trembling through tears, and I saw Patrick Ireland falling limp from a school window. It was so far over the line that Leslie's intention did not even matter to me.

"Um, no," I stammered after a few stunned beats of silence. "I don't think so, Leslie." I hung up the phone.

TEN

TOBACCO AND FIREARMS

T HE GENERAL PUBLIC CERTAINLY DID NOT NEED TO HEAR
Leslie Edelman's offensive joke to become disgusted with the
gun industry after the Columbine massacre. Most people in the country expected sympathy and gun-policy contrition. Many of us in the
industry quietly agreed, at least in part. We believed that the NRA was
being tone-deaf and should have done a better job with messaging—
at the very least, it could have at least been more empathetic. None of
us wanted to lose our jobs to more regulation, though, and didn't have
the courage to publicly criticize the NRA or its front man, Wayne
LaPierre. Certainly, no one dared to publicly speak ill of Moses.

To outsiders, our inaction probably looked like a lack of empathy,
but it was really driven by underlying existential fear. If you believed
that your culture and your job were under assault, it was easier to understand why the organization's "stand and fight" mantra felt necessary.
In time, it would be this same sort of existential fear that would cause
tens of millions of people to take what would appear to be uncaring
political positions and to vote for Donald Trump for president.

Back then, the growing fear of the imminent doom of our industry dominated trade shows, business dinners, and conversations, and it often boiled over in my own conversations with Leslie. For months his frequent, angry statements like "All of those asshole mayors are going to put us out of business anyway" echoed what I heard from other executives.

The "asshole mayors" to whom Leslie referred enacted the same strategy used in the 1998 tobacco liability lawsuits a year before Columbine. Those suits resulted in a settlement worth more than $246 billion and forced the tobacco industry to make major sales and marketing concessions. Those restrictions are still in place today.

Frustrated politicians who had spent careers working on gun control turned to mayors who represented citizens affected by gun violence. Mayors from places such as Miami, Chicago, and New Orleans had legal standing and knew how to use it. As they celebrated the success of the tobacco settlements, they re-crafted the arguments and then filed similar lawsuits against many of the nation's largest firearms companies, alleging broad liabilities.

Many people across the country, including most of us, believed that the lawsuits would provide the leverage to force the same sort of concessions agreed to by Big Tobacco, including a cessation of most paid marketing and mandates requiring new safety devices and graphic warning labels on gun packaging. We also had reason to expect massive compensation payments to governments for the violent impacts of guns.

By 2000, the list of entities that filed suits even expanded to include medium-sized cities such as Bridgeport, Connecticut, whose mayor, Joseph Ganim, went to court that January. Mayor Ganim made his case in a news conference on the same day he filed his $100 million suit: "We're saying to the handgun manufacturers that from now on, you are responsible for the cost of handgun violence, not Bridgeport families." Ganim also laid out the goals and tactics of the lawsuits, which focused on forcing gun companies to add safety modifications to their products by threatening court settlements.[1]

Miami mayor Alex Penelas also filed suit, and he laid the responsibility for dead children at the feet of our industry. "We will not allow the gun industry to escape accountability any longer," Penelas said at a news conference. "They have killed our children by the dozens."[2] By *they*, Penelas meant *us*. Me.

The lawsuits and corresponding press conferences sought to make advancements in two areas: improving safety devices on handguns and ensuring that companies controlled the distribution of guns to prohibit criminals from buying or stealing them. To reinforce the sales angles in the suits, the litigants also named three industry trade groups and several dealers who had sold guns that were used in crimes.

Back then, my thoughts on guns in general involved little nuance, and how I felt about the lawsuits was no different. I had a gut feeling that the industry should be proactive in preventing gun deaths, but I generally just stopped there. That's the way a lot of gun-industry people reacted. On one hand, there was agreement among us that there could be an issue, but there was also stalwart opposition to dealing with it, or at least opposition to a bunch of industry outsiders forcing action. Even though it seemed like none of us gave our position much thought, it probably came down to the simple fear of losing careers and compensation. The mayors suspected that it really was about even bigger sums of money.

When asked about the large monetary damage claims, Mayor Ganim explained that because the industry was in the habit of giving large contributions to the NRA to stop legislation, he believed it necessary to go after the industry's money: "That's the route that we're going because [the NRA has] always very effectively, with big money, lobbied the legislature and kept laws from being passed."

The lawsuits gained steam when, in December 1999, President Clinton and Andrew Cuomo, his secretary of Housing and Urban Development (HUD) joined the cause, adding a feared army of powerful federal lawyers to the fight. It would be expensive for the federal government to join, but Cuomo believed it was a sound investment because his agency spent more than $1 billion each year implementing policies to keep citizens safe from gun violence. Clinton reinforced the importance of the suit and let everyone know that the goal was to force the industry to end what he called "irresponsible marketing practices."[3]

The lawsuits. The constant discussion of more gun control. And now Columbine. A one-two-three punch seemed to collude against the industry at once. The pressure increased just days after the massacre, when Republicans in the Colorado legislature pulled two bills that would have expanded the right to carry concealed guns and limited the city of Denver's ability to restrict gun sales.[4] The last time the industry had been embarrassed like this was 1994. And this wasn't supposed to happen again to the most powerful lobbying organization in the country.

All of this frightened Leslie, but not as much as the owners of the companies named in the lawsuits. So far, Kimber had escaped being named largely because local mayors had relied on crime statistics to select the companies they would target, and Kimber products—just as Greg Warne wanted all those years ago—were not showing up in those stats. But of course we paid close attention. The lawsuits named all the largest companies, and we believed that if several companies went down, it could be the end of the gun business as we knew it.

Federal law required all gun manufacturers to maintain "acquisition and disposition" (A&D) books. These records carefully recorded every gun we built, then tracked the dealers we shipped them to. Whenever a gun is used in a crime, the US Bureau of Alcohol, Tobacco, Firearms and Explosives tries to obtain that gun's serial number, and then the agency researches the sales history by "tracing" the gun through the manufacturer's A&D records. Sometimes the trail peters out before it reaches the crime scene, but with a serial number, investigators always know where the gun was made. This is why removing serial numbers from guns is such a serious crime.

Kimbers were almost never traced, which meant that my promises of high-quality products to potential employees, and my quiet assurances to Sara, had so far proven true. I took some solace in that, but to Leslie it seemed like very cold comfort. "It's like they say about rising and falling tides," he said to me in an afternoon call. "We are a boat just like them. I mean, yeah, we are trying to take market share from Smith and Ruger and Glock, but if their volume is cut, it will mean the retailers go out of business, and that means we make less money. *You* make less money, Ryan." Leslie was right about the tides, but as usual he seemed to care only about the money. I wanted to make a living too, but I also cared about the promises I made. And I couldn't shake the feeling that we were heading down a dangerous moral road.

Ed Shultz, the CEO of Smith & Wesson, could not make the same assurances to his wife. And he certainly could not promise potential employees that the guns they sold would escape the attention of government criminal traces. Smith & Wesson produced more than 20 percent of the handguns sold in America, which meant that criminals regularly used them. That's why the company was named in every single lawsuit.

Smith & Wesson, which many people regard as an iconic American company, was, in fact, not owned by Americans. The British conglomerate Tomkins PLC had purchased Smith & Wesson for $112 million in 1987. The fact that foreigners owned Smith & Wesson often prompted the leaders of other gun companies to whisper doubts about the trustworthiness of the company.

Tomkins sought to remedy the trust issue by hiring Shultz, a self-described "rabid gun owner."[5] Shultz seemed right for the job. He had grown up in Iowa, where he attended a one-room schoolhouse, and he looked and even acted like former president Harry Truman. But if Tomkins thought it was hiring a CEO who would fall into line with the rest of the industry, it was wrong.

Shultz was an uncommon gun CEO who believed in old-fashioned negotiating. He believed in the give-and-take of the old political system. Shultz was outspoken, often claiming that there were business and moral reasons to justify proactive gun control. Importantly, he believed that the widening gap between gun-control advocates and gun-rights activists would eventually only hurt the gun industry. He was also the sort of man who did not just want to engage in the dirty business of debating adversaries. Shultz wanted to act. "Having grown up on a hog farm, I have always been aware that if you get into a wrassle with a pig in a mudhole, two things happen," he once told the *Hartford Courant.* "You get very dirty, and the pig loves it."[6]

If Shultz was tired of fighting in the mud, New York attorney general Eliot Spitzer, Connecticut attorney general Richard Blumenthal, and HUD secretary Andrew Cuomo offered a hot shower. They had been looking for a negotiated solution to put limitations on the gun industry for months. And as the liabilities from municipal lawsuits and the threats from the federal government became too much to bear, Shultz agreed to a backroom settlement.

The deal, negotiated with only one company and in secret, shielded Smith & Wesson from the threat of lawsuits in exchange for committing to mandatory trigger locks on all guns and the eventual development of "smart guns." *Smart guns* was a term that meant new technology to ensure that only the owner of a gun could fire the weapon had to be integrated in the fire-control systems. Perhaps more importantly, the deal also enforced strict limits on the marketing and display of firearms to the general public, and it all had to happen within three years.

On March 18, 2000, Shultz joined President Clinton at a surprise press conference to announce the agreement. To all members of the shooting industry it was a complete gut punch. No one, especially not the NRA, had any idea this was coming. Clinton, who had often criticized the gun-show loophole that led to the purchase of guns used at Columbine, triumphantly noted that an important component of the new agreement would force dealers to ensure background checks at gun shows and limit maximum daily purchases to a single gun.

Shultz had just announced costly and controversial new gun policies that might be extended to the rest of the gun business. And he shocked everyone. Immediately, the entire industry scrambled. Most of us knew that if one or two more big companies joined Smith & Wesson, the new restrictions would become de facto law, which is precisely what the Clinton administration had bet on.

First up was Glock, which found success as the largest supplier of firearms to America's police departments, and it had won most of that business by beating out Smith & Wesson over the previous decade. Glock executives knew that failure to comply could cost them their hard-won law-enforcement business. Indeed, the day after Shultz's surprise press conference with Clinton, and under pressure from the White House, the mayors of Miami, Atlanta, and Detroit announced that their police departments would purchase only Smith & Wesson firearms for their officers. Within an hour after that announcement the news leaked that Glock was strongly considering the administration's deal.

Dwight and I absorbed all these breakneck developments in disbelief. Talk of the settlement and its ramifications consumed every call with every dealer and every moment between us. "I was just on the phone with the guys at the NRA publications," Dwight said after ending an animated phone call in our office. He was furious. "I think we need to *boycott* these bastards. We need to make sure no one buys a Smith & Wesson gun no matter what. If this all becomes law, our lives are going to get a lot harder. The industry will be a shadow of itself." By "we," Dwight meant the entire industry. Back then, and even today, there is a kind of connection among all gun-industry members. The kind of subconscious link formed in a war, when many personal differences are ignored as the larger existential issues are addressed.

"I think you're right," I replied. I agreed we had to flex our own muscles. We could not let the industry fold like this and wreck everything we worked so hard for. I did not understand it at the time, but my quick response came from my own belief at the time that our industry *was* under serious attack. It came from the sort of fear that builds up over time. The NRA had carefully but aggressively fostered this belief inside all of us since the 1994 assault weapons ban, and like soldiers in a war, none of us ever stopped to question it.

"Delfay will be sending us all a message," Dwight added. "He'll let us know what we need to do."

Bob Delfay was a leader of the National Shooting Sports Foundation (NSSF), our industry's trade group, which is closely aligned with the NRA. Dwight and I eagerly awaited direction from the NSSF, and it didn't take long. The NSSF announced that all other gun companies would join forces to push back against the secret deal that Smith & Wesson had negotiated in what Delfay called a "coordinated effort." He relied on the strength and reputations of his organization's members, which included Kimber and all other manufacturers. "We are confident that no other major manufacturers will desert this coordinated effort in favor of their own individual deal," Delfay said in a public rebuke of Smith & Wesson.[7] And with that, Smith & Wesson officially became a pariah.

Both the NSSF and the NRA had been caught flat-footed. Nothing in the gun business was supposed to happen without their explicit approval or direction. This rogue behavior from a leader of a foreign-owned company did not have a page in their playbook. But the embarrassing defeat of 1994 had taught both organizations to play hardball: No dissent. No defectors. No prisoners. Never again would they allow anyone to step out of line.

ELEVEN

THE WAGES OF SIN

A S THE INDUSTRY ANGER OVER SMITH & WESSON'S ROGUE agreement grew and soon after the NRA caught its breath after the surprise attack, it became clear to all of us that there would be hell to pay. The headline of an NRA press release on March 20, 2000, left no doubt about what that hell would be:

THE SMITH & WESSON SELLOUT

The NRA first claimed that President Clinton had "declared his Administration's war on American gun owners." And with Vice President Al Gore gearing up for a run to succeed his boss in the Oval Office, the NRA heaped blame on him too: "Smith & Wesson, Inc., a British-owned company, recently became the first to run up the white flag of surrender and run behind the Clinton-Gore lines, leaving its competitors in the U.S. firearms industry to carry on the fight for the Second Amendment. Of course, there is no Second Amendment in Britain, where subjects are barred from owning handguns and many long guns."[1] Dwight and I pored over the angry statement, which also listed various ways in which the Clinton/Shultz agreement would essentially ruin firearms ownership in America. It did not call for any boycott, but we all read that word between the lines.

Leslie read the statement too and called us immediately, scared and seething. "We can't let these fuckers get away with this!" he barked through the speakerphone. "Dealers will go out of business, and sales will be cut in half."

"Glock is about ready to sign up," I said.

"I've already been making calls," Dwight replied. "Let's send Shultz a fucking message."

The unspoken truth, understood by all manufacturers, was that if new safety requirements, smart-gun mandates, and distribution regulations were forced on us, guns would become more expensive. And more-expensive guns meant that fewer people could buy them.

"Whatever has to be done needs to be done," Leslie mumbled, "and we don't have much time." Then he slammed down his phone. Dwight and I looked at each other knowing exactly what needed to be done. There was never any overt order at Kimber; neither Leslie nor the NRA explicitly directed a coordinated boycott. But they didn't need to. Everyone who worked in any gun company knew that the most effective way to send or receive any message was through cash flow. We also knew that a boycott was the fastest way to interrupt Smith & Wesson's supply of money.

I went to work calling and faxing dealers, imploring them to stop selling Smith & Wesson products and to send back the guns they already had. Because of the wartime camaraderie common even among dealers, none of this came off as a competitive play. There was an understood and shared common goal to just stay alive. I reinforced that message too: Smith & Wesson was out to hurt *all* companies that sold firearms. It did not matter if the message came from a competitor; it quickly resonated. And because of the dealer network I had developed, I enjoyed a direct line to accounts across the country and had hundreds of personal relationships. Dwight did the same with his extensive network of gun writers and publishers. "Holy shit," he stammered when he learned that one of Smith & Wesson's largest customers in Florida announced that it was joining the boycott. "RSR is out."

"Yeah, I just talked to them an hour ago, and I thought that's the way they would go," I told him. "I have at least fifty other big accounts that are doing the same thing."

In our minds we were the eighteen-year-old boys who had just learned about the attack on Pearl Harbor. We didn't need to be told; we just rushed to sign up for battle. There was something reflexive about the boycott, as if we had all been primed for just such an action. Dwight and I had begun the effort, but the hints dropped by Bob Delfay and the National Shooting Sports Foundation ensured that the effort to strangle Smith & Wesson took hold easily. By the end of the day, Dwight and I had made real headway in imposing an effective boycott of Smith & Wesson, and we were getting a lot of support from around the industry.

As sales dried up for Smith & Wesson, industry companies took notice, especially Glock. In a quick statement to the press, a Glock executive stated that the company had decided to back off on negotiating with the Clinton administration. It would rather risk "bleeding to death with legal bills" than experience the horrors being inflicted on Smith & Wesson.[2]

The NRA, of course, realized that all of this meant additional fundraising and membership opportunities. In what would become a go-to play for all controversies, the organization used the uncertainty to help stuff the coffers, and the NRA ended the year with nearly a quarter million new dues-paying members.

Large dealers and other manufacturers took note of my efforts. In an industry that had been conditioned to fear constant attacks, people wanted to cheer the brave warriors who counted coup on any enemy. The social adulation was sometimes subtle and sometimes obvious. "Great job on the Smith & Wesson deal" was a comment that we heard many times.

Seemingly all of a sudden, I became a prominent player in the gun industry. I had finally proven myself in the trenches. My peers saw I had made a difference; I was not someone to ever fuck with. No one could deny I played a key role in helping the NRA build the foundation for a new brand of national politics that demanded almost religious devotion.

There was only one unwritten but clearly understood line of scripture in this new political church: "100 percent loyalty and no one steps out of line. Period." The organization had learned to be unforgiving. Anything but strict adherence was an unforgivable sin, and Ed Shultz would soon realize the wages of that sin.

As our boycott took hold, national news reports highlighted the large red circles and slashes that gun-store owners drew over the Smith & Wesson logo in their shop windows across the country. Within days of the agreement, Shultz struggled to hold his multinational company together in the face of plummeting sales. In a statement the marketing director let the industry know that our efforts were working: "We've been getting beat up pretty bad, and the whole idea seems to be a boycott of Smith & Wesson products," Ken Jorgensen said.[3]

Shultz later described his almost instantaneous fall from gun-industry celebrity to outcast: "When I first came here in 1992, people were very excited when I told them I was with Smith & Wesson," he told the *Hartford Courant*. "They told me about all the guns they owned. Now, when I got on a plane to go somewhere and people saw the Smith & Wesson logo on my briefcase, they would look at me straight in the eye like they hated me. They made it real clear they just wished I would fall out of the plane."[4]

By the summer, our boycott forced Shultz to lay off hundreds of employees. In an attempt to explain his actions and stop the bleeding, he appealed to gun owners with statements that were part explanation and part plea for decency in the wake of Columbine. In a 2018 interview about it all, Shultz recounted the difficult nature of his decisions: "I changed I said, 'OK, we have to find another solution.' You can't just say, 'I made [the gun], I shipped it, it's out of my hands.'"[5]

Despite his pleas for reason in 2000, the NRA and gun owners would have none of it. For them, murdered kids at Columbine may have been bad, but they knew how easily it could result in the loss of their gun rights. They were hardened for battle. Many remembered how Ronald Reagan had used this same kind of sympathy in the wake of the Luby's and 101 California Street shootings as he successfully lobbied the last few Republicans to vote yes on gun control. The NRA knew that its members needed to watch a public spectacle. Now Ed Shultz had to be marched to the gallows.

As if it were a hanging at high noon in the middle of an Old West town, we all watched the bottom drop out from under Ed Shultz. He resigned as CEO of Smith & Wesson in late September, barely six months after standing on the stage with the president of the United States. The square-jawed CEO, who had grown up on a hog farm and who loved to hunt, was defiant to the end. In his final statement he both made the case for his actions and chided the rest of the industry: "I had to make those decisions based on the tradition of the company and my own beliefs of what's right. Would I put locks on our guns if it might save one child? The answer was yes."

The next spring, Tomkins accepted an offer to sell Smith & Wesson to a small group of investors based in Phoenix. They paid only $15 million. A few days later, the new ownership group traveled to NRA headquarters in Fairfax, Virginia, to make peace with the organization that now ran the industry. Like a great king assessing a casualty report from enemy territory, the NRA was confident that the sacrifice of Shultz's career and Tomkins's loss of a couple hundred million dollars had taught everyone an important lesson. The NRA forgave Smith & Wesson and allowed the company back into the fold.

All of us in the industry took note. Leaders from every company began making very large and very public contributions to the NRA, an unspoken requirement that only became more obvious over time.

By 2011, Smith & Wesson once again dared to embrace British leadership from a new CEO named James Debney, but James knew to study history rather than to make it. Debney made sure to buy the million-dollar Gold Jacket from the NRA, and he knew to stay off the stage with Democratic presidents.

In hundreds of subsequent news stories about the relationship between the gun industry and the NRA, there were many inferences to the fact that the NRA did the industry's bidding. The stories might say things like "The NRA is just an arm of the gun industry." In truth it is the opposite. The gun industry is an arm of the NRA, and the events of 2000 proved this to be true. Crushing Shultz and Smith & Wesson reminded all companies that the NRA ran the show.

All executives knew the unspoken org chart. Nobody would develop innovative new products without the NRA's approval. It even became standard practice to seek new-product-development and marketing advice from top NRA staffers. This kept manufacturers in the good graces of the NRA and ensured that the organization always had a bead on industry trends. The NRA may have overreacted to the Smith & Wesson betrayal, but it did not want to be surprised again. The NRA's control had far-reaching implications, including any advancements of gun-safety technology, for example. I saw it in our own leadership discussions too. "Why don't we quietly work on a smart gun?" one of the members of our team asked as we considered possible new projects. "If we could figure out a design that really worked, we could make a huge splash!"

"Yeah, that's a decent idea," Dwight responded before he winced and added, "but if the NRA ever found out that we were working on that shit, we'd get crucified too."

Dwight was right. For years there had been a lot of controversy around the idea of developing a "smart gun" with electronic security to prevent children or other people from firing a gun they did not own. Resistance came from many angles, and they were all magnified by the NRA. Some believed that the electronics would fail, causing the gun to be useless. Some believed a conspiracy theory that electronics might provide the government with a way to disable guns. Some resisted because the guns might be more expensive. All gun-company executives could see the promise in perfecting the new technology, but we were all scared to death to try.

I confirmed this fear with other executives who relayed stories about similar discussions in their boardrooms. In any other industry, pursuing this sort of new technology would have been the holy grail for business development, but the NRA made sure it was kryptonite for the shooting industry. For the NRA, one of the most inflammatory components of the Smith & Wesson agreement involved forcing integral locks on many pistol models. We all knew that something as revolutionary as smart guns was certainly out of the question.

It was as if the NRA had a seat on every leadership team of every gun company. Manufacturers even allowed NRA officials to name their products so that the organization had a vested interest in their success. And the NRA magazines mailed to millions of members every month, including *American Rifleman* and *American Hunter*, usually got the first crack at all new-product announcements.

There were dozens of other advertising venues, but most companies spent an inordinate amount of advertising budgets with the NRA. Kimber was no exception. Eventually, we wrote huge checks every year to advertise with the organization. This sort of industry spending got so out of control that the NRA had to invent ways to allocate the funds. Free videos, web ads, banquet sponsorships, then NRATV. Most of the advertising made no real business sense, but the last thing anyone wanted was to be marched to the Shultz gallows.

Just like the eventual Republican devotion to Donald Trump, the NRA's grip on our industry was nearly total. Whenever there was an opportunity for a gun company or executive to comment about some controversy or policy, we all knew to run it by the NRA in advance. In future years, when the New York legislature considered gun-related bills, Kimber and all other companies parroted the talking points from the NRA, and we stuck to those messages because we knew not to upset anyone in far-off Fairfax, Virginia.

Most executives never even spoke to politicians without the NRA's involvement. If you wanted to stay employed, you were expected to toe these lines. Just as in all authoritarian regimes, there was no official set of rules or a meeting to spell out the expectations. All subjects knew to pitch in and make a big deal of it if possible. The NRA staff, gun-industry executives, and a growing army of internet-fueled gun consumers all made sure to do the policing.

The NRA also expected us to help drum up membership. We firearms companies sold millions of guns each year, and the NRA knew damn well that each sale meant a potential new NRA member. Almost all gun companies happily sought more approval by adding NRA membership cards inside their packaging. Kimber placed the card in our boxes, like a Hallmark card tucked inside a birthday present. Many companies went even further in displaying devotion and paid for free NRA memberships with the purchase of a new gun. We all complied partially because NRA members had become the core customer base for us all, but mostly it was fear.

Individuals also began jostling for NRA affirmation. My overt boycott efforts went a long way toward securing a position of honor, and I regularly received compliments about my role in preventing the industry from becoming a shadow of itself. Some of those came from top officials at the NRA.

My role in the boycott helped cement me in the most trusted circles of insiders. They thought of me as a brave frontline soldier worthy of promotion. Together with my growing professional accomplishments at Kimber, I was on the fast track.

I did not know it at the time, but my actions had also caught the eyes of the powerful people who lost the Smith & Wesson battle. As Blumenthal, Spitzer, and Cuomo watched their plan crumble, they were also taking note of a gun executive from Montana who had played a leadership role in derailing the whole effort. Other gun companies patted me on the back, but these three rising stars in the Democratic Party were preparing to hit Kimber with subpoenas.

TWELVE

BUSTED

E LIOT SPITZER WAS SMART, MEAN, AND DEDICATED. AS A prosecutor, he aimed for big targets and hunted powerful enemies. While in charge of anti-racketeering in the office of the Manhattan district attorney, Spitzer even built an undercover sweatshop that he used to infiltrate and prosecute the Gambino crime family's trucking and garment rackets. After New Yorkers elected him as attorney general, Spitzer deployed his vast subpoena power to target fraud committed by the country's largest companies and wealthiest people. This dogged pursuit of financial crime earned him a fearsome reputation and the nickname "Sheriff of Wall Street."

In 2000 Andrew Cuomo served as Bill Clinton's secretary of Housing and Urban Development. His father, New York governor Mario Cuomo, was a perennial presidential hopeful. After Andrew's stint as a cabinet secretary, he also went on to be elected as New York attorney general, then governor, like his father. The younger Cuomo came from a family of political royalty, and he brought to the office smarts and determination: traits that would come in handy in 2020 as he battled

President Trump in televised daily sparring matches over the country's response to the COVID-19 outbreak, and then again as he fought to stay in office after multiple scandals plagued his administration in 2021.

Richard Blumenthal would one day be the senior U.S. senator from Connecticut, but prior to 2000 he made a name for himself as the Constitution State's attorney general. Blumenthal led the legal attack on the tobacco industry, and then he sued tobacco behemoth Philip Morris when it published a cartoon advertisement in *Rolling Stone*, on grounds that the ad violated the terms of the nation's huge tobacco settlement. Before that, Blumenthal sued Microsoft in a successful antitrust settlement that changed the rules of personal computing for the entire globe. He was smart, calculating, and ambitious. Having served as assistant to political giants such as senators Abe Ribicoff and Daniel Patrick Moynihan, and having clerked for Supreme Court justice Harry Blackmun, Blumenthal also had a long list of very powerful friends.

Clinton entrusted his administration's gun-control efforts to these three Democratic rising stars. These were the people who sat down with Ed Shultz as Smith & Wesson negotiated its secret deal. These were the men who watched in frustration as gun companies coalesced to resist a deal they hoped would remake America's gun culture. The outcome angered them, and they suspected that our boycott violated federal antitrust laws. These were the three people who zeroed in on the actions of a Montana sales office that looked like a hunting lodge and then used the power of the Federal Trade Commission (FTC) to file a federal antitrust action against Kimber and me.

Given the pedigrees of these politicians and the power of the federal agency they were about to use, it seemed clear that I would be at a disadvantage. I had faced the law only once in my life, in a small-town traffic court when I was in high school. I had broken a litany of traffic laws in an attempt to use a fast car to impress a pretty girl during a late-night street race in the small town where I grew up. Even though there were no big-time attorneys and certainly no cabinet secretaries to fight me in court, the result was still an embarrassing and expensive legal defeat, at least for a kid of sixteen.

My second brush with the law proved to be far more serious and involved Spitzer and Blumenthal, who let the threat of antitrust prosecution slip during a press conference in the spring of 2000. "We have issued subpoenas," Blumenthal said. "We are conducting interviews." Blumenthal did not give up specific names, but he went on to mention that they were looking at "companies in the industry." Spitzer added he was "intrigued by some of the things we have heard."[1] His quiet confidence worried me. This was the same guy that had taken down the Gambino family.

Dwight quickly fired off an email to the office. The subject line laid out the issue: "New York State Attorney General says industry reaction against Smith might be antitrust." That subject was enough to get the point across, but the email went on to give everyone in the office more explicit direction:

> A.G. Spitzer, who is one of the brokers of the Smith deal with Housing and Urban Development, says that an investigation might commence to determine if antitrust violations have or might be occurring. Smith says they might be forced out of business by the reaction to their deal. As an overview, a coordinated activity by the industry against Smith might in fact be antitrust. Such an activity would include a threat or suggestion of a boycott. Be advised that it would not be a good idea to suggest any form of action to a dealer or other industry member.

In other words, the feds had smelled a rat in our unofficial boycott. After Dwight sent that email, he walked into my office. "Uh-oh," I said. "Little fucking late for an overview of antitrust law, ain't it? If you haven't noticed, we've been organizing a boycott around here. That's what we're trying to do, remember?"

"Don't worry," he replied. "Just covering some asses. I don't think they'll really do it. They're just trying to intimidate us into stopping."

By May, Smith & Wesson was on life support, and no other company in the industry would budge. Spitzer, Cuomo, and Blumenthal decided to throw a Hail Mary to salvage their deal. Dwight was wrong; the Democratic trio of prosecutors wanted us to end our boycott, and they needed to make an example to show the rest of the country that the gun industry wasn't immune from future gun control. Our first subpoena was served to Kimber's Yonkers factory on May 2, 2000.

"Goddamn Democrats!" Leslie Edelman yelled at me. "Now they got the federal government to investigate us? How the fuck did that happen, Ryan?" I said nothing into the phone as I let him collect his breath. "And *you* are named. And a bunch of stuff you did is probably going to come out. Get ready to get on a plane. You'll be flying east and talking to a lot of goddamn lawyers. Go to the fax machine. I'm sending you some shit to read. Better study up." Leslie slammed down his phone, and I tried to swallow with a lump in my throat.

I had, in fact, helped organize a boycott of Smith & Wesson. I had sent multiple emails directing my staff to help. I sent faxes filled with explicit requests. I had initiated dozens of conversations with dealers. To make matters worse, I did it all without much consideration of any antitrust laws.

News of the federal antitrust investigation against Kimber quickly made its rounds in the industry, which prompted me to call up a couple of the executives I knew at other companies. But all those congratulatory back pats from others in the industry were not going to be much help now. In fact, what I heard from them only exacerbated my fears. "Those Democrat assholes are mean," one industry friend told me. "All they care about is putting us all out of business. They hate that we even *own* guns. They need an example, and I bet they rig the whole thing to hang you from a light pole."

The NRA had invested a lot in making the Clinton administration and its allies into bigger-than-life boogeymen, and it worked. When I called up another buddy, he added some conspiracy theory to the mix: "Shit, Busse, I bet they even have the judges in their pockets. That's the way these big-city New Yorkers work."

As I assessed my odds, I could only see that there was high confidence in a scenario where I would be subjected to some sort of white-collar torture followed by a public embarrassment and the loss of my dream career. But as worried as I was, I also focused on learning exactly what I needed to do to avoid that disastrous outcome. I studied up on tactics and legal tools—things like discovery, motions, and affidavits.

Leslie had hired an expensive attorney with an office in Lower Manhattan. That attorney further expanded my legal lexicon when he called to prep me for my upcoming trip to New York in August.

"When you get here, we will do a murder board with you for about half a day," he warned, matter-of-factly. *Murder board? That sounds terrifying*, I thought, making a note to look up the term. "Then we'll take a break, and then we'll do it again the next day, and then we will do it the next day until you are ready. You are not called to testify until Monday, so if we have to do them on Saturday and Sunday too, that's what we'll do."

The trio of prosecutors had plenty to murder me with. For weeks, a team of lawyers had scoured my phone and email records. They had copies of my files and had spoken with all of my sales team as well as many of the dealers I contacted. Those lawyers turned my professional life upside down. They collected all the stuff that fell out and sent it to the attorneys representing the Federal Trade Commission, as well as the states of Connecticut and New York.

During the weeks of back-and-forth with our attorneys, I had plenty of time to build up expectations about what the other side would be like. How would they talk? What would their hair look like? What would they wear, and how would they walk? Given the dark language from the NRA and the foreboding conversations with others in the industry, I believed that the federal attorneys would be an intimidating mix of movie stars and supervillains—probably a little heavy on the villain.

The week finally came for me to travel to New York, and I settled into a room in the Marriott tucked between the Twin Towers in Manhattan. Each day I got up and walked a couple of blocks to a legal office where a group of attorneys questioned me over and over, coaching me on what to say and how to say it. They took turns playing the opposing counsel.

"Did you send an email to Cecil Cahill marked URGENT?" one of them asked.

"Yes, if that's what the record says."

"And Mr. Busse, did that email read in part, 'Today's agreement by Smith & Wesson is tragic. Despite the press's gloss on the issues, it is clear that this is an endrun on our industry. I therefore ask that you immediately cease the retail of all Smith products and immediately return all unsold products direct to Smith & Wesson'?"

"Is this where I am supposed to say, 'I am not sure, but you have the written record, and we should rely on that—not my memory'?"

"Yes, good!"

"OK, here's another one," an attorney piped in. "Did the whole office get an email from a Mr. Dwight Van Brunt that read, 'I was told yesterday that the City of Bridgeport approached Ruger in an effort to get them to sign on, and Ruger told Bridgeport to have a meaningful sexual encounter with itself'?"

"Yeah, that sounds just like something Dwight would say."

"No, Ryan," another one interjected, patiently. "Remember, rely only on the written record. Do not offer a comment. And damn sure don't smile, even if you think it's funny. Dwight did write that, but just let the record speak for itself."

"Yes, sorry. Keep going."

This went on for hours and hours until we had examined every document and phone record a dozen times—until the attorneys had anticipated what they thought was every possible legal question. The legal team seemed confident that I may have been guilty of a lot of rabble-rousing and had done a good job with the boycott organizing but ultimately that I had not violated any federal antitrust laws.

Their assessment of my innocence hinged on the definition of *antitrust*, which requires official coordination between competitors to be considered a crime. Many people from different companies had, in fact, exacted their own punishment on Smith & Wesson, but none of us actually *coordinated*. Not officially, anyway.

What we did was apply another future tactic of modern politics, developed by the NRA and soon to be adopted by the political Right. That tactic was to summon legions of gun companies together to form a single, massive, unstoppable army dedicated to protecting the center of power that sold our guns and, more importantly, to build a culture that made those guns sacred. Every joke, every sideways glance, every comment about "fucking Democrats" kept all soldiers constantly at the ready. When the NRA dabbled with overt or covert racism, as they did in Marion Hammer's speech, all warriors got the message about what was acceptable and what tools were to be used. No one ever needed to give or receive an official order.

Years later, troll armies on the Right and enforcers in the Trump White House, like campaign manager Paul Manafort and fixer Michael Cohen, acted under the same unwritten enforcement rules. The directions came to all of us in quiet signals that we were trained to look for, from racist dog whistles to the subtle winks that empower White supremacists (just like Trump's directive to the White nationalist group the Proud Boys, during his 2020 debate with Joe Biden, to "stand back, stand by"). Whether the directive was written or not, everyone knew that we were called to protect our pro-gun leaders and attack everyone else. The same commands would be employed to maximum effect in the Trump administration, and the NRA was the proving ground for it all.

What the NRA did back then was far more effective than any direct order for an industry-wide boycott, anyway. We all feared losing our jobs, maybe even the cultures from which we came. When the hated Democrats struck a match and waved it over the gasoline fumes of that fear, we reacted en masse and with lightning speed to snuff out any flame.

I studied the case and the law enough to believe that I had not been involved in any official antitrust conspiracy. Even with that confidence, though, I still worried that the powerful prosecutors knew how to twist the evidence, and there was a lot of evidence: dozens of letters and emails from me and from Dwight. Piles of phone records indicating we had made or directed thousands of calls. Proven relationships between me and executives of other companies. Their warnings made me believe that crafty attorneys could take all of that and make it look like I coordinated the entire effort. In other words, I had good reason to be scared shitless.

When the day for the beginning of my testimony arrived, I remember I wore the same necktie I had worn to Vern's General Store. It was my favorite, and I considered it to be a good-luck charm. But unlike that day in Idaho, I had no expectation that I would bullshit some attorney into letting me off with an easy victory. I would not be dealing with a phone-book lawyer and a diner waitress.

The room in the large New York City courthouse was empty and sterile. Twenty chairs surrounded a huge table below bright fluorescent lights. If we had not been here for a legal proceeding, the room would have been perfect for an autopsy. As people filed in for the proceedings, I tried to pick out the supervillains or maybe the movie stars. Had Cuomo or Spitzer made the trip themselves?

I sat with attorneys on either side of me. Across the table there were five people, including a couple taking notes, and a stenographer at the far end. Directly in front of me was a middle-aged man in a suit with sleeves that were too short. He had messy salt-and-pepper hair and thin glasses.

This must be a mistake, I thought. This man could have been a high school chemistry teacher. This dweeby man could not be the attorney sent by supervillains to take me out.

For the first couple of hours the salt-and-pepper man asked me direct questions as he peered over his glasses and scribbled notes. "Did you call Bob from RSR?" "Did you make a plan with anyone from Ruger?"

"In your phone records, we see you called McBride's in Austin, Texas. What did you talk about with them?"

When he started to press me about a letter I had faxed, my attorney leaned over and whispered, "Bathroom."

"What?" I whispered back, trying to listen without turning my head toward him. "What did you say?"

"Piss. Tell them you have to take a piss. I'll meet you in the bathroom."

I asked for a restroom break, and the attorney followed. Defying polite men's restroom etiquette, he selected the urinal directly next to me. "They might be recording in there, and I'd bet they have this men's room bugged too," he whispered. "So keep it quiet. You're doing great. Just make sure to say 'I don't recall' some more."

Back in the autopsy room, the questions dragged on. One of the other Federal Trade Commission attorneys took over for a while, and the salt-and-pepper guy leaned back to stretch. I could see that there were holes in the bottom of his shoes.

My mind drifted off. This was neither a movie star nor a supervillain. He was not hell-bent on destroying me or my industry, as far as I could tell. He was just some middle-aged attorney who had been sent here to do a job. He probably had a family, or maybe he was thinking about what he would bring home for dinner. The scary government boogeyman that I had been told would be here never even came close to that courthouse. This guy had favorite comfy shoes just like the rest of us. Soon he took over again and asked several questions about my motives.

The whole ordeal took five hours. Then we all cordially shook hands and went our ways.

That evening the lights of the massive Twin Towers lit up my hotel room as I sat on the bed drinking a room-service beer. A week of murder boards and five hours of deposition left me exhausted. My mind wandered as I contemplated the events of the past few months.

Back then, as I sat in the Marriott, it all seemed clear. I had acted on instinct, and when questioned under oath, I answered questions honestly, based on what I believed at the time. It took a while, but a year later the FTC and the states of New York and Connecticut dropped the antitrust case.

Even now that I have had years to assess my role, I still don't fully recall what drove my actions. They felt instinctual. I was caught up in the fear of losing a career in an industry that was already prone to being irrationally fearful. Yes, it was easy to get sucked into the moment and to contribute to what felt like a wartime effort. Fear of loss was the key, but I also harbored the unthinking politics of aggrievement. I was ambitious and wanted to make a mark that people would notice. I wanted to knock a big competitor out of the game. Whatever the combination of reasons, I cannot dispute that I rushed into battle, sword drawn. And I drew blood.

I regret what I did. It's not so much that I am sorry about derailing the particulars of the deal that Shultz negotiated with the Clinton administration. The truth is that the policy prescriptions in that agreement *were* complex. Some were nothing more than uninformed ideas. Some would have been quite effective; some were probably foolish. Regardless, I still believe that our country should have considered them using the old imperfect system where pressures build and solutions are then debated.

What I regret is that I helped the NRA create a political world where that debate can no longer happen. The NRA fomented a hardline "you're with us or against us" position that left no room for common sense. I helped prove out a system where any criticism is met with insults, boycotts, trolling, and even the destruction of livelihoods. I helped the NRA perfect politics that bled into the Republican Party and conservative politics, and that ultimately crucified people such as former gun CEO Ed Shultz—but also more recently Lieutenant Colonel Alexander Vindman, national security expert Fiona Hill, Senator Mitt Romney, and Secretary of Defense Jim Mattis. I thoughtlessly donated my personal power and boyish dreams to the NRA as it twisted lessons from 1994 into an authoritarian scheme that would be implemented by the political Right. I deeply regret the resulting horrible impacts to the country and to many of the things that I hold dear.

In the coming years, although it took a while to get there, I experienced an epiphany: the industry I helped save became one with the NRA, and the organization would have no problem using the tools I helped it develop against anyone, including me *and my family*.

That night in New York City as I sipped on an expensive but well-deserved bottle of beer, I was just beginning to wrestle with my jumbled emotions and the truth of my experience. What had made me rush into battle so quickly, and why had I been eager to win the approval of powerful forces in the industry, including the NRA? The antitrust case was serious, but there were no supervillains. Had the NRA and other industry leaders inflated other dangers too?

People in our industry were not supposed to doubt the wisdom of collective persecution or question the existence of the evil on the other side. But something told me I had bought in too deep, rushed too quickly, questioned too little. I had done all of it willingly, yet I could not help wondering if I was a pawn.

There were times during the boycott effort that I really believed there was an existential threat, but why did I believe it, and did my fear have any basis in fact? While it was happening, I don't think I ever stopped to think about it, and I never heard anyone else in the industry talk about it either. No one ever questioned any of the NRA assertions. Maybe I was fighting someone else's fight. Maybe there were people who depended on willing warriors like me.

THIRTEEN

CENTER OF MASS

A LTHOUGH I BEGAN TO QUESTION THE FOUNDATIONAL myths of the gun business, I never doubted the growing power and partisan nature of the National Rifle Association. In the lead-up to the 2000 election, Wayne LaPierre cohosted a black-tie dinner that raised nearly $20 million to help elect Texas governor George W. Bush to the presidency, placing the NRA on the highest rungs of Republican politics. The organization, which officially claimed to be nonpartisan, picked the GOP side and never pretended otherwise.

The NRA, and by extension the entire firearms industry, made no bones about its disdain for Democrats up and down the ballot.[1] The philosophy was to go all in with one side to maximize power, a strategy confirmed by NRA first vice president Kayne Robinson, who suggested of a Bush victory, "We'll have . . . a President where we work out of their office."[2]

Sure, the NRA's public support of Bush was a gamble, but a win would return huge benefits. The firearms industry would lend money and deliver voters, then eventually hand over the road map for the authoritarian political tactics too. This authoritarian system realized its full power with the surprise election of Donald Trump, but sixteen years earlier, LaPierre had laid the groundwork with statements like "We must declare that there are no shades of gray in American freedom. It's black and white, all or nothing, you're with us or against us."[3]

Kimber and all other gun companies got on board and operated behind the scenes, powering the NRA machine as it tightened its grasp. This meant that industry sales and marketing teams like mine were playing an outsized role in US politics.

We helped the NRA develop a small but forceful demographic of single-issue voters who voted only for guns, thus wielding incredible influence in key races. Grover Norquist, the outspoken conservative anti-tax warrior, confirmed the strategy in 2000, just before he was elected to the NRA's board of directors: "Gun control is for the right, what prayer in school is for the left."[4] Norquist also said that "the question is intensity versus preference. You can always get a certain percentage to say they are in favor of some gun controls. But are they going to vote on their 'control' position?"[5] Both Norquist and the NRA knew that the answer was *no* and that at least a small number of NRA absolutists were reliable types who always voted against gun control. Gun-control advocates who spent their professional lives promoting legislation such as the Brady Bill and the assault weapons ban also knew that Norquist was right. Mike Barnes, the president of Handgun Control, often bemoaned the truth of the political equation. "They have a very vocal tiny minority of American citizens who overwhelm the majority because they are so vocal and they're so vehement," he said, describing the current and future arc of conservative politics with words that now seem prophetic.[6]

There were, at most, a couple hundred people like me across the country, selling and marketing guns. None of us thought of ourselves as high-level political power brokers. But whether we knew it or not, the members of my sales team were leaders in a movement that was remaking US politics.

People I met on vacations or at barbecues always had more questions when they learned what I did for a living. They wanted to know what it was like to be a gunrunner. At times I found it odd, but a politically astute friend opened my eyes when he told me that "guns are everywhere. The NRA makes or breaks races. They elect presidents and senators. Your industry is, in effect, running a big part of the country, and that's why everyone is so damn curious about what goes on inside your walls. It's *you guys* who make the NRA tick."

I realized that most people had a preconceived notion about what life in the firearms industry was like for us. Given our political impact, they believed we must have been highly regulated, working in white lab coats like doctors in a hospital. Or maybe we were buttoned-down military types with service academy degrees who snapped to attention on well-ordered campuses.

They were right to be curious about our influence, but they were surprised to learn that most of us were just ragtag gun enthusiasts. We were ordinary people with ordinary problems who just happened to end up selling and marketing tools designed to kill. For the most part, we were not highly trained, buttoned-down, or extraordinarily disciplined.

In fact, many were people like one of my salesmen, Darrell Stuart. "He'll be moving to Kalispell to work for you," Leslie mumbled. "He used to work at Nationwide out in Nevada, and when I shut the place down, I promised him a job if he ever needed one."

"I don't know the guy," I pushed back. "I want to build my own team, Leslie." My primary concern was building a company culture of trust and cohesion, but Leslie didn't seem to care about that. "How do I even know if this guy is any good?"

"Look, you'll hire him because I told you to fucking hire him. All you need to worry about is selling guns," Leslie replied. "Darrell did OK selling ammo and Daewoo shit at Nationwide. Interview him if you want. Talk to him about whatever you please. But you have a new sales guy, and his name is Darrell Stuart. Congratulations." *Click.*

A few days later a mustard-yellow Toyota pickup truck with a topper over the bed screeched to a stop in the office parking lot. Before I knew it, Darrell stood in my doorway, wearing cheap aviator sunglasses and an Ozzy Osbourne T-shirt that was a size too small. "Hey, boss," he said with a grin. "Leslie said I should come find you."

I looked up and said nothing for a moment. All I could do was stare at his hair, buzzed flat on top and long in the back. His world-class mullet truly left me speechless. "Good to see you, Darrell," I finally said, waiting for other words to catch up. "That was a long drive. Why don't you sit down and let's have a chat?" He plopped in a chair across from my desk. "Well, why don't we start with guns, huh? What do you know about nine millimeters versus .45 ACP?"

Darrell leaned forward with a wide, excited smile. "Well, boss, I can tell you that nine millimeters fucking hurt!" For the second time in a matter of minutes I had no words. "Took one to the chest. Knocked the shit out of me!"

I thought I should tread lightly around what must have been a very traumatic experience. "Wow, man, sorry to hear that," I said. "You know, I don't think I've ever spoken to anyone who's actually been shot."

"Yeah, man!" Darrell sat forward again. "Back when I was a security guard for the mall in Reno. Me and my partner decided that we ought to know if our equipment worked. So late one night, I volunteer to go first. We drive back in the alley, and I make sure my Kevlar vest is on tight; then I get about twenty-five feet from him. That vest only covers the middle of you, ya know, and I didn't want him to miss and hit me in the arm or neck or nuts or nothin'. So I hold my arms up and yell at him so he aims in the right place. 'Center of mass! Center of mass! Center of mass, you son of a bitch!' He points his Glock at me and *bam*! Shit!"

"Shit. Wow." By "center of mass," Darrell referred to the shooting term for the middle of a target. For a typical human, the center of mass is about where the heart is—and that meant there wasn't much room for error.

"Knocked the hell out of me! I was on the ground and couldn't breathe for damn near five minutes. Big fuckin' bruise right here, man. Couple weeks later, when the pain wasn't so bad, I got to shoot him back, though. So he knows what it feels like too. But anyway, yeah. That's what I know about nine millimeters, boss. *They fuckin' hurt!*"

My mouth just fell open as I realized I was about to bring aboard a man who thought pretending to be a target was a good idea. I didn't ask for more details. Nothing Darrell could say would change the fact that I had to hire him. All I could do was hope this might be another short-term experiment from Leslie; maybe Darrell would go away like Daewoo.

"OK, Darrell," I finally said. "I think that's enough. You're obviously quite an expert. Now let's find you a desk and a chair."

That's how Darrell became a member of the growing Kimber sales team, at least for a while. We were growing and needed more people, so I interviewed and hired new employees as fast as I could. I wanted a team that held to the same standards as our product: elite, high quality, classy, iconic. Hiring Darrell certainly didn't fit into any of those descriptions, but he loved guns. And that was the one common denominator for all salespeople on any gun-selling team.

When interviewing potential new hires, I always asked about calibers, like whether a .30-caliber rifle was better than a 7-millimeter, or cartridges, which refer to the size and shape of the brass that contains the gunpowder that propels the bullet. In theory I wanted sales guys with impressive professional résumés, but the truth was that fluency in this basic gun jargon was often more valuable. Gun-industry sales forces were largely made of die-hard enthusiasts who simply loved guns and knew exactly how to talk about them.

Darrell was never a great salesman, but his stories and charisma appealed to fellow gunnies. That cultural connection was enough to keep Darrell in the game for a while. But within months, he started to have marital problems at home. Then he started bringing those problems to work.

"I can't even trust her to watch Nugent," he said of his wife one day, before she left him. (Their yellow Labrador retriever was named for the pro-gun rocker Ted Nugent.) "So I have to bring Nugent to work and leave him in the back of my truck. That OK, boss?" Sure, I agreed. I felt bad for Darrell.

I did not know it at the time, but Darrell also brought a cheap Star .25ACP pistol to the office with him every day. The Star pistols were crappy and inaccurate. Darrell's model was small with a cheap shiny chrome finish and fake ivory grips. It was exactly the kind of gun that I hoped Kimber would never make. Unbeknownst to me, Darrell stored the thing, loaded, in his desk drawer: a direct violation of company rules, which prohibited all personal guns on company property. Especially loaded guns.

Darrell struggled to fulfill the basic duties of his job as rumors of his deteriorating personal life permeated our office. I tried my best to steer clear of the gossip surrounding him. But one morning Darrell's struggles boiled over in the parking lot, prompting our secretary to burst into my office. "Ryan! Call the cops!" I looked at her incredulously, not sure whether to panic or take her seriously. "Darrell is about ready to kill Nugent!"

"No one is going to kill anything. Just calm—"

"Ryan, call the goddamn cops right now, or I will," she said, shaking with intensity. "He's in the back with a gun!"

"OK, OK," I said, standing up. "Just take it easy." As I approached the back door, I had to part a line of sales employees leaning over each other to get a glimpse out the back window. They moved aside for me, and I saw Darrell outside, yelling and waving his arms around with what looked like a gun in his right hand. I approached Darrell just in time to see him drop into a combat pistol stance and take aim at poor Nugent with his shiny Star pistol.

"I've had it with that fucking dog!" he screamed. "It tore the carpet out of my truck." His eyes were wild and angry as he turned to look at me. "I'm gonna kill that fucking dog, boss!" The screech of his voice frightened Nugent, who trotted away in a confused but hasty escape. Darrell's unhinged ranting also frightened the shit out of me, and I made my own hasty escape back inside, closing the door behind me like a barricade. With me out of sight, Darrell took aim at Nugent as the dog bolted across the field. Darrell squinted, aiming his crappy pistol.

Bam! "You fucking dog!" *Bam! Bam!* "You fucking dog!"

After each shot a puff of dust exploded near the poor dog. Darrell kept shooting, and Nugent kept running, picking up speed with each puff. The screaming continued as Darrell reloaded. Our frightened secretary screamed too as she watched the drama through the upstairs window.

"Get in your offices and shut your doors!" I shouted to everyone inside. "Stay away from the windows! We don't need anyone catching a stray bullet!" I sat down at my desk and stayed low, following my own advice.

Thankfully, Darrell was an awful shot with his crappy Star. He eventually calmed down after he ran out of ammunition, then plodded out into the field to make nice with Nugent. A few minutes later I watched him give the poor thing a hug before he coaxed him back into the Toyota. Darrell then moped back to the office. I sternly motioned for him to come see me. He slumped into the chair in my office, on the verge of tears. "Sorry, boss," he said sheepishly. "I got some stuff going on at home. It won't happen again."

I wanted to fire him, and knew I should, but also knew I'd be overruled by Leslie again. "Look, Darrell. A few things have gotta stay at home from now on. The unhinged crazy? That stays home. Nugent, he stays home. And that piece-of-shit Star? That stays home too. Got it?"

"Yeah, I got it."

"You can't shoot your dog. You just can't, and it's also against the company rules. Take the rest of the day off, but leave your gun here. You can get it tomorrow. You're damned lucky no one called the cops, or you'd be explaining all of this to them."

Darrell agreed, then apologized a couple more times. After he left, I sat at my desk with my head in my hands. *Did I really just witness a workplace shooting while working at a gun company?*

I was not supposed to be shaken by an episode like this. Gun leaders like me were supposed to just accept the realities of guns and move on. After all, nobody was hurt. Neither was the dog. But despite the industry expectations, it was difficult to escape the fact that emotions and loaded guns were not the best combination for a safe workplace.

Anything could have happened. Darrell was a loose cannon. I certainly could have been the one running through the field, dodging bullets from Darrell's cheap Star pistol. And I was a lot bigger and slower than Nugent. I did what was expected of me by our industry. No one ever asked questions about the dangers of guns. Loyalists were not supposed to worry about reducing potential abuses or do anything else that might slow sales. I shrugged off the incident as a freak accident, but the attempted murder of a family pet in our parking lot was too much for our office secretary. She quit soon after the incident. I didn't blame her. A few weeks later, I went to work hiring her replacement.

Tonya Marsh was the fourth candidate I interviewed. Not long into our discussion I could tell that she would fit right in. Tonya was tough, crass, and witty. She'd proudly grown up on the wrong side of the tracks, and nothing fazed her. It was clear that she would not take any grief from the growing group of sales guys. As I spoke to her about her experience, I envisioned her marching up to Darrell, ripping the pistol from him, and then slapping him until he came to his senses. She was just what we needed.

"Your desk will be right outside Dwight's office," I told her when she came back the next day for a second interview.

"Oh, shit!" one of the other sales guys remarked to her. "You're gonna sit outside *his* office?" I shot him a look that meant *shut up*, but the guy went on. "Good luck. He reminds us about every third day that he wants to kill every last one of us."

"Is Dwight the guy upstairs?" Tonya asked. "The one with the 'Spike Lee Can't Jump' T-shirt?" The shirt, Dwight's favorite, was his personal retort to the popular Spike Lee movie *White Men Can't Jump*, and none of us thought much of it. Things like that shirt were common nods toward the subtle casual racism in the industry.

"Yeah, that's him," I said, trying to put her at ease. "Don't worry, Tonya. Dwight is just a little, um, intense. You can handle him."

"I bet he's a real peach," she said smugly, already pegging Dwight as a personal challenge.

Tonya was entering an industry that did not generally value women in anything other than minor administrative roles. This had its roots in the mindset of the thousands of dealers who were our customers. Within weeks, Tonya picked up on this unfortunate reality. "Hey, can someone talk to this asshole on line 3?" she might ask. "I already gave him the right answer, but apparently he needs to hear it again from one of you idiots with testicles."

Tonya joined our Montana team as Kimber's growth skyrocketed. But all the success also came with more stress. The growing sales expectations were getting the best of Dwight. He never wanted to work with a large group to begin with, and the pressures of "catalog season" made it worse. Tonya had the misfortune of arriving smack in the middle of that stressful time of year.

During the long and difficult work required to put together the annual Kimber catalog, Dwight spent entire days shut in his office, guns spread across his desk and papers strewn about the floor as he searched for inspiration. He often held guns up to the light, examining them as if he were a great artist pondering how to paint his subject.

Just outside, Tonya fell right into her job. Within days she was directing traffic and kidding the sales guys with off-color jokes so good that they borrowed them from her and then used them on the road. She was the office glue I was looking for.

The addition of Tonya Marsh wasn't perfect, though. She tried to tiptoe around Dwight and his volatility, but she was loud, and her gregarious personality meant more office noise and activity. The frivolity only added to Dwight's worsening tension.

On more than one occasion during her jocular conversations with other staff, Dwight got up from his desk and slammed his door so loud that the entire office stopped for a moment. People held their breaths, wondering if the loud, reverberating bang meant that Darrell had finally finished off Nugent. Activity resumed only once Dwight's string of muffled swearing confirmed that there was no office gunshot.

Sometimes Dwight's outbursts included chilling things like "I'm gonna kill every single one of these motherfuckers." If he was trying to frighten the staff into silence, it worked. People were more quiet after those outbursts. Even Tonya didn't know what to make of him. "Do you think he really wants us dead?" the sales guys would whisper to her.

"I don't know what the hell he wants," she'd reply. "All I know is he's got an office full of guns, and he is fuming pissed. I mean, it all sounds totally safe to me."

Tonya, like the rest of us, was too busy to give anyone's outbursts much attention. We all worked longer hours and tackled new projects. And our growth had produced yet another annoyance for Dwight: attention from eager advertising salesmen who wanted a piece of Kimber's increasing budget. Advertising was Dwight's responsibility, but he had no patience for these new "ad jockeys" who constantly called to sell him on the idea of spending money. So Dwight tasked Tonya with the responsibility of sorting out the existing advertising partners from the new, time-wasting ad jockeys trying to break in.

Like most other duties, she quickly became adept at figuring out how to discern partners from prospectors. Dwight's catalog deadline was fast approaching, and with Tonya weeding out the new sales calls, he could stay hard at work on his masterpiece.

Tonya had street smarts and usually guessed right, but not always. Once, her phone rang, and a polished southern voice greeted her: "Hey,

Tonya, it's Frank from NASCAR. Say, I need to chat with Dwight for just a second about a project we're working on."

Frank was smooth, and NASCAR sounded impressive to Tonya—definitely more partner than jockey. "Oh sure, Frank, happy to do it." She pressed a couple of buttons and passed the call through.

Moments later, her phone rang again. "Hey, Tonya. Gosh, we must have a bad connection. Sure do appreciate your help. Could you patch me back through?"

"Gee, sorry, Frank. I don't know what happened."

Thirty seconds later, Frank called back a third time. But this time, she thought to check with Dwight. She pushed the hold button and yelled into his office. *"Dwight! Frank from—"*

Dwight stormed from his office, throwing the door open. His face pulsed red as he hovered over Tonya, his right hand gripping the same Kimber Gold Match .45 he had just been using for catalog inspiration. Tonya could only hope the gun was not loaded: *"You tell Frank to go fucking kill himself."*

"Sorry, Dwight," Tonya said, terrified and leaning away from him. She was cowering and quiet, traits that were contrary to her very nature. Then she stammered, "I, I can't tell him that."

Dwight pointed at the phone just inches from Tonya. Furious, he yelled, emphasizing each word: *"You. Tell. Frank. To. Go. Fucking. Kill. Himself. Or. You. Are. Fucking. Fired."*

Tonya slowly reached over and took the call off hold. "Hi, Frank?" Her voice trembled. "Um, well, Frank, please go fucking kill yourself." Then she slowly lowered the phone to end the call, never taking her eyes off Dwight.

Dwight stood over her, glaring, for what seemed like minutes. He then spun around, pistol in hand, and marched back into his office, slamming the door behind him. He had to get back to writing about the same guns that I promised Sara would never end up in a crime scene. The same guns that would be sold to NRA members across the country.

Tonya was just hoping *that* gun would not end up in a crime scene in our own office.

I was in charge of the growing sales team. But Dwight, who preferred working on his own, was in charge of marketing, and we operated with the understanding that we shared responsibility for the office.. Even though we often cajoled each other and argued like brothers, I did not have the authority to even deal with the outburst, not to mention fire him. We had learned to coexist where our work overlapped, and I could handle the intensity, but I was not so sure about Tonya.

After that, I expected her to slide into my office and explain that telling people to "fucking kill themselves" in an office full of guns was not exactly in her job description. But Tonya didn't leave. Instead, she became the closest thing we had to an office manager. She was tougher than any of our sales guys and knew how to turn adversity into humor.

"Hey, Psycho," she would ask Dwight in the weeks after the incident. "Is there anyone who I need to tell 'go fucking kill yourself' today?"

Through it all, I kept adding salesmen. I hired Scott Gibbs because he could sell anything to anyone, a skill I desperately needed. Gibbs was prone to histrionics and would stop at nothing to close a deal. He even made up stories about having cancer to generate sympathy.

No one in the office cared for Gibbs's tactics. He made it worse by boasting about his shooting skills and prowess with handling a gun. Most of the other guys were competent shooters, which meant that they were suspicious of anyone who boasted. I could figure out ways to ignore it all because, shooting skills aside, Scott could put sales numbers on the board.

Another of the salesmen who claimed to be a good shot was Bobby Meyer. When I first hired Bobby, I thought he would bring maturity and seasoned stability to the operation. As a Vietnam veteran, he was older than the rest of us. He had been a C-130 crew chief and had traveled much of the world. At least he had stories about faraway places. In the time between his military service and Kimber he had worked in an upstate New York steel mill owned by a Japanese conglomerate that ran a tight ship. That's what I needed at Kimber: someone who knew how to manage people in the military and in a tightly run steel mill.

He loved guns and talked about all of the geeky specifics with us. But even Bobby had a few loose screws. "You goddamn kids don't know shit!" he'd say. "The Japanese wouldn't put up with you idiots." Or "Back in 'Nam all of you pussies would never make it a day." Or "People like me have been flying around the world saving weaklings like you for generations. Show some damn respect."

This rubbed everyone the wrong way, especially Allen, a young guy who was proving himself to be the best employee I had. Allen had grown up in Connecticut with three brothers who loved to hunt. He moved to Montana and, like me, found his dream job at Kimber. Allen was wound tight, but he was articulate, driven, and dedicated. And he especially distrusted Bobby. When Allen became frustrated, as he often did, he would barge into my office, shut the door, and unload.

"Busse, there's something wrong with him," he said once. His volume went up as he continued. "I've known blowhards like Bobby. You know it's just a show. He's unstable, and I want to be on record, if anyone ever goes postal in here, it's going to be *that* son of a bitch."

The phrase *going postal*, first used in 1993, was itself derived from recent post office workplace shootings that occurred in places like Dana Point, California; Dearborn, Michigan; Edmond, Oklahoma; and Ridgewood, New Jersey. Without even thinking much about it, we joked about "going postal" right along with the rest of the country because it did often feel like there was a danger of someone snapping. I don't know what I said to Allen, if I said anything at all, which apparently didn't sit well with him. "You can doubt it all you want, Busse, but I'm going to stay ready." Before I could ask Allen what he meant by "staying ready," he stormed back out of my office and went back to work.

On many days our daily work inside Kimber's Montana office was cordial and friendly. But just like any other competitive environment, pressure built up. We all worked in tight quarters, and our rapid growth only turned up the steam.

One morning Allen and Bobby bumped into each other in the kitchen. Allen wanted out before he got another lecture, and he hurried toward his office without cleaning up his mess.

"You goddamn kids!" Bobby called after him. "Can't even clean up! If you'd have been on the planes back in 'Nam, our boys would have kicked you out the back and sent you to vacation with the Viet Cong."

Allen stopped and turned around. His fuse had come to its end: "Meyer, we are all so tired of your stupid 'Nam stories! Just shut the fuck up and get to work."

"Listen, kid," Bobby screamed back. "You punks might just want to know that I have a cancer list. You know what that is?" The kitchen remained quiet for exactly three seconds as the rest of the office perked up. "Yeah, I didn't think so, you cocky little shit. It's my list of the people I'm gonna kill when I get diagnosed with cancer, and you are fucking on it. And just so you know, I had a goddamn doctor's appointment yesterday." With that, Meyer slammed a coffee mug on the counter, shattering it.

Bobby Meyer's threat was pretty damn clear. Everyone heard the exchange. Allen's warning seemed more important now: *"I am going to stay ready."*

Scott Gibbs walked into the kitchen behind Bobby and Allen, trying to stay out of the fray. Relieved to have avoided the fury, Gibbs put his lunch in the fridge, got a cup of coffee, then went to his own office that he shared with another salesman. It looked like things would settle down so we could have an otherwise normal day at the office. No one seemed to notice the holstered pistol on Gibbs's belt.

Then, moments after he went into his office: *bam!*

A powerful shot jolted the whole building. *Holy shit, it's happening*, Allen must have thought. Everyone raced to Scott's office, preparing to see a body on the floor. Standing in the office was Gibbs, looking at his Kimber Ultra Carry .45 as if it was a dog that just ate the carpet out of his truck.

"The trigger is faulty," he mumbled, shaking. "I think my holster's defective. . . . It just went off." Gibbs kept his eyes on his gun as he rattled off excuses. The staff circled around him. Gibbs had violated company policy by bringing a loaded gun into the office, but the issue for him was that it was uncomfortable to sit in his chair with the pistol on his belt. When he remembered to remove it, the gun discharged, sending a powerful bullet ricocheting off the floor and into a wall less than an inch from Gibbs's office-mate.

There was no serious injury, other than the shock and near deafness of Gibbs's office-mate. Gibbs was embarrassed and with good reason. Serious gun people were not supposed to screw up like that. Everyone checked to make sure that no one was hurt, and in the process it became clear that Allen was nowhere to be found. Another sales guy noticed that Allen's office window was wide open.

As soon as he heard that powerful shot, and with the precision of an orchestrated military operation, Allen spun his office chair around and executed a maneuver he had practiced dozens of times: he used both feet to kick open the window, then jumped out of it. He landed like a paratrooper, rolling into a standing position, then broke into a run through the open field to escape the shooting, just as Nugent had done. We finally found Allen on the far end of the field, just out of pistol range and waiting for an update from the battlefront. He had, in fact, stayed *ready*. "Did he get somebody?" he shouted at his coworkers as they gathered at his open window. "He's got a cancer list, you know. You guys are probably all on it."

When Gibbs's gun discharged, Allen had tapped into the same overwhelming fear that gave Patrick Ireland the strength he needed to climb out the window at Columbine High School. The irony of someone escaping a shooting in a gun company by rolling out a window was not lost on any of us.

Over time Tonya would make this into another joke too. "Shoot anyone yet today, Tex?" she'd ask Gibbs, who'd grown up in West Texas. He responded by scurrying to his office.

"Keep it up," someone else told Tonya. "At least it keeps him from bragging."

We were distracted by the urgent business of growing a company, and to avoid getting derailed from our jobs we used humor to plaster over the realities of guns in our lives. Just like in the rest of the industry, there was an unspoken battlefield camaraderie at Kimber. We overlooked personal shortcomings and worse because the team was focused on building up a company, although we did this at our own peril. HR protocols and discipline reports were not a luxury we could afford at the time. It was something we could bring on once we became a bigger, more profitable firm. I did not have much experience in other jobs, so I just figured that every workplace had its share of issues. Ours just happened to involve more guns than most, right?

We tried to laugh off the craziness, but the truth was that angry threats, failing marriages, and firearms accidents are never funny. We were supposed to be professionals. We were all gun experts. But we only served as proof that even people who were paid to know guns couldn't escape the danger that resulted from our products and the everyday stresses of life.

Dwight, Bobby, Gibbs, Allen, and Darrell were very different people, but they had one thing in common: they all loved guns. With the exception of Darrell, I always asked the same question in their interviews: "Why do you want this job?" Without exception, no matter how different the candidates were, they all gave versions of the same answer: "Because I love guns. And I just want to work in the gun industry. It's my dream."

As I traveled to trade shows and shared drinks with executives from other companies, we swapped stories. Not everyone had a Bobby or a Gibbs. No one else had a Darrell. But they all had similar tales that shared a common thread. Our industry was almost exclusively populated with people who were in it because they simply loved guns. Even guys at the NRA had stories about accidental discharges in their headquarters. Loving guns was the only common requirement for entry into the tight group of people who were fueling change in America. "It's the same for dealers," the other executives commented. "Most of them are not businesspeople. They're just guys who really love guns."

An almost unnatural affinity for firearms even reduced the pressure on gun companies to provide high compensation packages. "We all know we could probably make more money elsewhere," someone would say. "But we work here because we love being in the gun business." We all agreed on the existence of what we called a "gun-industry tax": the price of working in an industry that we had once dreamed about as kids.

The same common love of guns is how the NRA cultivated a few million gun customers to become single-issue voters. The organization was learning that one thing was more powerful than this deep, visceral love of guns: the threat of having those guns taken away. That, the NRA knows, is far more powerful than common sense, the safety of others, or even economic self-interest.

The NRA rightly sensed that this kind of extreme dedication could be juiced and then harnessed to change basic laws of US politics. It was learning that the cultural memories, like mine with my father, could be amplified and reframed to make the country laugh off accidental office shootings and minimize deliberate mass murders. It was coming to know that even political authoritarianism is more acceptable than the mere threat—real or perceived—of guns being taken away.

The NRA was reordering the country's political solar system by placing guns in the middle of it, forcing everything else to orbit around them. Guns became the new center of mass.

FOURTEEN

RESCUED BY THE SKY PEOPLE

"MR. BUSSE, THAT'S THE BEST FUCKING PART. WE CAN LIVE in Montana. *Montana!*" Those were Dwight's words on the night we decided to take a chance on Kimber. I knew that there were steep odds against making Kimber a success. Living in the state that many call "the Last Best Place," on the other hand, was no long shot. I had always imagined Montana as many people around the world do: full of wild, unexplored places and rugged landscapes, scarred by craggy mountains and badlands, and sculpted by clean, cold water.

My visions of the state were formed by stories that Dad told Cory and me about a trip he had taken to Montana as a young man. And then in college, those dreams were nourished by books I read— Theodore Roosevelt's *Wilderness Hunter*, Jim Harrison's *Legends of the Fall*, and Norman Maclean's *A River Runs Through It*—all narratives that romanticized the very Montana life that I yearned to live.

Throughout the first few years in Montana, I worked long hours at Kimber. But when I could break away, I spent every second of my time exploring the vastness in the millions of acres of surrounding public lands. I found new creeks and mountains almost every week.

Just after I arrived in Montana, I found a companion who tolerated all my adventures, and I named him after Robert Ruark, the vagabond 1950s author inspired by his iconic African safari. My Ruark was a Brittany spaniel, and he accompanied me on every journey. In the fall, Ruark trotted by my side as we hunted birds in places so expansive that I did not think I could see them all—even in a full lifetime. I had fallen in love with the land and water of the Big Sky State.

Back then, my love of hunting, nature, and exploring the unspoiled nooks and corners of Montana wasn't tainted by the inconvenience or weight of politics. Sure, I still considered myself a loyal Republican. Yes, I knew the Republican story line well, and I bought it without doing any comparison shopping. I had heard the rhetoric a hundred times: Richard Nixon started the Environmental Protection Agency, so he was an environmentalist, and that was good enough. George H. W. Bush helped close the hole in the ozone layer and reversed the damage from acid rain. Bush and many other notable Republicans were hunters, like me. That was the important part. They said the right things, and they liked to hunt. And if you liked to hunt, surely you cared about the importance of untouched public land. For me, it was a simple political calculus that gave me the freedom to comfortably call myself a conservationist without stepping anywhere beyond right of center: my comfort zone. Unfortunately, it would take me years to realize that actually fighting for the places and livelihood I loved would require me to step in the other direction.

That step began on a single August afternoon just a couple of years after I moved to Montana. That day, I simply pointed to a new spot on my map, then figured out a way to get there and explore it. This was the ultimate form of American freedom. That day, it was the Rocky Mountain Front.

I had heard and read about the Rocky Mountain Front a few times before. The front is a two-hundred-mile-long strip of wild land extending south to north in West Central Montana, where the knobby spine of the Rockies collides with the prairies, where rolling grassy hills suddenly spike upward into massive cliffs and limestone reefs, where cold rivers pour from jagged peaks out into the prairies of the Missouri River drainage.

"I'm gonna look for an elk-hunting spot," I told Dwight on the Friday before I struck out for the front, which required a long drive around the south boundary of Glacier National Park. "I hear it's really something."

"Take your gun," he warned. "There are some big-ass grizzlies out there."

I had also read about grizzlies and mountain lions, wolverines and wolves. Even a few lynx still roam the front. In fact, it's the last place still home to all of Montana's native predators.

The next morning I drove east a few hours with Ruark, and after flipping through pages of my map book and opening a few cattle gates, I found a narrow dirt game trail leading to a long mountain ridge that looked promising. To the east I could see distant island ranges such as the Bears Paw Mountains, Sweet Grass Hills, and Highwoods. I climbed through the bunchgrass, creeping juniper, and ancient wind-twisted whitebark pine, and crested the ridge. To the west I could see the same never-ending sea of solid granite mountains that had intimidated Meriwether Lewis and William Clark almost two hundred years earlier. The Blackfeet Indians call these mountains the "Backbone of the World."

The day was warm and windy, and Ruark pointed, then flushed native blue grouse as we climbed up. Sure enough, I noticed enormous grizzly tracks in the dirt as I picked my way through the rocks. *This is a long goddamn way from Kansas*, I told myself as I knelt to drink from a small spring. Ruark whined at me and cocked his head. Good dogs know exactly when to listen.

"Don't worry," I told him aloud. "We'll be at the top soon, buddy. Won't be too much farther."

A few minutes later, as I peered around a large limestone cliff, the world opened up into a place so beautiful that it actually made me weak. Shaking, I had to sit down on a log. A creek meandered far below me in a valley flanked by mountains so massive I could see only portions of them. Dozens more granite peaks towered above those mountains for as far as I could see, almost like a little kid's crayon drawing. Snowfields and glaciers streaked across all of them, even on this warm August day. The blue sky met purple mountaintops, which faded into dark green forests and gray cliffs, then tumbled down into a lush valley that lifted a gentle breeze full of the exotic, earthy smells: flowers, dirt, decay, and minerals. Ruark sat on his haunches and panted.

For the first time in my life, I found myself with nothing to say, even to Ruark. I had nothing to *think*. This place consumed me like a drug. This place, in the middle of nowhere, was—as former Montana governor Brian Schweitzer once told David Letterman—"untouched since God reached out his hand and made it."

I'm not much of a crying man. I wasn't before that literally breathtaking moment, and I'm not much of one now. But sitting up there, feeling small but alive and very much a part of it all, I began to weep.

Ruark whined and leaned against me as I wiped tears from my eyes, wondering what the hell was the matter with me. It was, strangely, a *relief*. I learned a lot about myself just sitting up there. My father's stories, Roosevelt's great adventures, novels by Harrison and Maclean were all bits and pieces of a ranch kid's idealistic dream. And they all became real in an instant. For years, I had taken them all to be like some ethereal religious parable that my mom had made me learn in church, stories that represented things that were not really true. But now I could see Montana was not some made-up tale passed down through the generations. No one embellished or imagined the wildness of this place. That wildness was beautiful.

Over time I came to appreciate the fact that I actually *owned* this perch and the valley below and the mountains above it, along with every other citizen of our country. This publicly owned land and the millions of acres like it changed my adult life in profound ways. Years later, I delivered a speech to more than two thousand people in the rotunda of the Montana State Capitol. In that speech I confronted the thoughtless right-wing politics that my industry had built and fueled, the same politics that eventually threatened this wild place. And me.

By then, the NRA had twisted the old Republican principles into a new religious fervor that was toxic to any environmental policy. The NRA even made room for dozens of powerful politicians and a national Republican Party platform plank that specifically attacked public lands. My speech in 2018 was one of the many times that I tried to push back against what I had helped create.

"Our public lands are the finest living example of equal justice," I told a roaring crowd of public-lands supporters in the capitol. The land we all own as Americans is the one concrete component of our great egalitarian experiment. The rights and laws that form our system are beautiful, no doubt, but they are only words. Our great public lands are not just ideas; they can also be touched just like any other physical object. The fact that we own them together as citizens is, for me, the single finest example of equality in our democracy.

I was not the first to be struck by this remote place in the Rocky Mountain Front. The Blackfeet believed this jumble of granite, trees, and flowing water to be the birthplace of their people. Having long ago given up on my own religious upbringing, I found a new appreciation for why a native creation myth would originate here, and I could even understand how generations of people considered it to be true.

The Blackfeet called this part of what is now Montana the Badger-Two Medicine, named for the nearby Badger Creek and the Two Medicine River. They believed that the "Sky People"—the Sun, the Moon, and the Morning Star—looked over the people who were created here. On that day, with tears still in my eyes, I knew that in a very important way I too had been born in this place. The Sky People were looking down on me as well. On that day I first discovered this place, I had not yet met Sara. I did not know much about reflection or meditation. But something larger than all of us came over me in that moment. I sat there and breathed in the rugged beauty, surrounded by ancient, twisted trees that were old even before Lewis and Clark ever laid eyes on Montana.

"This is our church, buddy," I mumbled to Ruark as the Montana wind whistled through the twisted trees and flapped his ears as he sat beside me. I would come back to the Badger-Two Medicine many times over the coming years. Each time, the Sky People watched over Ruark and me just as they had on that first day. This was the first place I ever camped with Sara; I brought my dad and Cory here on the day before Sara and I were married. I would hunt elk, catch fish, and see grizzlies on almost every trip. I adopted the Badger-Two Medicine as my own sacred home.

Over the years, as I made friends with the people who lived on the adjacent Blackfeet Reservation, I learned more about the place. "When the government made our ancestors give up our religion, our people escaped into those mountains to practice our ceremonies where the officers could not see us," a friend told me. "That's how we kept our religion and language alive." Not only had the place served as the spiritual home of the Blackfeet, but it also served as a sanctuary from brutal government persecution.

Sara and I became deeply connected to all our favorite places across the West. In 2005 we named our first son Lander, after our favorite small town in Central Wyoming. And then in 2008 we named our second son Badge, in honor of the place that became my church—as our way to pay homage to the Sky People. In the following years that connection became intertwined with Sara's moral influence, and it's her grounding influence that helped me begin to understand that my conservative facade was cracking. It all began with a request to help defend my sacred place in late 2003.

The call came from members of a coalition led by Trout Unlimited (TU), a popular conservation organization that boasts more than 150,000 members and focuses on protecting fish habitat such as the rivers found in the Badger-Two Medicine. "Ryan, will you come to

Washington, DC, to give a speech at the National Press Club?" the guy from TU asked. "We know you are a passionate advocate for the front and other places like it."

"I'll do anything to defend the place," I responded. "Yes, of course." That year I had been closely following the Bush-Cheney energy plan, which pushed for opening up untouched places such as the Badger-Two Medicine, the Valle Vidal in New Mexico, and the Roan Plateau in Colorado to massive industrial projects. As the news of the controversial energy plan leaked in 2002 and 2003, I became increasingly troubled with the idea that politicians who claimed to be on the side of hunters and anglers were instead pushing policies that would harm both us and the outdoor places we loved.

Those were the first cracks. Sara, behind the scenes, only encouraged them.

"Look, let's be honest," the TU guy said. "You're from a very conservative industry. Are you willing to criticize President Bush?" The forwardness caught me off guard. "It's an election year. The press hook is that you look like a typical Bush voter and yet you are not happy with his policies."

"I get all of that. What's your point?"

"Our point is that you are going to get *hammered* on this. People are going to come after you."

"I have a lot of street cred in this industry. They can't come after me!"

"I don't think they care who they kill."

"Listen, all I'm doing is speaking out for wild places where gun owners hunt. For God's sake, I cried when I found this place, and I hunt and shoot as much as anyone. How the hell can they criticize that?"

"OK, you've got balls of steel. We'll send you a plane ticket."

I did not consider myself brave or possessing any particular testicular fortitude. I just cared deeply about my church. It was naive. Or maybe deep down I knew they were right. Perhaps this was my own way to put the final nail in my old, uninformed politics. Regardless, I had no problem getting on that plane.

Of course, I should have seen what was coming. After all, *I* helped the NRA create an authoritarian system that required preapproval of any political speech. No industry member was allowed to praise a Democrat or criticize a Republican, yet here I was, doing both with a speech that got national attention. I reasoned that anyone who would attack me for protecting the places where we used our guns to hunt was not a friend of hunters or a friend of mine. *Surely, the NRA and the gun industry cannot be so nakedly partisan as to come after a firearms executive like me. I mean, crucifying Shultz was one thing; he was changing gun policy. I am only trying to help save places so we can sell more guns.*

I stood at the podium and delivered my remarks about the wild Badger-Two to an air-conditioned room full of DC reporters. I laced into the Bush administration for pushing an industrial plan that would irreparably harm several of the most iconic wild lands in the West, including the place most sacred to me and to countless others. A few of the reporters asked me probing questions: "The NRA is a big supporter of Bush, but here you are criticizing the administration. Aren't you with the NRA?" "How many other hunters do you think you speak for?"

I explained that I used to think of myself as Republican but that I could not vote for a president who thought it was acceptable to trample over our last wild places to punch oil wells. *That's edgy, but I'm just defending our hunting spots.* Not to mention, it was quite simply what I believed.

"That was great!" the folks from TU said after the speech. "There will be a bunch of attention from this." I worried my speech wasn't good enough because it did not seem like I got much of a reaction from the room. "These are professional DC reporters, Ryan. They don't cheer; they just write." The TU guys were correct; the reporters were paying close attention.

The next day as I flew home to Montana, newspapers ran stories about my counterintuitive speech in DC. The press hook had indeed found its mark: red-meat gun executive criticizes a Republican. My old politics were crumbling, maybe already turned to dust. I was finding my true calling as an advocate for the things I really cared about.

From this I learned one of my most valuable lessons: I could exert an outsized impact by staying *inside* the industry. The more capital I built up as a professional firearms executive, the more I could spend picking and winning fights in the policy areas that mattered to me. Everyone expected talking points from the competing sides of the gun debate, but no one expected someone like me to cross over the developing and predictable battle lines and make the war a whole lot more complicated. This single fact tethered me to the firearms industry for longer than I wished.

"Jesus, Ryan!" Tonya said as I walked back into my office. "What the hell did you do back east? The goddamn phone is ringing off the hook. Some reporter guy from the *LA Times* wants to chat with you about your little talk—whatever it was."

I had been careful to couch my statements in ways that made it *seem* like I would still consider voting for a Republican because I wanted very much to be effective in stopping the energy policy. But the truth was I had already made up my mind who I would vote for. The battle over the Bush-Cheney energy plan was only the last and most public straw for me. It was finally time for me to start actually thinking about my politics and to stop laughing at stupid, simplistic bumper stickers.

I spoke to the *LA Times* reporter and to dozens of others. The *Denver Post* ran a story that quoted me as saying, "Hunting and fishing isn't something we do. It's who we are. Someone who wants to take that away from us—we can't support." Stories appeared in dozens of other papers across the country too. As I suspected, the reporters used "vice president of a gun company" or some version of that label in every story. And that, of course, caught the attention of the people who ran our industry. I had not gotten their approval. I had violated a basic rule of the NRA police state.

"Ryan, ESPN is on the phone now," Tonya called out to me as she transferred the call. "They want an interview too. What the hell did you say back there?"

I did the ESPN interview, and soon industry websites and blogs took note. One popular blog posted the details of my activity under the heading "Kimber VP will vote against Bush." The post, which garnered instant online attention, received dozens of comments like "This guy ought to be fired for being so stupid."[1]

Just as I had hoped, the articles and interviews soon caught the attention of power brokers in DC too. And that caught the attention of Leslie Edelman. "What the fuck are you doing?" he barked through my phone. "Larry Keane from NSSF just called, and the guys from the NRA called too."

"What'd they say?"

"They told me that your statements about President Bush and the election are 'not helpful.'" Leslie paused to let the weight of his words sink in before he added: "You need to shut the hell up, Ryan. We don't need to elect a goddamn Democrat."

"Not helpful to what? I'm just standing up for the places where we hunt—the places where people use guns."

"The NRA cares about reelecting George Bush, and so do I."

The swift reaction made it clear to me that the NRA and NSSF were just fine sacrificing hunters and wild land in exchange for power. In this moment, I learned how the police state inside the industry was set to function. I never heard directly from the industry leaders. They made calls behind the scenes, they gave the nod to others to attack or threaten my job, but they kept direct evidence of their involvement in the shadows. Like the president who would one day adopt their tactics, they could sow disinformation, give speeches littered with lies, and even walk right up to the line of incitement, but they always had a path of deniability.

I knew I was on thin ice. I also knew that I had Larry Keane and Wayne LaPierre in a pickle. I was a rising star in the industry, and I had helped the NRA crush Ed Shultz. I had been a trusted soldier. My guess is that this meant they wanted me gone, but they didn't know exactly how to do it. Would it be a slow, public torture? Would it be a quick and quiet exit? Would it cost me my childhood dream of working for a gun company I believed in?

Because of the success of my Kimber sales model, I had lots of contacts across the industry and across the country, and that meant I was a leading candidate for the Shooting Industry "Person of the Year." Keane and LaPierre knew they could not put that sort of notoriety back in the bottle.

I had other connections too, and one of them was inside the walls of the NRA. Kyle Weaver, who had become a friend through our work on the NRA banquet system, would soon work his way up to become second in command of the organization. For many insiders, Kyle was the obvious heir apparent to LaPierre.

Kyle was the same age as me. He stood about six feet tall, with blond hair and a quiet, disciplined personality, and I always felt we had something besides business in common. Over the years, I pried personal details from him. I learned that Kyle loved fly-fishing in the wild country of Wyoming and Montana, and we often discussed fishing together if the opportunity ever came up.

"Want to come fishing with me in Montana?" I asked, believing that the Badger-Two Medicine could win over more advocates if they could only experience it like I had. I also believed no political affiliation was more powerful than the humbling beauty of the place. "It's a tough hike, but I think you'll love it."

Eventually, Kyle agreed, and on a warm summer day we sweated up the same route that Ruark and I had used. Near the top, where I had experienced a spiritual epiphany years before, I took the opportunity to try and bring Kyle in. "This is the place those fuckers want to drill," I told him. "The same place that your organization was OK throwing away. The same place that LaPierre tried to get me fired for saving." Kyle didn't say much as he scanned the view with his lips shut. "That's all despicable, don't you think? Now that you're here, don't you understand?"

"That political stuff is all Chris's baby," Kyle finally replied, referring to Chris Cox, the powerful head of the NRA's Institute for Legislative

Action. "Chris knows what he's doing. It's so much bigger than you or one place, Ryan. Chris and Wayne are smart. They know what they're doing."

I was so stunned I couldn't take my eyes off him. Kyle and I had just hiked together through one of the most pristine wild places left on our planet: a place so beautiful that an entire Native nation believed their ancestors were created there. Kyle was a friend; he was breathing the same fresh air I was. His eyes were seeing the same view that mine were. Yet it seemed to me that the power of the NRA kept him from even considering doing the right thing.

I believe then, as I do now, that it is simply not possible for any informed and decent human to believe that destroying a place like the Badger-Two Medicine is beneficial to our species, much less to gun-loving hunters and fishermen. And yet here I was, with an accomplished, educated professional who seemed to be just fine with punching holes in sacred ground as long as it advanced the larger political ambitions of the NRA. That is when I understood the true impact of the world's most powerful political organization. It disgusted me. Unfortunately for our country, this same sort of thoughtless devotion would soon grip tens of millions of otherwise rational people like Kyle.

In future years the NRA would become even more aggressive with the deception. In an attempt to prevent more people from seeing the light, they formed groups like the NRA Hunters' Leadership Forum and continued to make unsubstantiated claims such as "The NRA does more for hunters than any other organization, hands down."[2]

Despite my personal friendship with Kyle, the NRA turned up the heat enough to make my life very uncomfortable—at least for a while. Behind the scenes the high-ups at the NRA condoned a continuation of the smear campaign, which meant that Kimber regularly got calls and letters from hundreds of angry NRA members threatening harm to the company by parroting the absolutism of the NRA talking points. They attacked me because of my unconscionable stance against our Republican president. In the world of the NRA, just that simple dissent was enough to prove I was a dangerous subversive who was not 100 percent loyal. Over the following weeks we got hundreds of messages, most of them along the lines of "I will never buy another Kimber because of that asshole Busse's attacks on the Second Amendment, and I'll tell all my friends to do the same. He supports communists."

This troll attack was an important piece of the NRA's political machine that eventually manifested itself in armies of MAGA hats, armed amateur militias, and resistance to mask mandates during the COVID crisis. The NRA's goal was intimidation, and it hoped that the attack was powerful enough for Leslie to fire me. The NRA at least needed me to squirm enough in public discomfort to remind all other executives not to step out of line.

But stepping out of line is how I became a leading advocate for our country's wild places, for the clean water that flows through them, and for the creatures that thrive in them. I fought for the policies and bedrock laws that protected all these places, and I believed that all hunters have a duty to do the same. I reread Roosevelt's books—this time with an eye for the importance of conservation efforts. I added books like Aldo Leopold's *A Sand County Almanac*, and I explored new literature like Tim Egan's *The Big Burn*, a book that opened my eyes to the pitched political battles over our environment and the creation of America's publicly owned lands.

I look back now and wonder why events like Columbine did not trigger me to change. Why now? Why had I been so willing to excuse workplace shootings or participate in the persecution of Shultz? I look back at the NRA's refusal to allow consideration of closing the gun-show loophole after Columbine, and I am embarrassed that I turned away. The truth, as I believe it now, is that I wanted to believe in and belong to something so badly that it took an attack on something personal from the team I thought I was on to shake me from my stupor. The experience taught me to look for the same sort of personal conflict in others as a way to convince people to begin their own separations.

I also learned valuable political lessons about how best to wield influence and create opportunities. Many times over the years people asked why I stayed inside the gun industry. Perhaps you're asking the same question as you read this. Why was I working for a business that in turn fueled a political system bent on destroying so many of the things I held dear?

It was never an easy decision, and it was one I considered often. I stayed for two reasons. First, this was my industry too. I didn't want to forgo my dreams and ambitions just because the NRA had ulterior motives. I believed and still believe that Americans have the right to own firearms. I believed then and still believe in reason and responsibility. There was nothing that forced the industry to remain thoughtlessly devoted to the NRA, and I knew I should stay and fight for an approach that I believed in. The second reason had to do with what I learned around my appearances at the National Press Club. I learned that journalists don't cover dogs that bite men. Speaking up from the inside was me biting the dog. It was power. And that meant I could get attention not afforded to others if I offered an unexpected perspective. My life and career would remain on a knife's edge, and I constantly worried about whether powerful executives and their trolls would catch me. But it also meant that I had a rare opportunity to make a difference.

Just like that night in the Manhattan Marriott after my Federal Trade Commission legal proceedings, doubts and emotions took over, but they were much stronger now. I felt betrayed and embarrassed that I had been duped into believing I was a part of an industry that shared the values of my childhood. I had realized that for the NRA and its disciples in the gun business, much of the talk about conservation and hunting was just another ruse to get people like me into the culture war and to write checks supporting it. I was correct about the perilous existence I had chosen, and in the days that followed my speech, it seemed like my job hung by a thread.

"How's it going today?" Sara would ask during her regular check-in calls. "How many letters and calls did you guys get?"

"A shitload," I'd answer. "And I know Leslie is under pressure to fire me, and I know that Dwight doesn't support me either."

"You gonna make it?"

"I think so? It was the right thing to do. I'll have to be smart about it, but if I make it through this, get ready because I'm doing more of it, not less."

"Ryan, no matter what comes of this, I'm *glad* this happened." She paused. "I am proud of you. Now at least you can stop pretending."

FIFTEEN

TUPPERWARE PARTY

D ESPITE SARA'S COMFORTING REMINDER THAT I COULD "stop pretending," my problem was that I chose to stay inside an industry that required someone like me to be good at pretending. The angry reaction to my advocacy made me realize that I was witnessing a growing move toward radicalization. Much of it was subtle, but there were important public events that highlighted the slide too, and I should have seen it coming well before my epiphany in 2004. I had even been witness to many of those events, including at the NRA convention two years earlier.

"You are why Al Gore isn't in the White House!" Wayne La-Pierre yelled to the packed ballroom of nearly five thousand people at the 2002 NRA convention in Reno. I was there along with Leslie, Allen, Dwight, Bobby, Gibbs, and the rest of Kimber's growing team. Even Darrell made it. Every other industry leader was there too, and many of us listened closely as the crowd applauded at the power that the NRA had wielded in the 2000 presidential election.

The NRA had, in fact, played a central role in that contentious election. In the weeks leading up to Election Day, and in a harbinger of the 2016 and 2020 elections, Charlton Heston embarked on a sixteen-city tour through America's presidential battleground states. Heston's NRA events were passionate and raucous precursors to Donald Trump's furious MAGA rallies. Attendees held up signs like "Gore Communist Scum," and Moses spoke openly about finding a rope so that he could form a lynch mob for Democrats. The cultural fervor combined with Heston's celebrity to form powerful and emotional events. The crowds swelled and swooned, and soon more people attended NRA rallies than Gore's own campaign events. In one of them, Moses highlighted the power of the NRA and offered a prediction: "Some papers have said if Gore loses those swing states it will be because of the NRA's effort."[1]

As I watched in Reno, I thought about how far the organization had come in just three years. After Columbine, this big annual convention had been canceled; the only events were a few business meetings and the resulting protests. Back then, the mood was much different. The industry faced potential waves of new gun regulations, a traitorous Smith & Wesson CEO, and reactions to what was then America's deadliest school shooting. But by 2002, many of those concerns had dissipated, and the atmosphere in Reno was celebratory. Because of W's big electoral win, there was even talk about passing a law to make the municipal lawsuits go away too.

LaPierre felt the energy surge, and so could Jim Baker, the organization's longtime lobbyist and resident Washington insider. Baker, a dead ringer for John Slattery's character Roger Sterling in the AMC series *Mad Men*, wore tailored suits and dined in the finest restaurants. He was a smooth old-school lobbyist with a huge Rolodex who worked in the halls of Congress as the director of the NRA Institute of Legislative Action (NRA-ILA). Baker made no bones about being a partisan, but he also had a reputation as a dealmaker. He was the last of a dying breed: the type of insider who fought with Democrats during the day and then sought them out to share drinks in the evening.

However, LaPierre used a worsening partisan tone when he spoke to the NRA faithful, and that ran contrary to Baker's political style. In fact, it was Baker who recruited and introduced the keynote speaker for that 2002 convention, conservative Democratic US senator Zell Miller of Georgia. Both Baker and Miller stood on the stage and received polite applause, even though they symbolized exactly the sort of political compromise that the NRA was working to stamp out.

Baker probably knew his time in charge was coming to an end, but he also had a keenly honed sense of self-preservation. So during his speech he tossed the crowd a bit of ego-boosting red meat: "No other group could do what we did collectively in 2000. Now it's time to finish the job! The Senate is our battleground."[2]

With that, Baker welcomed Senator Miller to the stage, one of his last moves as director of the NRA-ILA. He remained associated with the organization, returning on occasion as a behind-the-scenes fixer and backroom adviser. But within weeks, Baker handed the reins of the NRA-ILA to Chris Cox, who soon proved to be a very different kind of power broker.

Cox was a fresh-faced operator destined to become the most powerful lobbyist in the country. He wore the same kind of tailored suits as Baker, but he had none of the affinity or patience for bipartisan deals. Cox, then almost exactly the same age as me at just thirty-two, would never dream of introducing a Democrat at the national convention—even a staunchly conservative one like Zell Miller, who openly supported Republicans.

For Cox, winning the game was just the first step. He also insisted on running up the score and, if possible, not just beating but *destroying* the other team in the process. Cox hastened the end of the old American system of wheeling and dealing, which relied on people like Baker, who knew better than to completely alienate a potential political ally.

The growing power of the NRA excited the organization's leaders, and it worked as long as they could keep their members cheering. But it did negatively affect our industry. True, gun companies supported Bush's victory, albeit one claimed only after a drawn-out, thirty-six-day battle that culminated with a controversial decision by the Supreme Court. But this did not mean that anyone relished the resulting business conditions.

We had just endured a six-month sales boom in the lead-up to the November 7 election as fearful consumers bought up guns in anticipation of a possible Gore presidency. The NRA-fueled Bush victory removed that threat. And in a classic case of "be careful what you wish for," this meant that our sales tanked.

In fact, we all settled in for what we anticipated would be a long, four-year slog of stagnating gun sales. We'd need to fight for new business, just like any other industry that had to find success without the aid of fear-driven booms. I thought that Leslie would want to take market share from other gun companies by producing or importing lower-quality, cheaper firearms. I continued to insist that Kimber stay focused on premium, classic models. I knew I'd win that debate as long as I could keep selling our existing product lines. I just had to keep our existing business strong enough.

Keeping Kimber's brand image stable while growing the company at the same time required another highwire act. We pulled it off by tapping into the growing "concealed-carry" market. Talented gunsmiths and engineers in our Yonkers factory modified our larger, century-old 1911 design into shrunken versions—small enough to carry in a pocket, in a purse, or in a concealed holster. Our new Pro Carry and Ultra Carry models kept the basic attributes of the venerable old gun but shortened the slide and frame: same guns, just small enough to carry concealed.

Up until the late 1990s, the only legal way to wield a gun in most states was to display it—usually in a holster—for all to see, called "open carry." In many places, especially in rural, western states, there were no laws prohibiting it. Open carry was rare because social norms made it taboo to walk around with a loaded gun. In keeping with those norms, no one really encouraged open carry because neither responsible gun owners nor gun companies wanted to frighten average citizens with other regular people carrying loaded guns in, say, a mall or a grocery store.

For years, the industry itself upheld the social norms that labeled open carry as a historical relic and the people who used guns to intimidate as dangerous outliers. Even the NRA understood the potential blowback, and as late as 2014 the organization took a strident public position in opposition to the practice when it posted an unambiguous statement on its website: "Let's not mince words, not only is it rare, it's downright weird and certainly not a practical way to go normally about your business while being prepared to defend yourself. To those who are not acquainted with the dubious practice of using public displays of firearms as a means to draw attention to oneself or one's cause, it can be downright scary."[3]

Of course, by 2020, when my son was verbally attacked by angry men openly carrying guns in public, those long-held norms had been fractured and forgotten. It might indeed have been weird, but open carry had become yet another intimidation tool and a power statement of the political Right. It became acceptable and even celebrated for heavily armed people to exploit the laws, march into state capitol buildings, disrupt civil rights rallies, and intimidate people with loaded semiautomatic rifles as their main tactic. But even with the increased visibility of publicly displayed guns, open carry was mostly a social statement. It was not widespread enough to be transformational from a market standpoint.

Concealed carry, on the other hand, which is now widely accepted and ubiquitous, was almost universally prohibited in the United States prior to the late 1990s. Why was it legally acceptable for citizens to carry visible, loaded guns but not to carry concealed ones? The answer has its roots in the Old West. Back then, a gun worn on a hip was common and unthreatening, but slipping a gun into a boot or hiding it inside a coat pocket was what criminals did. That was the accepted norm for well more than a century in our country, right up until the late 1990s.

Revising those old concealed-carry laws had been a major objective of the NRA. By the early 2000s, the organization made significant headway, and with advocates such as Marion Hammer, the NRA racked up the wins state by state. As governor of Texas, George W. Bush had played his own role in creating the new market. It was not easy, even in a state that boasted the largest gun market in the country. Many citizens opposed allowing more concealed guns, fearing increased gun violence. The battle for legalization of concealed carry in the Texas legislature was fierce, but Bush campaigned on the issue and prevailed. As governor, he signed a bill legalizing concealed carry in 1995, making it a signature win for his first term.

Across the country, other legislative battles played out with similar results. The entire process took a few years, but eventually almost all states passed legislation allowing some form of concealed carry. A gun-market transformation followed. And so did more success for Kimber.

Prior to the passage of the new concealed-carry laws, most small pistols were considered pariahs, not unlike the shiny Star .25 that almost killed Nugent the dog. But within a few years, small handguns became the backbone of the gun business. The practice of carrying small, concealed guns became not just tolerable but also respectable. Kimber sold hundreds of thousands of them, and none were cheap. Many inside the industry were both hopeful and skeptical at first, believing that mixing more guns into places like grocery stores might prove to be disastrous. But as long as prudent and responsible regulations, such as permitting and background checks, were adhered to, it became obvious that most of the fears about what concealed carry might become were overblown, and it was difficult to deny that many Americans needed to be able to defend themselves and their families.

The right of law-abiding Americans to defend themselves with concealed handguns created entirely new business segments. Concealed-carry classes for new "self-defense customers" popped up across the nation. Accessories, such as inside-the-waistband holsters, fanny packs, and purses modified for carrying pistols, exploded into the market too. The resulting "carry market" permanently transformed the firearms industry, eventually composing 50 percent or more of all firearms sales in the nation.

For those of us in the business, this emerging market was about the only highlight for most of 2000. The business boom certainly was not enough to counter the sales slump resulting from Bush's win. Through the first eight months of his presidency, gun sales fell by more than 25 percent compared to the previous year.

Downturns like this usually meant more anxious chatter among company leaders. The industry was still small, we all knew one another, and that meant we talked openly about general trends and specific customers. We asked each other questions like "How's that new pistol selling for you?" Or "Is Gander Mountain paying you guys on time?" We met in bars or made phone calls to get business reports, hoping for a glimmer of new activity or a promising new lead. I kept an industry intel notebook in which I recorded important notes from these conversations.

We used the information to help guide pricing and to market new products, but there were bits of chatter I knew not to record or repeat. After Bush's win, I started to hear dark whispers that sounded a lot like Leslie's "back-to-school special" Columbine quip. These statements were usually hushed, and they almost always occurred after one too many drinks at an industry trade show. Firearms salespeople knew they should not utter them, but slow sales often prompted revealing frustrations. "What we need—I mean, I hate to say it," someone would say, realizing halfway through he shouldn't complete the sentence. "But if there was another *shooting*, boy, business would take off—"

"Shit, man!" someone more sober would cut in. "Ears are everywhere. What if someone recorded that and it hit the news?"

"We'd be fucked!"

"Fuckin-A! CNN would crucify the shit out of us. Button it up."

And then people laughed it off or ribbed the guy who said it. The truth was that everyone knew damn well that a national tragedy was the quickest remedy for slow gun sales. Even if we internally discouraged talk about the sales benefits of mass shootings, people didn't shy away from discussing the *impacts* of tragedy on our sales. "Cheap polymer pistols and ARs—that's what sells like crazy after a shooting," someone would usually say into a glass of bourbon. "That's when the Tupperware party starts! They just buy the cheapest piece of plastic that goes bang." I always detested any discussion of tragedy or the resulting spikes. To me, the roller-coaster business cycles driven by politics and tragedy seemed unsustainable, and they discounted the hard work of companies like Kimber, which focused more on the fundamentals of quality assurance and strong relationships. Whenever the talk turned to another sales spike, I'd try to change the subject.

In an industry populated by century-old companies with long histories of building metal guns, "Tupperware" quickly became a derisive term for any gun built using plastic parts. These plastic ("polymer") guns were a relatively new phenomenon in the world of firearms manufacturing. Their existence challenged the notion that any serious firearm was made of hardened metal. Plastic was for toys and kitchen containers.

But then in the late 1980s, Glock changed the gun world when the Austrian company introduced a handgun built around a molded polymer frame. Before long, consumers considered Glock pistols legitimate and serious, and many of the country's largest police forces armed their officers with them.

The term *Tupperware* never went away, but gun companies took notice of Glock's commercial success. Among other advantages, polymer-framed guns could be produced at much lower costs. Profits could be higher, and retail prices could be driven down. Those business advantages were too much to pass up, and eventually almost every company developed its own "Tupperware" guns.

At Kimber we still believed in the workmanship and *weight* of firearms. My sales staff had even developed their own "anti-Tupperware" pitches and proudly used them as they convinced dealers to focus on higher quality. "Don't settle; buy metal!" they would often say as they encouraged dealers to buy our more expensive guns.

As polymer guns became more available and more acceptable, they too spurred a cultural movement that resulted in dramatic growth. Rap artists glorified the guns. Famous hip-hop songs specifically mentioned Glock in their lyrics. Some artists bragged of owning the guns, and some, such as Tupac Shakur, died from bullets fired by "Tupperware" pistols.

The plastic pistols were also central in other tragedies, such as the Luby's shooting and the 2007 Virginia Tech murders, both of which were committed by people shooting high-capacity Glocks. Years later, Jared Lee Loughner would take his own "Tupperware" gun to a political rally at a Safeway in Tucson, Arizona. The plastic frame of his Glock 19 held thirty-three rounds, and Loughner used it to murder six people, including a federal judge. He wounded fifteen others, including a sitting congresswoman. Gabby Giffords bravely fought for her life, and after a partial recovery she became a powerful spokeswoman for legislation aimed at reducing gun violence. Much of that violence increasingly involved polymer-framed pistols.

Without a spot in that "Tupperware" market, it was true that Kimber was not heavily affected by most tragedy-driven sales, but fear-driven spikes on a national scale hit all of us. The sort of broad national catalyst for Kimber's success in the sluggish first few months of Bush's presidency happened suddenly on a clear Tuesday morning in September.

Like millions of other Americans that day, the Kimber staff watched the terrible events of September 11 much like we watched the massacre at Columbine High School. We quietly huddled in my office, leaning in to hear or see updates.

"Well, fellas," one of my salesmen said with a sigh. We looked at him, and he looked back at us. What he said next seemed inappropriate, but he was spot-on: "Get ready for a run on guns."

SIXTEEN

COUCH COMMANDOS

I N RACIALLY TINGED, HYPERBOLIC LANGUAGE THAT IS NOW AN NRA hallmark, Wayne LaPierre's convention speech just a few months after 9/11 stoked the fears of a nation that had been shocked by the heinous mass murders committed by foreign terrorists. La-Pierre began by artfully piquing the indignation of the NRA audience, most of whom had flown on commercial flights to attend his speech: "Walk through any airport today and you see red-faced, teary-eyed women, singled out to endure security wands orbiting their breasts, while electronic squeals detect the metal in their underwire bras. You see grandmothers shaken down and stripped of their cuticle clippers and knitting needles."[1]

As LaPierre pounded his podium and as the audience added its own anger, he shifted to racism. "No, we don't want to risk offending an Islamic ex-con with two aliases, no job and no luggage, paying cash for a one-way airline ticket, whose shoes are packed with plastic ex-plosives," he added, imploring the crowd to fear "people who are not citizens of our homeland, who don't belong in our homeland along with aliens on work visas, or green-cards, or student passes."

The country had a new tragedy and new villains who conveniently fit into a frightening racial and religious profile. It all added up to a simple solution for the industry's dipping gun sales and sliding NRA membership. NRA spokesman Andrew Arulanandam framed the reasoning as scared, innocent Americans protecting themselves from *the other*. "Post 9/11, we've seen an increase in interest in firearms particularly for personal protection," Arulanandam told *ABC News*. "It's a natural feeling that after 9/11, people want to be proactive and take necessary actions to protect themselves and their loved ones in these uncertain times."[2]

I did not agree with the fear-driven ugliness and increasing authoritarian control of the NRA. But if I wanted to stay inside the industry, I had to figure out a way to walk the line. That wasn't going to be easy, especially when I had to attend the big conventions and trade shows where much of the ugliness took place.

Once each of those events were over, after all the typical trade-show glad-handing and late-night meals, I was relieved to board the Delta flight back to Montana. My schedules from conventions almost always meant that I arrived home after midnight. After the weeklong show in 2002, I tried to enter the garage quietly so that I could slip into bed without waking Sara. But when I pulled into the driveway, I could see the lights on in the kitchen. She stood behind the counter waiting for me. I dropped my bags and barely got a hello in before she dug in. "I saw some of that asshole's speech," she said, referring to LaPierre's address, which earned national press coverage. "They're trying to frighten everyone. It's not right for the whole country to be afraid, and it's damn sure not right for your business to profit from it."

"We're both tired," I replied, but I knew she wasn't going to let it go.

"No, let's talk about this. Now."

"I agree," I said, after a sigh. "It is stupid." Sara crossed her arms. "But I'm keeping Kimber above all that. Can't we just talk about this in the morning?"

"My god. He made fun of the Million Mom March, Ryan. Moms wanting to protect their babies, and he gloated about them going out of business!"

I knew she was right. Indeed, LaPierre thanked his members for laying off most of the thirty-five employees of the Million Mom March, the group responsible for organizing a Mother's Day march in 2000 in response to mass shootings and other gun-related deaths. But a week of being constantly on my game at a convention had me worn out. I just did not want to think about it, much less talk about it.

In retrospect, my response to Sara that night was like that of Republican US senators who looked away from the racism, incompetence, and misogyny of the Trump administration. Those lawmakers tolerated it because they were in the club and because they wanted a conservative Supreme Court and a tax cut. Because they believed themselves to be different from Trump. In 2002 I simply wanted to help build a company and sell guns that I could be proud of. I was still naively hanging on to dreams first formed during those childhood days with my dad. None of those dreams involved irrational fear, hate, racism, and boycotts. But here I was, still participating in it all, and the NRA did not care what I or anyone else had signed up for; it had much bigger plans.

As conspiratorial and irrational as it was, the racial animus fomented by the attacks of 9/11 and then exacerbated by the Iraq War *worked*. It helped reverse the inevitable sales slide produced by a Republican win and provided a long-lasting source of healthy gun sales. I don't remember a single other firearms executive who questioned the approach of feeding fear with more firearms.

However, there were more-rational payoffs from President Bush's victory, but they came in his second term. The first occurred ten years to the day after Bill Clinton signed the assault weapons ban. In a classic play to hold on to the political middle, George W. Bush spent much of his first term indicating that he agreed with the ban and might even renew it. But after his reelection, he changed his mind in what looked like a payback to the NRA. All he had to do was . . . nothing at all. By taking no action prior to September 13, 2004, Bush allowed the sunset provision of the law to take effect.

We felt the impact immediately. Even though the 1994 legislation never specifically banned the AR-15, the law codified the same important societal resistance that the industry wise men upheld at the Southwind Classic. The day after Bush let the law expire, the same rifles used in Iraq and Afghanistan were suddenly legitimized for sale in gun stores across America, and they could be accessorized and improved without limit. The industry rushed to gear up for mass production.

This, of course, proved to be another wildly profitable development, and it came as my own career got the attention of the other leaders—this time in a positive way. In 2005 I was recognized as "one of the most influential people in the shooting industry."

I had also been nominated the year before and would make the list again in the future, but that year I was one of three finalists. That meant that I was expected to appear at a fancy awards ceremony patterned after the Oscars, complete with tuxedoed hosts handing shiny trophies to winners who gave emotional acceptance speeches and bowed to loud applause. Categories included Pistol of the Year, Ammunition of the Year, New Product of the Year, and Manufacturer of the Year.

By that time, Kimber had received awards and had its share of nominations. Those company awards were feathers in my cap, for sure. But the final award each year—the most coveted—was the Industry Person of the Year.

The gun business took this honor very seriously. Wayne LaPierre, Bill Ruger, and Moses himself were among the previous winners. And so on April 15, 2005, I stood onstage in Houston in a carefully choreographed ceremony. A couple hundred industry leaders watched from their white-cloth-covered tables. There was a fog machine and bright lights. Loud music played as my picture flashed on huge screens above the stage. A deep voice boomed through the fog as it announced my bio. A spotlight illuminated my face.

"Ryan Busse. Kimber. For charting, developing, and directing Kimber's dealer-direct sales program from inception to over two thousand Master Dealers, making it the most successful direct-sales program in the firearms industry."

It was all so ironic. Just as I was flirting with serious doubts about the entire industry, here it was, recognizing me as one of its top leaders. This was different from the unofficial attaboys I got for helping lead the Shultz boycott. This was a very official recognition of my role in the industry. I did not win, but the mere nomination and participation in the ceremony meant that I finally earned my place in the upper echelon of the gun business. My staff was proud, and they gave me a good-luck card signed by everyone on our team.

Internally, I was conflicted. Externally, I was proud to be recognized but not necessarily for the business reasons. I was already calculating how I might use my new status to help effect change from within the industry.

Just months after I stood on that stage in Houston, President Bush delivered on his own mission to remake the gun industry, and on October 26, 2005, he signed the Protection of Lawful Commerce in Arms Act. This controversial bill shielded firearms companies from liability claims arising from the unlawful use of their guns, meaning that cities no longer had standing to sue for the impacts of gun violence in their limits and that victims of mass shootings were barred from suing manufacturers or dealers. The new law had massive ramifications that were not lost on the NRA. In a press conference celebrating the passage, LaPierre accurately described the law as "the most significant piece of pro-gun legislation in twenty years."

"It's a monster, Ryan!" Leslie proclaimed in a call to me shortly after the White House signing ceremony. "Those fucking Democrats can't touch us now."

Even Wall Street took notice. For professional money managers, the risk of investing in companies that might be sued because of urban gun crimes was gone. Eventually, financial gambles like the one made by the small group of investors who bought Smith & Wesson paid off with incredible growth and lucrative public offerings. Within a decade, retirement funds and 401Ks included stocks from Ruger, Smith & Wesson, and Alliant Techsystems—a conglomerate that owned several industry companies.

The less obvious gift from Bush to the industry was the cultural change to America brought on by Operation Iraqi Freedom and Operation Enduring Freedom. As the conflicts raged on throughout the Bush presidency, America sent hundreds of thousands of troops to fight in what the gun industry pejoratively called the "sandbox": the derogatory term we used for the Middle East and Afghanistan. The impacts of war on our country were immeasurably terrible, but the upsides to firearms sales were huge.

For nearly a decade, pictures of soldiers fighting with, or posing with, AR-15s and other tactical weaponry dominated cable news shows, creating an entire generation of Americans who became fascinated with high-powered firearms. Far too many of those soldiers did not return. Those who did had an affinity for the guns they relied on in combat, which meant yet another potential new marketing opportunity.

The NRA immediately understood the power of patriotic messaging: the use of military weaponry and returning American heroes. Just like that, gun sales became synonymous with supporting the military; conversely, opposing guns or even supporting gun control became—to many Americans—*unpatriotic*.

Medal of Honor recipients were sought out to give invocations at NRA banquets. Politicians stood on stages to give emotional tributes and then hand out awards or commemorative guns to war veterans. Heartfelt speeches about heroic acts in war brought crowds to tears. Top NRA leaders walked trade-show aisles with weary soldiers who had just returned from battle. The message was clear: patriotism means respecting our flag, our soldiers, and the *guns* they used to protect America.

As for the guns these (mostly) men used, some were handguns. Many of those "battle pistols" became leading sellers for American gun companies. But the focus of the emerging patriot gun movement was on the rifles of war. The industry referred to these AR-15s, and the many models and variations inspired by them, as "black guns." The term even came to occupy slots in official sales reports for many dealers and companies. "You ask what is selling," a typical sales report from a dealer would read. "Well, black guns are hot; pistols are OK."

In the world of military rifles, better craftsmanship strictly meant increasing the efficiency of function. Most buyers frowned upon any artisan adornment on these serious tools of war. Everyone in the firearms industry used the "black rifle" market category to set these guns apart from traditional segments because everyone believed that an AR-15 would never really become an heirloom or a collector's item. We all used the term because, like a hammer or shovel, the AR-15 was a *tool* that required only a simple flat-black finish.

It would take a few years for the impacts of the Iraq War and George Bush's presidency to become clear, but eventually returning soldiers like Sergeant Major Kyle E. Lamb found a home in the industry. Men like Lamb popularized the black rifles and were elevated to celebrity status by the gun business. The industry called on such men to speak or to sign autographs for long lines of fans at trade shows and product launches.

Sergeant Major Lamb was a decorated Delta Force officer who had spent more than two decades serving the United States in war zones such as Iraq, Somalia, and Bosnia. Despite his thick, menacing beard, Lamb was engaging and charismatic. He looked like a covert military badass from central casting, and he had an innate sense about how to sell firearms products. To many NRA members, Lamb embodied the brave, masculine soldiers they had been watching on TV for a decade.

Lamb and dozens of others like him eventually returned from the conflicts initiated during the Bush years. Many of them capitalized on the industry's growing desire to use patriotism and bravado promulgated by the war to market guns, ammunition, and accessories to consumers who had only watched or read about their heroics. In short order, the marketing tactic worked, and the spokesmen like Lamb built up powerful social media followings and served as celebrity endorsers for a wide range of products, almost all of which were originally designed for military deployment.

A few years after Lamb, Mat Best, also an Iraq War vet, followed suit. Best capitalized on the wave of patriotism and the growing affinity for Special Forces operators to build a powerful platform from which he endorsed guns, became friendly with right-wing political figures, and even developed a *lifestyle* centered around military weapons.

Despite the fact that Best had personal experience with the deadliness of military guns, he became famous for popularizing the viral term *pew pew*. The playful phrase reduced the distant sound of gunfire into descriptive cartoon words that a toddler could say. "Just kind of a funny noise for shooting a gun," as Best himself described it. "Pew pew!"[3]

Gun consumers across the country used the euphemism as a substitute for shooting everything from small pistols to .50-caliber rifles that could blow holes in vehicles nearly a mile away. The phrase *pew pew* eventually became one of the most popular tactical hashtags in the world and was attached to millions of social media posts.

Even if guns were not supposed to be playful, no one dared criticize soldiers who had fought for our country. That gave men like Best and Lamb the freedom to create edgy brands and trending hashtags. Best made a habit of posting pictures of himself sleeping on a bed made of his large collection of AR-15s. With each post, likes and clicks and retweets skyrocketed. Best eventually boasted one million Instagram followers and nearly 1.5 million subscribers on YouTube.

As people like Lamb and Best grew their influence, they branched out into more mainstream areas of American pop culture, and the NRA knew that this would attract even more potential gun consumers. Best helped launch a multimillion-dollar coffee company inspired by military guns. He and his partners promoted Black Rifle Coffee with videos that looked like a rollicking combination of war zone and frat party. Each video featured bikini-clad women, lots of shooting, and plenty of caffeinated beverages. The coffee became the preferred morning drink of millions, and Black Rifle Coffee handed out tens of thousands of free cups at the big firearms-industry trade shows.

Best, an energetic and talented marketer, even used the feedback loop created by the Iraq War, the NRA, and his newly created gun culture to help launch his memoir, *Thank You for My Service*, a book that debuted at No. 5 on the *New York Times* best-seller list. The industry took notice; we could all see the marketing power of these ex-military guys and their black guns. Companies big and small lined up to spend money with them because an endorsement or a mention on their social media sites could mean thousands of sales.

In people like Best, the NRA and gun industry saw a clear path to expand gun culture from an aging and relatively small slice of the country to a new generation that could change the mainstream of social consciousness. The marketing power of these former warriors became so powerful that when Best, a man who played a guitar for fun but had no history of musical success, created a music video titled "Bitch, I Operate," it debuted at No. 36 on the Billboard charts. In the song, Best raps through a day of his life, setting the tone with the first verse:

Wake up in the mornin' and I'm feelin' kinda fresh
Five pounds of bacon on my motherfuckin' chest
Carbon-stained pillows, hands smell like lead
Under my mattress, gun safe is my bed
Loaded up mags just ready to blast
ISIS flag when I wipe my ass[4]

In his introductory YouTube video promoting Black Rifle Coffee, Best looks into the camera and says, "A lot of people call my videos offensive. Well, fuck you!" Then he catches an assault rifle. As he pulls the trigger, the blast comically blows the clothes off two women standing next to him, leaving them standing in their underwear. "People ask us why we have so many guns. I just tell them, 'How 'bout over two hundred years of freedom, *bitch*!'"[5]

Best and Black Rifle Coffee helped normalize an edgy brand of tactical bravado that celebrated the AR-15 as a necessary component of manhood and militaristic patriotism. Before long, shirts and hats bearing the company logo, which included the outline of the AR-15, would be proudly worn across the country, popping up at Little League games and church barbecues. The sight of the rifle in that logo also sent a message of solidarity and intimidation that became powerful enough to play a role for many who stormed the US Capitol on January 6, 2021. On that day, many proudly wore their Black Rifle Coffee logo gear, including a man who carried zip ties through the Senate chamber as he sought out members of Congress to apprehend.[6]

All of this flew in the face of the NRA's carefully curated image of conservative respect for social norms, which used to mean a common understanding of basic politeness. After all, for decades NRA members were the proper churchgoers who did not tolerate the coarseness of people who minimized the effects of violence, swore, and used explosions to remove clothing from young women. When I saw the embrace of people like Best, I knew this was no longer the same organization that sent my grandpa his favorite cap or that had once mailed *American Rifleman* magazines to my dad back on the ranch. The glorification of violence, the utter rejection of political correctness, and the freewheeling masculinity and objectification of women had shifted the organization's members to gladly accept a new cadre of brash militaristic ambassadors. With the embrace of Lamb and Best and the dozens of others like them, it was now obvious that people who once claimed to care deeply about polite etiquette and responsibility now gave zero fucks about that old insistence on traditional morality.

The desensitization to violence, overt misogyny, and intimidation proved to be another of the many political tools developed by the NRA and then handed to the Right. Years later that same desensitization would come in handy for Republicans when, during the 2016 election, candidate Donald Trump demeaned women, called Black athletes "sons of bitches," and regularly urged his rally-goers to physically attack journalists. Just as the NRA embraced surprising new brand ambassadors a decade earlier, culturally conservative voters and elected leaders who once recoiled at such offensive activity cheered on the valuable political payoffs in 2016.

Powerful media outlets, like those being developed by the growing number of influencers, might have seemed like a competitive threat to the NRA marketing machine. But unlike other media companies, this new crop of influencers was very careful not to actually compete with the organization. Instead, they made sure to work *with* it. They made money building their own platforms, but they also knew that a big part of their success relied upon the largesse of the world's largest gun-rights organization. And so they made sure to support that organization with membership drives, social media posts, and political statements that only reinforced the NRA's stances on hot-button issues.

Eventually all these outspoken and controversial advocates endorsed or supported candidates like Donald Trump. Once Trump was elected, they functioned like sheepdogs, keeping strays like me in the herd. They even weighed in on tangential policies such as environmental conservation and national monument designations, topics that were very important to me. People like Lamb always took the strident Far Right stance, parroting administration talking points and making sure to fuel the profitable feedback loop. There was no room for dissent, even on topics that had nothing to do with guns. It was all part of the "completely destroy your enemy" political game of Cox and LaPierre.[7]

The wars of the Bush administration, of course, made this all possible. An entire generation of people who had watched the Afghanistan and Iraq conflicts play out on TV were ready to worship these returning heroes and collect their memorabilia. Loyal fans were ready to discard their affinity for politeness and social norms. Just as there was no room for dissent among gun companies, there was no room for pansies or anyone who dared to question the importance of defending American *freedom*—nuance be damned.

In response to influencers like Lamb and Best, developers designed new video games such as *Call of Duty*, which used the same weapons that had been deployed against "sandbox" terrorists. New companies sprung up to capitalize on the growing demand for high-capacity AR-15s and tactical pistols. Where there was once only a tiny handful of manufacturers building military-style guns, soon there would be hundreds.

The industry's century-old companies also adjusted, and eventually my friends at Smith & Wesson capitalized on the demand by selling hundreds of thousands of their own AR-15s. We all knew that there would never be enough military contracts to suck up even a small percentage of the new guns on the market, but I asked about it anyway. Once, while talking about these guns with my friends in the Smith & Wesson booth, I asked, "Where do you think you'll sell them all?"

A man behind me who I recognized as a veteran industry sales rep jumped in. "C'mon, Busse," he said with a laugh. "You know they're gonna sell them to the couch commandos. That's where the big market is!"

Couch commando was industry slang for the millions of consumers who had never fought in a war, much less joined the military, but who nonetheless considered themselves experts simply because they scrolled through the social media feeds of people like Lamb and Best, and knew how to play first-person-shooter video games from the comfort and safety of their couches. "There are people out there that couldn't serve for whatever reason, but they want to put on the body armor, they want to run down the range with their AR and do a fuckin' transition drill," Best himself told the *Washington Post* in 2019. "A little taste of the drug, you know."[8]

The wars in Iraq and Afghanistan and the resulting expanded market changed everything about the gun business—even the *color* of guns in America. Many of the handguns used by the US military were finished to match the color of the sandbox, and the new "desert tan" finish became an important feature for successful new gun launches. I realized how important it had become as I called big accounts to see what was selling. The answer was clear: "Anything in desert tan." The color switch caused a conundrum for one particular market segment because "even black guns are selling in tan."

Kimber, back then, was not positioned to capitalize in a meaningful way. But we did make a feeble attempt with our own "sandbox-colored" 1911 pistol. We patterned the Desert Warrior after the models we made for military units that still carried 1911 pistols. Most companies sold hundreds of thousands of their sandbox guns to civilian consumers; Kimber sold only a few hundred. An expensive metal gun like ours just did not have the same mass appeal or high capacity of the less-expensive polymer battle guns.

I never liked the term *warrior* being associated with Kimber, but the explosion of tactical culture changed the rules of naming guns too, and because it was such a tiny part of our market, I gave in. It was just another thing I would endure so that I could fight the larger battles.

I remembered just a few years earlier, before the industry started marketing directly to the couch commandos. Back then, people like me in the industry were paid to worry about insensitivity and liability at every turn. Gun companies carefully avoided developing or marketing products that broke the rules of decency.

That meant when a company developed a new product, marketing teams suggested a name, but attorneys and corporate leaders then conferred to make sure that the name did not encourage dangerous behavior or expose the company to potential increased liability. For decades this resulted in gun models like the Kimber Custom Classic, the Remington 870, and the Smith & Wesson Model 629. But the new tactical culture removed that filter, and soon the industry would embrace guns like the Ultimate Arms Warmonger and the Wilson Combat Super Sniper AR-10 without so much as a second thought. There was even pressure to celebrate this bold approach because the industry had to feed the emerging market.

Even though the direct sales impact for Kimber was not large, we certainly felt the gravity of this new kind of gun consumer. Through the Bush years, when all these building blocks for the new market upheaval snapped into place, the industry still felt small, and we could only guess about how massive it would become.

NICS background check totals would eventually shed light on the growth. Before the wars, before the sunset of the assault weapons ban, before 9/11 and Kyle Lamb, before Muslim bashing and Black Rifle Coffee, and before the Protection of Lawful Commerce in Arms Act, the gun industry sold between five million and eight million guns per year. After 9/11 and George W. Bush's wars, the industry's annual sales would shoot up to between thirteen million and sixteen million units per year between 2013 and 2016.

The Bush-era cultural shift meant that the components for this sales explosion were in place. Now all we needed for final detonation was a pinch of Sharia law conspiracy theory and a Black president with a Muslim-sounding name.

SEVENTEEN

ZUMBOMANIA

W HEN George W. Bush took office in January 2001, the gun industry sold only about 1.5 million rifles in the United States each year. Those firearms, for the most part, were bolt-action hunting guns, lever guns like my little Browning, and .22 rifles like Cory's Model 60 Marlin. Virtually none of them were AR-15s.

Today, people hold a common misconception about sales of AR-15s, many attributing the lack of AR-15 sales back then to the assault weapons ban. But even during the decade in which that law was in effect, which extended through Bush's first term, the manufacturing, buying, and selling of AR-15s were still perfectly legal as long as the guns did not combine two or more of the extra features enumerated in the legislative language. Contrary to popular belief, the actual AR-15 rifles themselves were never specifically banned like the Tec-9 and many other weapons, yet well into the Bush years gun companies built almost none of them, which meant that consumers purchased almost none of them. Why?

By the time Bush left office, the US public bought nearly seven thousand AR-15s *every single day*.[1] The country soon embraced even larger numbers of the guns as symbols of freedom, symptoms of fear, and statements of patriotism. But before that explosion in sales, the guns did not sell largely because *the firearms industry itself resisted them*.

That was when a handful of reasonable, experienced, and morally conscious people unofficially moderated our industry as thought leaders. These were the people who grasped the societal dangers of open carry. They understood that just because something was legal did not mean it was right. In other words, these people functioned as risk managers. Many of them were respected columnists and reviewers who wrote extensively about guns, ammo, and gear. Many also wrote about hunting: about the ethics of fair chase, about protecting outdoor places. These people partnered with seasoned industry executives to form the unofficial group that functioned as the guardians of the industry flame. They didn't live in constant fear of politicians taking guns away or repeat baseless conspiracy theories. They didn't feel the need to link gun ownership with patriotism or divorce it from responsibility. They did not minimize the seriousness of guns or ever dream of using them to intimidate. They probably didn't regularly vote for Democrats, but they also didn't wear partisan politics on their sleeves. They didn't need to. And for the most part, gun consumers followed their lead. These were the *wise men* of the gun industry, and every company sought their blessing and approval whenever new products were launched.

Dwight and I knew that if we could impress the wise men with the high-quality guns that we built and believed in, they'd likely write favorably about them and readers would buy them. That part was basic marketing. What we needed was something *better* than basic. We needed a way to make Kimber stand far apart from our competitors. "Kansas!" I said one afternoon as we brainstormed ideas. "What if we take them to my place? Where I grew up?"

"Really?" Dwight scoffed with a chuckle. "There isn't even a motel there to stay in."

I explained that everyone could stay in one of those towns sixty miles away that I could see flickering in the dark as a kid. "Each morning we'll drive 'em to my parents' ranch. Spend the day shooting where I learned how to shoot. Plenty of prairie dogs. It'd be perfect, man."

After chewing on it a bit, Dwight agreed. And that's how we kicked off what became a famous annual event for Kimber between 1997 and 2008: "the Southwind Classic." The prairie-dog hunt at the Busse Ranch became one of the largest shooting promotional events in our industry. The idea sounded pretty good to our target audience too. More than twenty big-name writers attended Southwind, representing such magazines as *Outdoor Life, Field and Stream, Guns and Ammo, Shooting Times*, and *Petersen's Hunting*. Of course, writers from the NRA's magazines, *American Rifleman* and *American Hunter*, expected invitations too. Before long, gun writers *begged* for invitations. Even other companies took note and cosponsored our event—brands such as Leupold optics and the ammunition manufacturers Winchester and Federal. In fact, Dwight and I made Southwind into one of the most prestigious shooting events in the industry, complete with logo-embroidered shirts and custom luggage, gifts that the writers could display as they advertised for us on their travels.

For each event, I was in charge of coordinating the delivery of truckloads of guns, optics, and ammunition to my parents' ranch shop, temporarily displacing tractors and ranch supplies, effectively turning my childhood home into an armory.

Both Dwight and I also had to carefully determine who got invitations. We always invited people like *Outdoor Life*'s Jim Carmichael and *American Sportsman*'s Grits Gresham: larger-than-life wise men Dwight had idolized as a kid. And we'd have to sort through new names too.

"J. Guthrie," Dwight told me as we planned the 2004 Southwind Classic. A last-minute cancellation had opened up a slot for the event, and Dwight scrambled to fill it. "Know him?"

"Heard the name. Don't know him."

"Well, the NRA guys say we should invite him. A real up-and-comer, they say."

Of course, Dwight had to call the NRA about our open slot. I made some calls too, and Guthrie checked out. He was not yet thirty, but we figured he'd too be among the wise men someday, so we sent him an invitation.

"You care if I bring my own gun?" Guthrie asked when we called. Dwight shot a look at me. Bringing a personal gun to Southwind violated normal protocol. The whole idea was for writers to use *our* gear.

"Oh, hell, I don't care," I whispered to Dwight. After all, Guthrie was young, he checked out with others, and I didn't see a downside.

"We just really want you to have a good time," Dwight told him.

"If you want to bring a gun, that's OK," I added. "But just make sure you shoot ours too!"

A few days later, as rented Suburbans full of writers pulled into the Busse Ranch from Denver, I greeted them all. As we loaded thousands of dollars' worth of guns and ammo into the vehicles, I made sure everyone understood the plan, including when to be back for the big barbecue that evening. On the first day of the hunt, I held everyone's attention for a few minutes for a safety speech. It was a matter of instinct; I learned early on that any daylong hunt should begin with safety reminders.

"We're here to have fun and to shoot a lot!" I told the dozens of eager visitors. "But safety first! Keep your rifle actions open inside the trucks. Fingers only touch the triggers when you are certain. Be safe. *No gun is worth losing a life over.*"

Then it was time to send everyone into the field.

"Guthrie, you get to go with me and the big-timers today," I said to the newcomer as I gave the final directions. It was my job to take the most-important writers to one of the best locations on the ranch, and our last-minute cancellation meant that Guthrie caught a lucky break.

After my group's Suburban rolled into the pasture, we all started preparing our gear. I carefully laid Kimber rifles on the ground for members of my group to inspect and test. I knew that some of the writers fired so frequently that their rifles became hot to the touch. That meant I also needed to have hundreds of rounds of ammunition ready to load.

As Guthrie walked his rifle out to his spot, I caught what sounded like an audible gasp from the other writers. Guthrie was preparing to shoot his AR-15. *A black rifle.* Within minutes, the wise men huddled around the new kid to explain the unwritten rules of their polite gun society. Guthrie had screwed up by bringing a legal, post-ban firearm into a group of gun-industry opinion makers.

"Look, son, 'normal' people don't use or shoot that kind of gun," one of them explained. The national assault weapons ban was still in place, but the issue was not legality; it was self-restraint. I felt the same way—suddenly embarrassed by my decision to allow Guthrie to bring his own gun without even bothering to ask what kind of rifle it was. After the huddle, I sheepishly asked him to put his AR-15 away. Over drinks that evening, many of the other industry leaders talked about our unspoken AR-15 prohibition.

"We're not like those *tactards*," someone said, referring to the politically incorrect term for gun enthusiasts who, at the time, were fringe consumers who believed more in the rifles of militia building than the art and craftsmanship of the fine guns we were trying to sell. Guthrie seemed perplexed.

"Look, just a few years ago I worked my ass off to get a really important contract for Kimber," I told him over a glass of disappearing whisky. "It took me two years, but guess what kind of guns the LAPD SWAT team uses for their new official pistols?"

"No shit?" Guthrie said. "*You* got 'em to use Kimbers?"

"I sold them on Kimber, man. But the industry was not all that cool with it."

"Is this a pitch? Because that's a big one."

"Not a pitch. I'm just trying to let you understand the blowback over your gun. The LAPD SWAT team is the first and most famous special weapons and tactics team in the country. These guys are real operators. Well trained and highly respected. I mean, they are real badasses."

"They're the best."

"This should have been a monster deal at the SHOT Show, right? You would think half our booth would be dominated by an endorsement like that."

"For sure," Guthrie replied. He lit up with excitement.

"But that's not how our industry works. We weren't allowed to even display the LAPD stuff. Nothing 'tactical' or military is even debatable at SHOT. There is a law-enforcement section for that stuff. Not many people go in there, and if you want to get into that part of the show, you have to be a cop."

The Shooting, Hunting, Outdoor Trade (SHOT) Show is the gun industry's most important event each year and one of the largest trade shows in the world. SHOT was governed by the National Shooting Sports Foundation, the firearms-manufacturing trade group, which meant that the gun business itself set the rules for the show. There was a closed-off law-enforcement section where a few companies had small police-focused booths, but in the main part of the show none of the big companies were allowed to display even a bulletproof vest or a tactical glove, much less an AR-15. There was no law mandating this, but the industry policed itself by determining what could or could not be displayed to thousands of hungry customers with money to spend.

"That's just the way the industry works," I added. "We all have to worry about how the general public perceives us. That means we don't wave military guns and tactical shit in people's faces. There are going to be a lot of photos taken on this shoot, and that's not the kind of stuff our industry is trying to sell. It's just not a good look, OK?"

Guthrie was five years younger than me, but he looked down on me with the intensity of a young man who knew the world was changing. He seemed to understand what the rest of us at this event just did not know yet. Somehow he sensed that people like Mat Best and Kyle Lamb were soon to exert their own influence. Nonetheless, the long black case containing his semiautomatic black rifle stayed locked up at the shop for the remainder of the event.

A few years later, in 2007, another larger controversy over AR-15s dominated the discussion at the Southwind barbecue. "How 'bout that crazy Zumbo shit?" one of the other industry executives asked as we drank our beers. The crazy shit to which he referred involved one of the wise men, the successful and respected *Outdoor Life* writer and TV personality Jim Zumbo. He was a former wildlife biologist whose fans lovingly referred to as "Mr. Elk." He had written nearly two dozen successful books on hunting, and he regularly spoke at industry events and signed autographs in show booths. This meant that Zumbo also frequently attended hunting events like Southwind. And after one of these events in 2007, he wrote about it on his personal blog. The words that Mr. Elk published that February changed his life forever:

> I must be living in a vacuum. The guides on our hunt tell me that the use of AR and AK rifles have a rapidly growing following among hunters, especially prairie dog hunters. I had no clue. Only once in my life have I ever seen anyone using one of these firearms. I call them "assault" rifles, which may upset some people. Excuse me, maybe I'm a traditionalist, but I see no place for these weapons among our hunting fraternity. I'll go so far as to call them "terrorist" rifles. . . . We don't need to be lumped into the group of people who terrorize the world with them, which is an obvious concern. . . . Let's divorce ourselves from them. I say game departments should ban them from the prairies and woods.[2]

Even though many industry leaders quietly agreed with Zumbo, news of his blog entry landed on our shores like a Category 5 hurricane. It ripped the roof off America's rapidly changing gun culture and created tremendous blowback.

"Most people I talk to think he's right," one of the executives told me. "Hell, I think he's right!"

Others shook their heads in agreement. One of them commented on the reaction that had held the attention of all industry leaders: "But goddamn! Right or not, is he paying the price from the tactards or what? They're crucifying the guy, and none of us dare say anything, or we'll end up like him!"

What was the price Jim Zumbo paid for writing about assault weapons and hunting? Within a matter of weeks, he lost his popular blog for Remington. Then the iconic sporting-goods chain Cabela's ended its sponsorship of his TV show. Zumbo then offered to end his role as hunting editor of *Outdoor Life*, and the magazine accepted. The severe reaction surprised many of us. Just a few years earlier, this same group would not allow J. Guthrie to shoot an AR-15. Now we were witnessing the slow assassination of Mr. Elk by pissed-off gunnies who didn't agree with a few words he wrote.

Dave Petzal, a highly respected firearms editor at *Field and Stream*, had attended our Southwind events several times, and I had spent many days shooting with him. Petzal, famously witty and acerbic, watched along with the rest of the outdoor press as Zumbo was whipped mercilessly. In a piece titled "Zumbomania," he shot an admonition toward the increasingly powerful trolls who took their orders from the NRA:

> For 40 years, Jim has been a spokesman and ambassador of good will for hunting. Through his tireless efforts as a teacher and lecturer on hunting and hunting skills, he has done more for the sport than any 250 of the yahoos who called for his blood. . . . To all the chatroom heroes who made him unemployable, I have a word of warning: You've been swinging a two-edged sword. A United States in which someone can be ruined for voicing an unpopular opinion is a dangerous place.[3]

As usual, Petzal's biting commentary was on the money. Zumbo's "unpopular" opinion destroyed his own career, thanks to the inexperienced opinions of the chat-room heroes who suddenly became a dangerous threat to anyone not fully devoted. Just like that, Zumbo stopped singing in our coal mine.

But Guthrie's song only got louder. Just a few years before Zumbo, it was Guthrie who had his finger on the pulse of American gun culture and politics. Before his untimely death at the age of thirty-seven in 2013, it was Guthrie who became a widely beloved and respected writer for several magazines. He succeeded despite those early warnings by the industry leaders at Southwind, and he emerged as an energetic advocate for AR-15s and other black guns. In doing so, Guthrie helped create a culture where flamboyant showmen such as Mat Best could attract millions of fans and Smith & Wesson could sell millions of guns to couch commandos.

Mr. Elk, a man who served as an example for the passing era of industry wise men, did not fare so well. In an attempt to salvage what was left of his long career, Zumbo made a painful round of apologies on various forums. "I hold no grudges," he wrote in June 2007. "I will continue to stand as firm on pro hunting as I've ever done. But what's different now is that I'll do all I can to educate others who are, or were, as ignorant as I was about 'black' rifles and the controversy that surrounds them."[4]

Despite other attempts to retain something of his pre-scandal life, Zumbo never fully recovered. In fact, his most lasting contribution to the industry was his very name. In the industry the term "Zumboed" is still used to describe career-ending attacks that follow any criticism of tactical culture. He did not survive the same sort of attack I endured after speaking out at the National Press Club three years earlier.

Both the NSSF and NRA saw a new set of industry norms in the aftermath of Zumbo's demise. On one hand it must have been encouraging for them to witness the unquestioning loyalty of their foot soldiers. They must have realized that this was not like the old days of Ed Shultz, when they relied on press releases and public statements to incite action from the ground forces. For the NRA and the NSSF, what happened to Zumbo was far better. This time a man had been attacked without so much as a nod from organization or industry leaders. Automatic and ruthless persecution: another industry-developed product that would come to dominate our national politics.

But the NRA also realized that Zumbo's words highlighted a dangerous branding problem. His description of *terrorist rifles* was troublesome. Even if the NRA could manage to unbrand that name, they still had to deal with the term *assault rifles*, which is what almost everyone else called the AR-15. Neither term was palatable for a gun that the NRA and NSSF wanted to brand as "America's Rifle."[5]

America's Rifle needed some good old-fashioned public relations work. After marketing studies and a whole lot of internal industry discussion about the subject, the NRA and NSSF launched a plan to remake the image of the weapons that created so much controversy. Through a quiet internal messaging campaign, we were all encouraged to accept the new rifles as if no negative stigma had ever existed.

"They are no different than an old double-barrel shotgun," the guys from the NRA magazines started to tell everyone. "That's the way we all need to think. There can be no daylight between sporting guns and an AR-15. We have to let everyone know that we all stand together on this." The NSSF paid for glossy print ads in traditional sporting magazines to hammer the point directly.

I saw the conversion happen in everyday conversation and in actions such as the naming of our industry's black-gun buyer's guide. The 2008 version was called the *Gun Digest Buyer's Guide to Assault Weapons*. Just two years later, the same publisher changed the name to the *Gun Digest Buyer's Guide to Tactical Rifles*.[6]

Focus groups suggested that the NRA and NSSF needed an even better name for a rifle that scared the general public. The adjective *tactical* was cool, edgy, and part of the new evolving culture, but the rebranding effort needed to be even more aggressive. The industry settled on a professional media campaign to change the name of assault rifles to "MSRs" (modern sporting rifles). The NSSF bought ads and even updated its website to proclaim that "AR-15-style rifles are NOT 'assault weapons' or 'assault rifles.' If someone calls an AR-15–style rifle an 'assault weapon,' then they've been duped by an agenda."[7]

AR-15 companies got the hints too and began applying sporting terminology to their rifles, softening the image of guns designed for military units. Daniel Defense named one of its AR-15 rifles the Prairie Panther. Remington built the VTR Predator. Wilson Combat offered the Ultimate Hunter. All these guns were just the same rifle with a new name, but even the big companies got on board. Smith & Wesson sold the M&P Sport. The names sounded better, but this did not make the rifles into hunting guns, a fact that we would all realize not long after one of those models was sold in a gun shop near Parkland, Florida.

This industry-funded MSR rebranding effort irked many other companies. Many of us had worked hard to build up product lines based on traditional guns, and now the industry trade group was essentially funding a massive competitive effort aimed at making our guns obsolete. Such companies as Kimber, Browning, and Weatherby did not build AR-15s, and the NSSF campaign was essentially converting sales of our guns into sales of MSRs from our competitors. When any of us raised reservations, we were told that accepting the AR-15 was the key to expanding the entire firearms market.

The second and more important reason for my frustration was that the social acceptability involved with hunting, and with the culture I shared with my father, was being appropriated to make AR-15s more acceptable to the general public. The industry needed the cover from the sporting culture to make this all work. As the years went on, I watched the NRA return to this well time and again as it used the acceptance of hunting to help sell products and politicians.

The NRA supported the industry's MSR branding effort, but the organization wanted to take it one step further. With the benefit of savvy research and a multimillion-dollar ad agency, the NRA knew that wrapping an American flag around anything would make it sell. And so the NRA decided to give the MSR a moniker that no patriot could argue with: "It's time to eliminate the misconception that AR stands for assault rifle, and tell the world what AR really stands for: America's Rifle."[8]

Industry leaders like the old-timers who had been at our Southwind events may not have liked the strategy, but it worked. Company owners like Leslie Edelman took notice too. He soon realized that the campaign to normalize AR-15s was effective. As assault rifles became MSRs and then "America's Rifle," barely a couple of weeks went by without Leslie calling me to suggest that Kimber should get into America's AR-15 business.

Many other companies jumped in, but I stayed steadfast. As I endured the constant pressure, I thought back to all of Greg Warne's stalwart admonitions about fighting to keep Kimber a respectable company that sold *craftsmanship*. I resisted the industry pressure at every opportunity, and I knew that my resistance to both Leslie and the industry rebranding would have made Greg very proud.

Greg would have had colorful commentary for sure, probably after chugging a warm beer. But he was missing out on all this controversy about military rifles. He also missed out on the booming business of a company he once led. Unfortunately for Greg, and for classic-gun aficionados everywhere and probably for the adult-entertainment business, he was found dead in a Costa Rican hotel room in 2006. The short newspaper story from San José hinted at his colorful life but offered only the generic "heart attack" as the cause of his death.

For such a rich character, Greg's final tribute seemed woefully short and unemotional: "Warne had an Australian accent, but much of his career was spent in the gun business, first in North America and later here. He identified himself as the retired president of Kimber, the rifle and pistol manufacturer in Clackamas, Oregon."[9]

I speculated with Dwight about Greg's last days, of course, but we never knew exactly what happened. I could buy that he died in a hotel room. I could not buy that he died of a heart attack. Certainly not while relaxing or watching TV.

In the weeks and months after I got the news about Greg, I realized that I actually kind of missed him. I didn't miss the days of bouncing paychecks or the wine-chugging stripper parties. But I did find myself wishing that Greg's product vision would have taken more purchase in our industry. I wished that Greg would have used his magnetic personality for something constructive.

In some ways it was sad for me that Greg Warne would never make a bigger impact on the world. He died as he lived: a man of unrealized and squandered gifts, too wrapped up in short-term personal gratification to develop a real legacy.

Greg's death also represented a passing in the industry. Gone were the days when a playboy could bootstrap a company based on classic guns and birthday parties. Gone also were the days when an industry had the sense to worry about public perception. Gone were the wise men who guarded against breaking social norms or frightening average citizens. And gone were the days when people like me could risk publicly criticizing the worship of AR-15s, even when it meant questioning the use of semiautomatic weapons of war for something as unwarlike as wiping out prairie dogs.

What happened to Jim Zumbo landed like a thud on all our careers. From these days forward, everyone in the industry understood that using a word such as *terrorist* or *assault* to describe AR-15s was not in keeping with approved terminology. Even when the guns were used in mass shootings, we all knew to avoid any discussion about the wisdom of proliferating a culture centered on those same guns.

There was no debate. The industry became consumed only with the promise of "growing our market." And it spent millions in advertising dollars to reinforce it all. The market-tested industry messaging campaign took hold, and the guns became ubiquitous. Soon AR-15s became the backbone of the gun industry. The not-so-old consensus and the concerned warnings from the industry wise men were in the past. Sales climbed into the millions.

The result was a country forced to endure *pew pews* from wannabe operators in places such as Las Vegas, Aurora, El Paso, Orlando, Sutherland Springs, Parkland, and Sandy Hook. With an impressive nationwide distribution like that, even I had to admit that the NRA had succeeded.

The NRA had indeed converted the AR-15 into America's Rifle.

EIGHTEEN

THE BEST GUN SALESMAN IN AMERICA

"CHECK IT OUT, BUSSE! JIM'S PAWN AND GUNS IS QUOTED IN this story!" I looked down at a printed copy of a national Associated Press story that one of my sales guys had tossed onto my desk. A manager from Jim's Pawn and Guns, a large Kimber dealer in North Carolina, had told a reporter in the days following Barack Obama's election that his store was an "absolute madhouse" because of gun sales. "Everybody, and I mean everybody, is buying guns right now," the manager added.[1]

The report from North Carolina could have described every one of Kimber's two thousand dealers across the country in the fall of 2008. The huge sales numbers should have produced a celebratory mood for gun executives, but leaders in the business were not celebrating. In fact, they were terrified.

Unlike in past years, when I got the feeling that industry leaders knew that at least part of the NRA hyperbole was for show, now people in the gun business believed it like gospel. The NRA did its best to keep it at a fever pitch. Every day during the election of 2008 the entire industry received emails, phone calls, and mailers reminding us that our livelihoods—our very freedoms as Americans—were under direct attack. I heard the fear in the breathless conversations with dealers and in the heightened concerns of other industry executives. Barely a day went by in our office when the issue of race was absent. On more than one occasion I had conversations with dealers who forced me to speak up. I'd hear frightened statements like "that Black Muslim son of a bitch is coming after our guns. Obama ain't from this country. He hates America!"

In conversations that foreshadowed the MAGA movement of 2016, I could hear the palpable fear in industry voices. For them, the only thing worse than losing a culture was having it taken by a Black community organizer from Chicago with a law degree from Harvard. The NRA and its most loyal mouthpieces, always looking for an opportunity to profit from fear, kept everyone on edge with a constant hum of dire existential warnings.

In another precursor to the Trump campaigns, the NRA painted a foreboding vision of an America ruled by a powerful federal government hell-bent on taking away rights and freedoms. In this imaginary dystopian future, which ironically looked much more like Trump's authoritarianism than Obama's America, the stakes could not have been higher. And a single man, we were told, was responsible for all of it. This man had never been given a Winchester shotgun for Christmas, never "operated," never even fired America's Rifle. Of course he was also a fucking gun-grabbing Democrat.

No matter how crazy the claims, members of the gun business believed these things because the NRA drops said they were true. Time and again during the run-up to the 2008 election, Wayne LaPierre reinforced his members' distrust of Obama with emphatic statements, and the organization spent millions to ensure that they were amplified across the country.

And just like that, these assertions and fears became the gun industry's own set of alternative facts. Even when the industry had good news to celebrate, such as the exploding gun sales, LaPierre stayed on message, tamping down any enthusiasm and replacing it with more fear. "The reason gun sales are rising is that gun owners and Second Amendment enthusiasts are justifiably suspicious," he said, referring to the skyrocketing NICS totals.[2]

Of course I believed none of it, but I could see how a frightened mental spiral could quickly consume a willing mind. Like those who believed it all, I had worked hard to build up a vibrant business based largely on the sale of pistols. If LaPierre was right, all that work was sure to go down the drain given that President Obama—as the NRA falsely claimed—would "ban use of firearms for home self defense" and "ban the manufacture, sale and possession of handguns."[3]

If that happened, I would certainly be out of a job. The grim NRA advertisements let us all know that even basic hunting was going to be a thing of the past, given that an Obama administration had, according to the NRA, developed plans to "ban virtually all deer hunting ammunition."[4] Cox and LaPierre told us that all this remaining slice of joy, along with our right to self-defense, was sure to disappear because President Obama was ready to "erase the Second Amendment from the Bill of Rights and exorcise it from the U.S. Constitution."[5]

And just to make sure that the unhinged messages permeated a patriotic country, the NRA tapped into the same trend that motivated millions of couch commandos. It wrapped its threats in an American flag and enlisted war heroes from the sandbox to appear in dramatic videos. This was a deft move because just like Trump's political base in 2016, many NRA members had not graduated from college and had certainly never been constitutional law professors like Obama. The combination of Obama's race and education provided a perfect foil for LaPierre, who had spent years deriding the elitist professors and liberals found on college campuses.

Military service, on the other hand, was tangible and honorable. Many NRA members had served or knew someone who had, and this provided the institutional validation that the NRA needed to reinforce its message. In one of the many NRATV ads in 2008, a White Iraq war veteran speaks to the camera with the intensity of a man entrusted with the responsibility of deciding who lives and who dies. "Like all the guys I fought with in Iraq, I was honored to defend my country and our freedom," Marine veteran Kurt Rusch says. Then the ad switches to quickly edited images of war and shooting—a lot like a video game: "But when I got back stateside, I learned that Barack Obama opposes my right to own a handgun for self-defense. It's ridiculous. Out there in the desert, defeat was not an option. Sure, combat was hell, but on the front lines, I knew I served a real purpose: Defeating terrorism. Protecting our way of life. That's what it's all about. There's no way I'm voting for a president who will take that away."[6]

I was not afraid of losing my guns or my hunting; in fact, I was very hopeful that an Obama administration would enact conservation measures critical to habitat and hunting. I was certainly not afraid of losing my country and least of all my job. Unlike almost everyone else in the gun business, I was happy that Obama was going to become our forty-fourth president.

Obama had pretty big shoes to fill because even though the Bush years initially produced the typical Republican dip, the truth was they had been very good for our industry. It took the worst terrorist attack in US history and the resulting wars, but during the first seven years of the Bush presidency, gun sales in the United States averaged about seven million units per year. That was 40 percent higher than sales during the Clinton administration. In an early sign that the NRA's racially tinged fearmongering had legs, gun sales shot up in the months before a possible 2008 Obama win. NICS checks for that year totaled nearly nine million units, 19 percent higher than the average of Bush's first seven years in office.

I had few doubts about Obama winning and no doubts about the impact of an Obama presidency, but everyone else in the industry believed the NRA's fear machine, and that created perceived volatility in our business. Executives like me spent a lot of time forecasting and speculating about the possible outcomes. Leslie was on pins and needles, and he often called to get a read on my latest sales and political forecasts. No matter how many times he asked, my response never wavered: "If Obama wins, there will be four or eight years of growth. He is not taking anyone's guns. We will not be able to keep up. And I think Obama is going to win."

Leslie seemed to skip over the positive impacts for him and instead responded with a version of "Yeah, maybe. But I hope the fucking Democrats *don't* win. They hate gun owners." He then rambled into longer diatribes about the imagined evils of an Obama administration, which were really just regurgitations of the NRA's election alerts.

Never once did I get the feeling that Leslie was putting on some sort of act. He knew how to spot even the smallest business opportunity, yet he was blinded to the reality of an Obama administration. I could see that he genuinely believed the NRA's rhetoric, no matter how fantastical or hyperbolic it was. For me at least, this was a powerful example of how easily voters could be convinced to act against their own self-interests. Within a decade, there would be tens of millions like Leslie.

However, I made no bones about following through on my National Press Club promises to vote against Republicans who actually threatened my own interests, such as access to public lands. As the election approached, I even reinforced my decision in office conversations with my sales team. My support of Obama perplexed my staff. I understood why. I was pretty sure they didn't know a single other member of the industry who would openly admit holding such opinions. "Busse, you work for a gun company," they often said. "How the hell can you vote for a Democrat? Especially *that* Democrat?"

I welcomed the curiosity, though, and wanted a team where we could be honest and debate our differences. "I'm tired of being lied to," I'd respond. "I don't believe any of the crazy shit that the NRA says about guns or Barack Obama."

On the surface, my staff did not share my doubts about the veracity of the NRA's claims, so I always added a footnote that gave me just a bit of leeway with them: "Don't worry; I'm voting for the candidate who will make your jobs easy. Obama is going to sell guns like you never imagined. Just think of it that way." Even if none of them wanted to vote for Obama or doubt the NRA's alternative facts, I knew they did not want to argue with higher sales and bigger paychecks.

This was my way of poking at the collective industry belief in conspiracy. Just like a future Republican Congress that held on to obviously false election-fraud claims, everyone in the industry was supposed to believe the NRA conspiracies, especially the one that said Obama would remake America into a gun-free zone. The real reason was that the NRA needed to keep up the act so that millions of consumers would believe the same thing and then send money and vote accordingly. I was dubious that my guys really believed it deep down. Maybe I just hoped they didn't.

My sales staff was careful not to allow my perplexing politics leak out of our small circle. Most of them had been with Kimber through the blowback from my National Press Club appearance. They knew that any further mention of such treasonous ideas from Kimber leaders would only encourage more trolling—maybe eventually even a boycott or a Zumboing.

For those reasons, I was also careful with Leslie. But I found ways to resist his politics too. Once, after I subtly pushed back on his "fucking Democrats" statement, he finally started to pick up on the cues. "You aren't telling me that you're *for* that asshole Obama, are you?"

In an industry that operates under an authoritarian code that does not allow people like me to voice contrary opinions, I considered my answer carefully: "I can't stand the conservation and environmental policies of the Republicans, and I don't buy all of these crazy scare tactics." In what had become common for me, I had to figure out a way to hide the true nature of my politics just so Leslie did not fire me. And so I posed questions meant to leave him with doubts: "Leslie, my job is to sell more Kimbers. Wouldn't you want me to vote for that?"

Leslie responded with an odd half laugh, not sure what to make of my questioning of industry fears or a potential fucking Democrat as a vice president of his company.

Of course, contrary to LaPierre's promises and Leslie's irrational fears, the country did not crumble under Obama's presidency, nor did gun sales suffer. Nobody took any guns away. I was not forced to give up hunting, and my job did not evaporate. Instead, I sat back and watched an industry capitalize on a long-simmering pot of racism first placed on the stove by Marion Hammer all those years ago. For more than a decade it had been slowly steaming, but when a Black man finally rose to power, the NRA racism pot boiled over.

Never again would the industry return to the sales totals during the previous presidential administration, which were under seven million units per year. During the first four years of Obama's presidency, gun sales exceeded forty-three million units, a staggering *52 percent* increase.

This all meant that times were pretty easy for a gun-sales team like mine. We were busy, but the hardest work of drumming up orders was no longer our main challenge. The truth was that "selling," at least in any traditional sense, was not difficult at all. With Obama in office, our days consisted of maintaining a back-order list of more than a hundred thousand guns. Just as with most other companies, we could never catch up. Dealers just had to get in line and wait for their deliveries. Often they waited for several months, sometimes for more than a year.

The news reports of constantly high gun demand attracted investors to an industry that had long been stifled by the assault weapons ban and threats of liability settlements. With those limitations out of the way, investor money started to flood the gun business, and we all monitored the results.

Most companies, like Kimber, were (and still are) privately held, and that meant any inside news came from calls and conversations at bars between people like me and other executives. But we could monitor a few companies. Sturm Ruger had been publicly traded since the 1980s. The company whose tagline was "Arms maker for responsible citizens" traded in a range of around ten dollars per share right up until 2008. But by the time the Obama presidency was over, the stock symbol RGR had been folded into countless retirement plans and investment strategies, and the company's average stock price increased nearly sevenfold, rising as high as eighty dollars per share.

The steady growth in gun sales also caught the eyes of big retailers. For decades, most of the gun sales in the country happened in small independent gun shops, pawn stores, and a few regional sporting-goods chains. People in the gun business had always looked longingly at the big shiny cornerstone stores in suburban shopping areas, partially because of the sales potential but also because of the social acceptance they represented. Up until the Obama boom, many of those large retailers had been reluctant to go all in on guns. Some might carry a hunting shotgun or two, maybe a .22 rifle, but not handguns or AR-15s. The liability and the potential social blowback were just not worth the risk.

But gun sales expanded so fast under President Obama that even big chains could no longer resist. Stores like Cabela's and Bass Pro Shops that already had gun counters expanded them to include entire new sections of AR-15s and other tactical guns. National chains such as Dick's Sporting Goods, Academy, and even Walmart opened or expanded gun counters in hundreds of stores too.

Almost all gun-company executives marveled at the result. The same man whom the NRA warned would ruin our industry had done what none of us could ever accomplish. The best gun salesman in America had taken the industry mainstream.

NINETEEN

BULLETPROOF GLASS

L IKE ME, DWIGHT FELT NEW PRESSURES AS THE INDUSTRY growth accelerated. We both sensed changes coming, and even though our politics did not align, we still shared the same basic vision for Kimber. When we started, we both had dreams about what the company might become, but Dwight never dreamed of a loud office, a big staff, and technological changes.

"I hate the internet," he often told me, referring to the growing power of influencers and social media sites that fueled the industry's transformation and market change. I distrusted these people because of the societal and policy implications to our country. Dwight disliked them because they represented a new kind of industry that did not rely on expertise, glossy catalogs, and famous old gun writers.

All the changes finally got to Dwight, and he resigned from Kimber to make a go of it on his own. Including our time at Burris, we had worked together for more than twenty years, but now he got his wish: he no longer had to play well with others. He became a solo gunrunner of sorts, forming his own company and brokering guns from his home. He built a gun studio where he examined, photographed, and then bought and sold all the obscure guns he loved. He and I had been through a lot together, and somehow we managed to keep the whole operation afloat without killing each other—or being shot by someone else in the office. Those things alone were major accomplishments.

Dwight's departure meant that Kimber had a big hole to fill, though. Unlike the other companies that focused on branding "Tupperware," which the industry now called "commodity guns," Kimber depended on our carefully honed brand and handcrafted quality. This meant that our company relied on top-notch marketing, and that had been Dwight's bailiwick.

We found our new department leader living not far from the center of the marketing universe in downtown New York City. Thomas Daybrik III had grown up in the moneyed business world of Wall Street. Unassuming, likable, and outgoing, Tom was in his midthirties when he joined us with bright eyes, a dark beard, and a booming laugh.

Tom was not a typical industry leader. He had not been raised with guns. He was not a hunter. He had never dreamed of working in the gun business as a kid and probably never volunteered to take a center-of-mass shot from a Glock. But Tom loved adventure, and when he heard of an opportunity in the gun business, he was instantly curious. "I used to travel a lot for my other jobs," he told me soon after becoming Kimber's new director of marketing. "The CIA recruited me to do some work on a trip to Africa once. I would have loved to do that, but I think I had one too many drinks that night and scared them off."

Tom and I had very different backgrounds, but I soon realized that I could work with him because, like me, he cared about keeping our products at a high level of quality and centered on proven traditional designs. Tom worked out of our offices in New York, which meant that we spent a lot of time on the phone. In those frequent conversations he and I strategized on how to form a bulwark against the continued pressure to get into the "America's Rifle" business. "I'm with you, Busse,"

Tom often said. "We need to make sure that Kimber doesn't just follow the herd or cheapen our image."

Most people in our industry distrusted big-city businessmen with no gun experience. But Tom quickly learned that the way to make friends in the gun business was through long bar tabs. Despite the fact that he could have easily passed for one of those "fucking Democrats," within a year Tom had bought most everyone in the industry several rounds of drinks and earned their friendship—one late-night whiskey at a time.

Leslie was making other new hires as well. Even though he continued to play a vital role at Kimber, the rapidly growing and complex corporation needed full-time operations leadership. With expanding manufacturing facilities in New York, dozens of vendors, and hundreds of suppliers, he hired a new chief operating officer to oversee our company. In his midfifties, Greg Grogan was tall and bombastic, and he had a background in the storage-locker business. We could all see that Grogan liked to be loud and in charge, and this created a lot of tension within our team. It was Tom who first noted the unease we all felt about our new COO. "I'm not sure we should trust this guy—pretty sure he has never owned a gun," Tom confided in me.

Grogan may have not had any experience with firearms, but I would soon learn that he did possess the increasingly important industry qualification of being politically aligned with Leslie and the NRA. Grogan also claimed to have an expertise in finishing out buildings, and Kimber was in the middle of expanding into yet another new facility in Yonkers. One of our new COO's first projects involved incorporating office space in that new factory, and it was taking longer than expected. Tom knew that he had to move into an office in this facility, and he continued to complain about the delays during almost daily calls to me.

"Well, I'll get to see it firsthand," I replied. "I'm coming to New York next month for the leadership meeting. Hope you're not sitting on a bucket under a light bulb."

"Oh, forgot to tell you," Tom added. "Now Grogan wants to install bulletproof glass between the executive offices and all of us. Does he have any idea how that looks? He gets to decide who is on the safe side of the glass? What the fuck?"

By the time I arrived in New York, most of the space had been finished, but Tom was still trying to debate Grogan over the final decision about the placement of the bulletproof glass. "You mean that if some son of a bitch from pistol assembly goes postal and comes up here with a gun to shoot the shit out of everyone, those motherfuckers get saved while I have to sit out here and get filled full of holes?" Tom yelled, waving a floor plan shortly after I arrived. The office plans proposed putting Grogan and a small group of other senior executives behind the thick glass. Notably for Tom, the plan left the marketing team exposed to possible workplace violence on the unprotected side of the barrier. Tom looked at me in anger as he pointed around the open office, at the product managers and marketing assistants. "Can you fucking believe it?" he seethed. "I guess all of us are just gonna be sitting ducks."

I saw a lot of irony in the fact that senior gun-company employees were arguing about who was safe from gunfire and who was not. I tried to get Tom to laugh about it, but he didn't think it was funny. He was angered by the slight and probably worried about the potential danger too. But over drinks that evening I got him to loosen up, and he finally embraced the irony: "Busse, you are right. This is all so wild. This whole gun-business thing is like a dark-comedy Netflix series, and I don't know if I should laugh or cry."

The next day we met up again at the factory so that we could put our hands on some of our new products. "We're gonna do some shooting down in the range," Tom explained with excitement. "We get to try out the new pistols today! I know you're a senior employee and all, but you still gotta sign these forms, and when you're down there, they are strict as shit. Safety glasses at all times. Ear protection never comes off.

Bulletproof vest always stays on. No exceptions. Any little safety hiccup and it's over."

A few minutes later, I joined Tom at the front of the heavy safety door of Kimber's indoor range, which was located in a secure area along the back wall of our huge industrial facility. The men in charge chatted with me for a few moments, then went through the checklist. "Safety glasses? Check. Looks like we have a vest for you. Good. Now the rules: Nothing in the chamber until you're in the shooting bay. Muzzle stays downrange always. If someone else is shooting, you always stay behind them. Finger only touches the trigger when you are ready to shoot and sure of the target. Got it?" Although to me this was a familiar safety briefing, I nodded my head in agreement before we entered.

As I flew home to Montana the next day, I considered the wisdom of the safety precautions mandated by Kimber and by all other gun companies. It was difficult to escape the obvious reality: guns and the people who wield them are inherently dangerous. Commonsense safety precautions were not optional; in fact, adherence to them was strictly required.

Within a few weeks, Tom called me with another update about the marketing team: "Grogan fired one of our guys today, right out in front of my office. But then, of course, he damn near ran back behind his bulletproof glass the second it was over. Everybody knows the guy he fired carries a Glock to work, and he was scared the place might get shot up."

"That's gotta go in the Netflix show," I told Tom.

Tom tried to be funny when he explained that he had been left to deal with potential violence on his exposed side of the glass, but I knew he was also angry. "I don't get the comfort of being safe behind that thick glass, you know."

Tom and I bonded through seeing the gun industry for what it was: ironic, duplicitous, self-serving. Often we did this through the use of more humor as we built out more scenes in our imaginary TV show.

We could both see the hypocrisy. On one hand, gun companies opted for, or even demanded, arduous safety procedures. And on the other hand, the industry marched loyally behind the NRA as it fought laws that would have required background checks for all gun sales. That bond between Tom and me allowed me the rare opportunity to be honest with a close colleague. And so, in the following weeks, I also decided to be more open about my politics with him: "It's not that I don't like our products, and of course I want to build a respected gun company. I want to be proud of all this, but I really detest the politics of this industry. Way too much of the business is built on bullshit fear and ugly conspiracies. Let's be honest, Tom. The reason people are buying guns right now is because a Black man is our president."

Tom agreed, not because he supported Obama but rather because my assertions were obviously true. Tom was a long way from considering himself a Democrat, but because he had not spent years being indoctrinated by the industry, he could see the truth a lot more plainly than others. In Tom I found a friend who would at least listen when I dared to discuss how fear and racism drove much of the market from which our entire industry benefited.

Tom and I talked even more frequently as we prepared for any upcoming trade show. As we discussed the logistics for the NRA convention in 2012, I let him know that the show in St. Louis troubled me. For many years I had found ways to focus only on our company, but the national gun scene was now so intertwined with the nation's politics that we all knew it was impossible to untangle the two.

As I prepared to travel to St. Louis, I thought about my position. I was an accomplished executive, proud of the company I had helped build. For people like me, the convention was a place for adulation, even worship, but I no longer prayed to those gods.

I specifically took issue with the NRA's distortion of truth, constant encouragement of racism, and detached conspiracy theories. Sure, I would go to St. Louis, but I would not go as a loyal pilgrim, like most. I had once been that person, but not now. I would not go as a groupie looking to have fun and adventure like Tom. I was not going to rub shoulders with political leaders like Leslie. I would not go to win awards, which were no longer important to me. I would attend as a conflicted person, still proud of my powerful company but also troubled and determined to have a positive impact on our country. After all, I had unique insights and access. I went to St. Louis agnostic if not outright atheist, harboring distrust about an industry that had proudly abandoned its principles and would embrace anything, just so long as it fed the growing power machine of the NRA.

TWENTY

DEAD OR IN JAIL

"**B**EST DAMN GUN I OWN. AND LET ME TELL YA, I GOT A bunch of guns." I looked up to see a stranger speaking at me in the crowded Marriott elevator. He was excited, as if I were famous. I said nothing. "Well, you *do* work for Kimber, don't you?" He pointed to the large exhibitor badge hanging from my neck: *Ryan Busse, Kimber, Kalispell, Montana / Yonkers, New York.* Shit. Right. There it was: an open invitation for any Kimber fan to accost me in an elevator at the NRA convention. Most everyone on the Kimber team knew to avoid wearing name badges outside the convention floor for this exact reason.

He was a large man dressed in khaki cargo pants, an untucked Wisconsin Badgers polo shirt, and a black baseball cap emblazoned with "NRA" in block gold letters.

"What gun do you own?" I asked, squeezing away from the door as another person got on.

"I bought your Ultra CDP .45. The Custom Defense Package. And that thing is sweet. My buddies slobber every time I get it out and show it off. I got a Glock and Springfield, and I got an old Colt and a bunch of other stuff too. Those guns are OK, but damn! My Kimber. Now that's my baby."

"Thanks, we take a lot of pride in them." Glancing at his shirt, I changed the topic. "You're from Wisconsin, huh? I have friends there."

"Close to Milwaukee. Bought my gun from the Cabela's north of town on I-41."

He looked at my badge again, this time zeroing in on the words above my name: "NRA St. Louis—2012." The 2012 was printed in deep red—a color chosen for good reason. "Hope your Wisconsin friends ain't in Madison. That's where we keep all our Democrats. Thinking maybe we should build a wall around the place. I carry my Kimber when I go into that town. Never know what them liberals might try and pull."

I looked up to see two other men on the elevator snickering in agreement. They wore stickers urging other convention attendees to "Trigger the Vote." One of them took the opportunity to speak to the small captive audience as we descended. He was excited. "Did you hear what Ted Nugent said? He said he's gonna be dead or in jail if Obama gets elected again!"

The less-than-subtle threat to President Obama earned Nugent a visit from the Secret Service. Most Americans found the threatening intimidation detestable, but in our stuffy convention elevator, the comments only produced chuckles of agreement. I tried to slip away, but as we all spilled into the lobby, a woman tugged on my sleeve. "We have a friend who named their daughter Kimber!"

"Oh, great," I replied, not knowing what to say next. "Thanks."

The large man from Wisconsin confidently grinned and nodded at me as we parted. A sign of understood solidarity. I had seen that look many times, and I knew it conveyed a rich message: *It's OK to hate the others. We're at war with them.*

I turned to take the most direct route to a tall black coffee, shoving my name badge in my back pocket so no one else could see it. I knew today would be another long slog, that I would struggle to wear a heavy disguise. And I'd do it while enduring thousands of people who took me to be something I was not anymore. I could not blame them, I suppose. Sameness, solidarity, unanimity, lockstep, freedom, patriotism, us versus them, stand and fight, God and guns, good versus evil. These were powerful verses in hymns that were written here, and they were catching on across the country. Someone like me was supposed to know them by heart. I slipped into the hotel restaurant hoping for a quiet breakfast. No such luck. A small group of executives from other gun companies immediately recognized me. "Busse! Sit with us!"

I usually found these guys at a bar after the shows, but today it was breakfast. We began discussing the Shooting Industry's Academy of Excellence Awards. "Weren't you nominated for Person of the Year again last year?" an acquaintance from Federal Ammunition asked.

"Yeah, I guess so," I said, wanting to shirk the recognition.

"We are sitting with royalty," one of my friends from another company chuckled. "None of us have even been nominated." He elbowed me. "Shit, Busse, you're big-time. You pick up the tab."

"You boys know I'm just a ranch kid trying to make a living."

It felt strange to hope *not* to win an award or to have my peers rib me for my success, but the weight in St. Louis that year was becoming painful. It meant that I would be a puzzle piece, snapping exactly into my numbered spot with the others.

I slugged down my coffee and swung my old Filson bag onto my shoulder—my security blanket of sorts. Rough, worn, and tattered, it had been with me on every single business trip I had ever taken. The other executives had modern laptop bags and travel backpacks. They joked about my old canvas bag, but it had become a reminder to me that I should chart my own course.

They all thanked me for breakfast, and we parted ways, making our own paths into the giant convention hall. I stepped out of the hotel for some fresh air. A sign across the street on the outside wall of the convention building read "Acres of guns and gear." I crossed the street into a small group of protesters slowly walking in a circle beneath the giant sign. Maybe twenty people, most carrying their own signs or wearing T-shirts with political messages. One woman held a poster that read "There Is Blood on NRA Hands!" Another read "Shame on You NRA!"

A Black man wearing a McCaskill for Senate button looked at me as I passed him on the sidewalk. I was rooting for Claire McCaskill, who was then running for her second term in the Senate, so I tried to connect with him. He made eye contact and gave me a nod, but it was much different from the confident nod of solidarity that I encountered outside the Marriott elevator. This one was fearful.

I turned into the America's Center Convention Complex and began the long walk down the hall to the main-floor entrance. The walkway was a hundred yards long, with fifty-foot ceilings. Along the left wall hung a long line of photographs, each more than fifteen feet tall. All NRA convention attendees passed below these giant banners to enter the main convention space, as if paying homage to the great leaders of the gun movement. On each portrait were the words "I am the NRA." Nugent. Tom Selleck. Oliver North. Chuck Norris. And, of course, Moses himself. I could almost hear Charlton Heston saying, "From my cold, dead hands."

The new message for all who walked below these pictures was not as succinct, but it was more powerful: *You are one. You are the same. You cannot be different. You are just like Chuck, and Charlton and Tom and Ted and Oliver. YOU are the NRA. THEY are the enemy.*

The hall also funneled everyone past attractive women waving their hands in encouragement as they sold tickets. They surrounded a large display showcasing dozens of brand-new guns. "Get your tickets! Win a gun from the Wall of Guns! We're giving one away every hour. Win a Smith & Wesson, or a Glock, or maybe a Kimber. If you win, you get your choice!"

Dozens of people scrambled to buy tickets before the next drawing. A man waving his credit card said, "I want that Kimber! I'll take some tickets." A woman in tight jeans and a cropped shirt approached me and asked if I wanted to buy any.

"I work for Kimber," I chuckled. "But thanks."

"Oh, everyone is hot for your guns," she said with a wink.

Just beyond the Wall of Guns a large crowd had formed, bottle-necked by the main entrance doors. As I pressed through the waiting gun enthusiasts, I pulled my badge from my back pocket. People stepped aside as if I were an entertainer going onstage.

Convention rules barred normal NRA members from entering the show floor before 9:00, but as a major sponsor and gun exhibitor I had special access. We could enter at our leisure. This small sea of people represented a typical cross section of NRA membership. Just about everyone was White, and almost all were adult men. There were a few younger boys, probably with their fathers, and a few women with their husbands. I could see the security guard at the door checking the badges of exhibitors like me who filed through the crowd. He was an older Black man with glasses and a slight build, the lone person of color serving a White audience. "Thank you, sir," he said, bowing his head as he checked each badge.

As I shuffled toward the guard, I noticed a heavily muscled man with tattoos on his large arms. With a shaved head and a tan, he wore a short-sleeved black T-shirt that read: "Don't blame me. I voted for the white guy."

The guard looked at the shirt and then at me in slow motion. I knew that I should say something. I should have apologized to the guard for the indignity. I wanted to tell him that I did not believe in that shirt, that I knew it was wrong, and that I respected him. I should have called out the racism and those who supported it right there so that everyone within earshot knew it was not acceptable. But I did nothing—the fear of judgment kept me from it.

I considered the loneliness of the guard and the embarrassment of my own inaction. I thought of all the people who had seen that shirt and said nothing or, worse, the ones who had laughed. Sadness gripped me. The guard's face then went blank, as if checking his emotions to finish a job he promised to start. *It's not the first time he's been forced to endure this,*

I thought. Through his glasses he glanced at my badge and murmured, "Thank you, sir." I passed by him and entered the hall just like all the others.

The bright lighting of the convention floor poured down on the red carpet of the first and grandest booth in the building. The NRA booth stood two stories. Large TV screens were positioned around the exterior, with NRA hunting shows and commercials blaring from each monitor. In the middle of the huge structure were three immense banners, each twenty feet tall: headshots of the organization's great triad. Or was it a trinity?

On the left was Chris Cox. In his picture he looked young and polished. On the right was Kyle Weaver. Now in his early forties, he had a slight but serious grin. In the middle and a few feet above Weaver and Cox was Wayne LaPierre. No person entering the convention hall could miss these three portraits.

The show floor felt like a small city with unfamiliar streets, and I was often disoriented as I made my way toward our booth. I found the main aisle and walked past Ruger, Smith & Wesson, and Sig Sauer.

Almost every booth displayed AR-15s or their variants. The same sort of tactical gear that was prohibited at events like this only a few years earlier now dominated the spaces around the guns.

Not that long ago it would have been hard to find an AR-15 at a show like this, but by 2012, nearly five hundred gun companies produced countless, customizable versions of America's Rifle. Like Lego sets for anyone old enough to shoot a machine designed for offensive military operations, the guns came with unlimited accessories: shorter stocks and shorter barrels for shooting in tight spaces like buildings or cars, heavy barrels for longer-range sniper accuracy, rails for add-on lights and lasers, forward handles, barrel shrouds to protect shooters from burning their hands during rapid fire, scopes, camouflage, stars and stripes, engravings, and, of course, bump stocks. The bump stock used the force of a fired bullet to reset the trigger, thus cheating the prohibition on fully automatic machine guns with a simple loophole: physics.

Anyone looking for innovative ways to increase the lethality of their AR-15s could find hundreds of options in the morass of accessory booths at the edges of the show. The rifles had become the bread and butter of gun sales in America, and the industry's largest companies were focused on selling their versions too. Ruger had the AR-556. Smith & Wesson built the M&P15 in more than a dozen configurations. Sig Sauer had the Sig516 and a long list of others. However, Kimber still had none of that market.

Cerberus Capital, a large private-equity company named for the mythical guard dog of hell, owned Remington and Bushmaster. As I approached this booth, I stopped at a large advertisement. It pictured Bushmaster's successful version of the AR-15 with the words "Consider your man card reissued," a slogan that would soon create tremendous controversy.

From there I found my way to Kimber's booth. For the next three days I would be here with Tom, Allen, and the rest of our sales guys as we greeted and small-talked with nearly seventy thousand Kimber fans and customers.

Our booth was impressive, a sort of cross between a ski lodge and a Tiffany store. Instead of diamonds and blue boxes, we had guns. Impressive columns lined our large space, and we displayed our pistols and rifles everywhere we could. We printed large images of shooters and hunters, and hung them from the rafters of the building. A few of those billboard-sized signs depicted me holding a shiny Kimber rifle or pistol, and I realized that I had posed for those pictures back when I was still hoping to win big awards.

At 9:00 sharp the dam at the entrance broke, and NRA members flooded the show floor. During show hours the Kimber area and the aisles around it were so crowded that it was nearly impossible to move. Questions came from all directions. After helping two men from Iowa, I turned to see a middle-aged man from Oklahoma in starched jeans and polished cowboy boots. His wife was dressed in a long skirt and a well-pressed western button-up blouse. Ribbons adorned their name tags, making it clear they had donated huge sums of money to the NRA.

This was their place to tithe. "We need to get a gun for my wife. Sometimes she goes into Oklahoma City, and I don't like her being there without a gun."

As I helped the man's wife find a concealed-carry pistol, he grasped my arm. In a hushed tone he worried that the future of the country was in great peril. "We gotta buy these guns now. I should get a new one too," he said. "If that Obama gets in again, y'all might be forced to close up shop."

I just looked at him and handed him a Desert Warrior, the Kimber with the "sandbox" color. He seemed struck with reverence when I explained, "This is the same pistol carried by some of our Special Forces in Iraq and Afghanistan."

For most Americans the sentiments of people like this couple were difficult to understand. Over the years, as I had strived to decipher my own issues with my career, I made a little more sense of it when I read a statement from former NRA vice president Warren Cassidy: "You would get a far better understanding of the NRA if you approach us as if you were approaching one of the great religions of the world." I knew that these Oklahomans were believers in Cassidy's great religion. Later in the week they and hundreds more would attend the star-studded NRA prayer breakfast. They'd be moved to tears, and to make donations, when a retired Special Forces commander earnestly asked the congregation to consider making a personal sacrifice for the cause, perhaps even die for it: "What price are *you* willing to pay?"[1]

Then large men wearing black suits barged down the aisle only a few feet from us. Curly wires protruded from their left ears. Former Massachusetts governor Mitt Romney, the soon-to-be Republican nominee for president, walked by with perfect posture. He received a polite welcome, but he did not generate the rapturous excitement for a presidential candidate that Donald Trump did just a few years later. Earlier in the day I sensed that Romney was not fully trusted after I heard many attendees quietly whisper their suspicions about his Mormon faith. He greeted some attendees and quickly moved on.

A few minutes later a short man with a very large belly pushed himself into the booth. He wore a short-sleeved shirt featuring a lion with a bushy mane on top and a picture of President Obama on the bottom. Over the top picture were the words "African Lion," and over the president's picture were the words "Lyin' African." This shirt might as well have been the St. Louis 2012 version of a pointy hood and a white robe. And no one batted an eye.

If the convention was a church, Kimber was a money changer. We were here to sell guns to all pilgrims. It was a hell of a marketing opportunity. Thousands of rabid influencers assembled in one place ostensibly to worship our product. Or maybe all the guns were just the pretense?

The throngs of people were also in St. Louis to hear the battle cries from the organization's leader. I met Wayne LaPierre a few times at private events, but also when he visited the Kimber booth, dutifully greeting us as he made his rounds to the most-important gun companies. As usual, LaPierre found me and shook my hand. He was a nervous man who spoke in short, staccato sentences. Of average height with thinning hair and tight skin, he looked like a stern junior high school principal on the downhill side of his career, but with a much nicer suit. When LaPierre spoke, he blurted rehearsed lines and waved thin bony fingers in the air as if summoning an evil spell. People crowded around us, and I stood to the side, trying to move from the scene.

"It's a big election, you know," LaPierre told them. "We all have to vote! You want to keep all of this?" He waved the thin finger around the booth, pointing at our products displayed under bright lights. "Then you have to vote! And contribute. *Make sure to contribute.*"

The guy knows his audience, I thought.

"Hope you're all going to the Friends of NRA banquet tonight," LaPierre went on. "It's a big year. We have to beat Obama."

I heard a man bark excitedly into his phone: "Get over to the Kimber booth! Wayne LaPierre is here!" Several NRA members in the growing crowd leaned in to shake LaPierre's hand.

"Thanks, Wayne!" another shouted. "Give 'em hell!"

The crowd applauded loudly as LaPierre slightly bowed and then nodded, waving a final thank-you to his fans like a rock star. Then he summoned his multiple security guards stationed strategically around the booth. They had the same curly ear wires as the Secret Service guys. And just like that, the entourage marched off to another booth to perform the same lines for a new audience. Once LaPierre left, the people in the Kimber booth quickly returned to admiring our guns.

As LaPierre left one side of the booth, I quietly slipped out the other, bumping my way through the mass of people for a scheduled meeting with Chris Cox. Jim Baker was back at the NRA helping Cox behind the scenes, and he would be there too.

As I moved through the crowd, I got stuck behind a large group of machine-gun enthusiasts. They were holding back the crowd to keep us from walking through a photo op unfolding in front of them. A proud mom and dad had placed their young son on a fully automatic helicopter gun as if he were the operator.

This had all been encouraged by the emerging popularity of tactical influencers. I could see the seeds of the "man card" movement here as several onlookers encouraged the young boy to aim the huge machine gun. His small hands stretched to grasp the large handles, and he leaned his right eye toward the sights, pretending to kill enemies on the ground. The gun weighed nearly eighty-five pounds, capable of firing nearly twenty rounds per second. It was chambered in .50 caliber and was designed to devastate any target up to a mile away. Each round was nearly as large as the boy's forearm and powerful enough to shoot through vehicles and armor. The young boy flashed a big smile as he looked up from the sights. His parents snapped photos as they voiced approval. His father beamed.

I squeezed my way around them, walked down another aisle, and then turned right into an area on the edge of the convention hall. There I found Cox and Baker. I greeted both and shook their smooth, manicured hands as we settled into a corner for a conversation in hushed tones.

This meeting was dangerous for me and maybe confusing for Cox. In the ten years since his promotion to head the NRA-ILA, he had become the most powerful lobbyist in the nation. Through Cox the NRA wielded immense influence. He was the sort of man who said no to meeting requests from US senators and who made or destroyed political careers. As he must have thought, *Why would a rising star in the gun industry want a clandestine meeting to talk politics?* The rules of the industry clearly prohibited questioning Cox. I had pushed the envelope before, and I'm sure he had a feeling that my politics were possibly on the fringe of this religion, but he granted me an audience.

Whereas the convention floor buzzed about the possible reelection of President Obama, Cox and Baker agreed to talk with me about their other priority: winning back a majority in the US Senate. I knew that to the NRA, it was no longer about guns; it was about power. That meant swaying races to Republican wins so that the winners were beholden to the NRA. Lots of pundits had focused on Montana, where a moderate, pro-gun Democrat named Jon Tester was fending off a Senate challenge from our state's longtime at-large congressman, Republican Denny Rehberg. For Cox, Tester stood in the way of the mission to deliver Republican sameness that they could control. But I knew Tester had done more than his part on guns. In fact, few if any Republicans had championed as many NRA bills as Tester.

The rest of the industry cheered every move that Cox made, but I was here working to influence the political outcome for one of the most important races in the country. This meeting was a turning point for me. I was ramping up my activism, using the street cred earned from awards ceremonies not to sell more guns but rather to fight for the things that mattered to me. I also knew that I was capitalizing on the respect granted to me after the Shultz boycott. The truth was that there were few industry veterans with a pedigree like mine, and as far as I knew, no one else would dare to stick their nose in the political decisions of the NRA.

"You guys picking a horse in Montana?" I asked bluntly. "You know the water Tester's carried for you, and don't even tell me he's not pro-gun."

Baker looked at Cox, then back at me. The smooth Washington insider was calculating just the right words. "I don't think we have as much influence as people think," he replied softly. This is what Baker or Cox said when they wanted to pretend they weren't DC kingmakers.

"You can bullshit a lot of people here," I shot back, "but you can't bullshit me, Jim."

We knew damn well that the NRA could manipulate all these people to influence Montana's Senate race by a point or two at least—simply with an endorsement. An endorsement for Rehberg might mean the Republicans could take back the upper chamber, even if it meant turning on a reliable pro-gun Democrat.

"Tester's solid," Baker admitted, violating Cox's practice of never speaking favorably of a Democrat. "But so is Rehberg. And the Senate's key for us if Obama gets four more years. You know that, Ryan."

Rehberg had earned a reputation for ineffectiveness during his six terms as a member of Congress, and important hunting organizations had good reason to doubt his support for conservation and public lands. That meant that his popularity among pro-gun, independent voters in Montana had taken a hit. Baker and Cox knew that Rehberg was not "solid," but they were working hard to appropriate hunters in the same way the industry had used "sporting" to help legitimize the AR-15. They knew that cultural connections to hunting could be used to convince sportsmen and -women to vote against their own self-interests. All the NRA really cared about was Rehberg's political party and the power it would cede to them.

"Tester's a champion," I told them. "He actually *is* solid. He's sponsored pro-gun bills, and he's been a leader on hunting issues. I thought this was about guns. Or is it about something else?" They said nothing, but I could tell they had discussed it before I even arrived.

These men helped spread conspiracies that demonized the president, but I had a hunch that they secretly *wished* for a second Obama term. In the twisted world they had built, the opportunity for more gun sales and more power that an Obama victory would create was just too lucrative to pass up. But that would also mean they would be forced to inflame even more hate and fear. I had seen their ruthlessness. They had no problem dismembering even the largest companies in the industry over the slightest hint of compromise. Tester was on the cutting block. Hell, I was on the cutting block.

I sensed that Cox just wanted out of the conversation, not wanting to be pressed into a corner or confronted by someone like me who saw through his maneuvering. "Stay in touch, man," Cox said. "I gotta run." And with that, we all departed cordially, and I reentered the crowd as it slowly flowed into a huge ballroom next door.

There, LaPierre spoke to a massive crowd. He began by heralding the importance of the NRA's "Trigger the Vote" effort, reminding everyone again that this was an election year. The Oklahoma couple, the large man from Wisconsin, Lyin' African Guy, and the rest of the over-capacity crowd got the message: be afraid of what Barack Obama and the Democrats might do. The "I voted for the white guy" fella definitely got that message.

"This year's election could prove the most disastrous in the history of this country!" LaPierre waved his bony finger again as he bellowed. A family of six with matching American flag shirts stood and cheered as he spoke. A giant screen behind LaPierre enlarged his image, and his voice boomed over huge speakers. LaPierre finished by juicing NRA members' fears, but the firearms executives like me in the room just heard *cha ching*. He knew that fear sold NRA memberships, and we all knew that it sold guns.

As if he was searching for just the right conspiracy recipe, LaPierre continued with the invective: "Obama has spent his entire political career engaged in a stealthy assault on your right to keep and bear arms. If he wins re-election to the White House, he will be immune from elections and free to misuse his ever-increasing power."[2] I could almost feel my sales forecast increasing with each word. And just as I reentered the booth, I got word from Allen that Leslie was looking for me. He had an important customer I needed to meet.

Leslie came to find me with a younger man in tow. I recognized him as former Pennsylvania senator Rick Santorum, who had come to address the NRA faithful. In his speech that day Santorum explained that his wife, Karen, wanted to attend the event but had to stay back in Washington with their ailing three-year-old daughter, Bella. Santorum's speech brought the crowd to tears and applause with an emotional announcement in which he proudly proclaimed that he had purchased a $1,500 gift for his young daughter. "Now Bella is a life member of the NRA," he said. "And I hope it's a long life!"

"Rick, this is Ryan," Leslie mumbled. "He's our vice president, and he'll take care of you."

Through Kimber, Leslie had spent $200,000 on Santorum's failed 2012 presidential campaign. Spending that money proved to be a poor investment when Santorum dropped out of the race just days before the convention, but it earned Kimber the distinction of being the first gun company to officially contribute to a presidential campaign.[3]

"I'm looking for a gun for me and one for Karen," Santorum told me with excitement in his voice. "Show me what you got."

Her name rang a bell. In the same speech where he announced his daughter's life membership, he had also introduced Karen to the crowd: "When it comes to gun-rights advocates, I have to say, I don't hold a candle to my wife," Santorum said. "I am a hunter and a gun owner, but she owns way more guns than I do. And she has a chance to shoot 'em more often than I do."[4]

"I hear Karen is quite the shooter," I said.

"Yes, she is, and she needs a new pistol. What do you recommend?"

I took several minutes to show Santorum around. He thought the Ultra Crimson Carry 9mm would be a good fit for Karen. Senator Santorum thought he needed something bigger for his own use. Maybe a Custom TLE model chambered in .45ACP.

"A .45 is the best round for protection, right?"

"Yes," I replied. "It's a bit morbid to discuss, I guess, but the cartridge was designed to expend enough energy to slam a two-hundred-pound man to the ground as he's running at you."

He looked at me and nodded approval as he held the gun with both hands, pointing it in the air, aiming through the sights.

Santorum had the polish of a sanctimonious, silver-tongued televangelist you just don't trust. He earned himself plenty of controversy during his political career, and I got the feeling he missed the thrill of offending millions. Sure enough, years later, after the massacre in Parkland, Florida, Santorum leaned too far over his pulpit when he said on CNN: "How about kids, instead of looking to someone else to solve their problem, do something about maybe taking CPR classes?"[5]

In the booth the former senator engaged me with a bright smile. He assumed that I was the same as him and the tens of thousands of others crowding around us. I was not, but I treated him as I would any other Kimber customer. He gave me his card and made me promise to follow up as he left. This was the professional service Leslie paid me to provide to a VIP.

"Busse, Kyle is here to see you," one of my sales guys called. I followed him to the side of the booth, where Kyle Weaver waited for me.

"Damn, man, you are really famous," I poked. "I'm thinking I need to get your autograph." He knew I was referring to the large banner with his picture hanging overhead.

"Yeah. Not really my idea, but that's the game now. It's what they asked me to do."

"How are the banquets going?"

"Great," Kyle said. "Scary good, in fact. Obama might be horrible for the country, but he's great for raising money. He's driving membership like you can't believe. Your guns are bringing huge dollars."

"You gonna come out to Montana and fish with me again?"

"No, man. You almost killed me off last time." He was referring to the trip into the Badger-Two Medicine a few years earlier. "You planning to attend the Glenn Beck deal this afternoon? I think we're calling it 'The Celebration of American Values.'"

"That guy is nuts. That's not my crowd. I just can't go along with the whole birther bullshit."

However, Beck was right up Kyle's alley. In a rare display of emotion, Kyle became excited as he spent a few minutes extolling the virtues of Beck, trying to convince me. I certainly did not plan to attend the Celebration of American Values. I was positive that they had misnamed the event. As far as I was concerned, the values to be celebrated there should not have the exclusive marketing right to the "American" brand.

What I said next I dared not say to anyone but Kyle. We had known each other long enough that I could strip away some pretense. I whispered it to him, loud enough to be heard over the buzz: "Kyle, this shit is getting out of control. I feel it. These people believe insane things. I see overt racism that no one questions. I hear about birth certificates and other insane conspiracy theories. Obama is not proposing taking a single gun. We all know it, and yet people here believe he is ready to rip BB guns from kids and impose Sharia law. It's nuts. Where does it lead? Cox is using that hate to attack things that I care about and that you should care about."

Kyle kept calm. He listened but did not turn to look at me as I spoke. A central tenet of the organization was that no one could ever recognize fault in the tactics of the NRA, much less speak them aloud. Never. If anyone but me had said those words to Kyle Weaver, the NRA would have taken swift action to ensure that he no longer had a job. But my friendship and industry status gave me *just* enough leeway.

I came to understand how professionally risky my actions were. In future years, as I studied the principles of authoritarianism, I learned that in order for a leader to maintain power, all subjects need to know that even trusted members of the group can be persecuted for anything at any time. Real authoritarian power, as I came to know, relies not on the actions of leaders but rather on the unthinking enforcement from average people. Leaders simply empower and encourage the volunteer armies.

Kyle's emotionless response was exactly what I expected. It was the same response I had seen on that ridge in Montana. "It's just the time we live in," he finally said. "It doesn't matter if I agree. Wayne knows what he's doing, and so does Chris. It's all bigger than just us. It's about the *country*." Kyle seemed to have given himself up to the NRA. He was born again. As I would with many friends in the coming years, I found myself hoping he didn't really believe it all. But my hopes did not matter. Kyle's response told me that he was just fine with empowering anything as long as it served the NRA's purpose.

I too believed it was about the country, but not in the way Kyle did. Even though I thought we were friends, I decided not to push the conversation any further. I knew that I needed to keep him close if I hoped to apply any influence.

The tight cultural filter of the industry had mostly succeeded. No one else like me had slipped through. I might have been the only one on the whole floor who found conspiracy, racism, and hatred troubling.

I did not know then the precise destination of the country. But it was obviously an issue. I believed that the long roots of the country's hateful downward spiral were spreading across the nation from this hall in St. Louis. I could see that people were being encouraged to do and say dangerous things. The warning lights for what might happen to the country were flashing red.

But rather than heed those warnings, the NRA wanted more. Gun sales, membership, and big fundraising hauls could go up only if the NRA created more fear. In order to perpetuate the system, they would have to create new demons out of people like Tester and millions of ordinary American citizens.

The NRA was setting an example of authoritarianism that could be easily replicated. The only things needed to make it explode on the national stage were rising fear and a candidate who knew how to twist it into religious devotion. I knew then I needed to put more on the line to stop it.

TWENTY-ONE

KEEPING SCORE

"**W**HY'D YOU WANT TO BACK A LOSER?" IT WAS MID-morning, and I was driving out of town for a day of fly-fishing. I knew I would soon lose cell service, so I pulled over to finish my conversation with Chris Cox, who had made good on his promise to at least stay in touch with me. He was still hell-bent on endorsing Denny Rehberg in Montana's 2012 Senate race and wanted to finish the conversation we started in St. Louis. "Look, Tester's gonna win this one," I added. "Don't you dare endorse Rehberg. You're gonna lose an ally."

"I don't know, Ryan," Cox replied, seeming to relish toying with a candidate's destiny. "Tester's a Democrat. I don't know what you're looking at, but our polling says he's the loser. And there are those Supreme Court votes."

Cox was referring to Tester's confirmation votes of Elena Kagan and Sonia Sotomayor, both of whom the NRA considered anti-gun, even though both had earned bipartisan support in their confirmation votes. I was becoming incensed with the game. "Really, Chris? You can't find anything bad on the guy, so you're going with 'He voted yes on those Supreme Court justices'?"

Tester was a proud progressive Democrat, but he had sponsored several pro-gun bills, including one that allowed people to carry firearms into national parks. He also led the Senate's amicus brief in support of the case to allow firearms in the city limits of Washington, DC. I knew that kind of legislative accomplishment was rare, especially for a Democrat. It was rare enough that few Republican senators could even match Tester's record. With no other reason to attack Tester, the Supreme Court confirmation votes were all Cox could find.

I stood my ground, but I'd already suspected that Cox and the NRA didn't care that Tester had sponsored bills or voted their way on gun policy. That was currency from an old, naive, bipartisan era; what mattered far more was that Tester had a *D* after his name. Cox did not value reaching across the aisle. He cared only about building a one-party machine that the NRA could control, so I stuck to the political calculus. "Well," I continued, "people in Montana love this guy, and I'm telling you he's gonna win. Your polls are wrong."

Cox paused as he thought about it. Then he sighed. "OK, man," he finally said.

"What does that mean?"

"We'll stay away from endorsing Rehberg. You'd better be right about Tester. I gotta go."

A farmer with a simple flattop haircut, Tester looked and acted like the people I had grown up with. He had an unvarnished political style; he laughed easily and spoke with his constituents with ease. I first met him in 2006, when I served on the board of Montana Conservation Voters (MCV), a political organization I had joined not long after my speech at the National Press Club. Tester impressed all of us as I chaired MCV's endorsement committee for the US Senate race, and he spoke as if holding court in a small-town coffee shop.

"I met a guy I think will be our next US senator," I told Sara that evening. "This guy Tester—he's got something I can't quite put my finger on."

"What's your gut say?"

"I've spent enough time around cattle shows and farm sales to know that he connects with people. I don't think the guy even knows what bullshit or pretense is."

Tester went on to win that first race in 2006 against incumbent Conrad Burns by a 3,562-vote margin, and over time we became casual friends, sharing drinks and swapping farm stories between political discussions.

"Cox says the NRA will stay out of your race," I told him. "They won't endorse you, but they won't endorse Rehberg."

"Hmm," Tester replied, knowing damn well how powerful an NRA endorsement was in a state with a lot of gun owners who had the power to shift elections. "They're up to something, right?"

"Cox spouted some bullshit about your Supreme Court votes, but I told him you were going to win."

"That's a bold prediction, Busse." We both knew how difficult the 2012 race would be.

"I told him only a fool would want to back a loser."

I was proud of the fact that I had exerted influence from the inside. Only someone trusted from the industry could have reported intel like this to a US senator. *This is why I stay here*, I thought.

Tester, who had lost three fingers in a childhood meat-grinding accident, often highlighted the fact that he was a dirt farmer from North Central Montana. But he was also politically shrewd. He took in my news with measured optimism: "I damn sure hope you're right about the winning part. But I don't trust any of those guys."

A few days later I understood why Tester had been skeptical. Allen walked into my Kimber office with a copy of the NRA's *American Rifleman* in hand. "See this?" he said, flopping the latest issue onto my desk. The magazine featured a glossy photo of Rehberg, which accompanied a glowing profile of the candidate. "I thought they weren't endorsing?"

"Those bastards," I muttered, flipping through the story. "They promised me they weren't gonna do this."

Part of any NRA membership includes a subscription to its monthly magazines, *American Rifleman* being the largest. I never received one because I was not an NRA member, but the fact that Kimber was a big advertiser meant that we always had several office copies. Features in *American Rifleman* were usually reserved for advertisers like us, who spent millions of dollars with the NRA. In lieu of an endorsement, Cox had secured the valuable space for Tester's formidable Senate challenger. He knew damn well the magazine was landing in the mailbox of tens of thousands of Montana members.

"You son of a bitch!" I yelled at Cox a few moments later, with my door shut. "What the fuck is this?"

"Ryan, Ryan," Cox said calmly. I suspected he had a condescending grin on his face. "Did you even read the article? Did you see any endorsement? I don't think you did." Cox was technically correct. He had devoted the NRA's most valuable advertising space to Rehberg, but the organization had not made an official endorsement. This was an NRA sleight of hand that I had never seen before; only endorsed candidates got this kind of press coverage. Even without an official endorsement, Cox knew that most NRA members would get the message.

"This is some dirty fucking pool, Chris. I promise I'm gonna do everything in my power to make sure Jon Tester wins this fucking election." And with that I slammed down the phone, assuming that I would never speak to Cox again. After I had a couple of minutes to cool down, I also knew that I had probably pushed too far and that the NRA was probably on to me.

Luckily for me, and for Tester, my Hail Mary promise of a victory came to pass. Even despite the *American Rifleman* article, Tester narrowly won his second term in the US Senate, but he beat Rehberg more handily than he had beaten Burns.

"The NRA show is in Houston next year," I told Sara after Election Day. "I hope Cox and Baker stop by the booth so I can rub this in their faces!"

"Don't get cocky," Sara said, as she often did during political seasons. Sara and I almost always talked politics at dinner, and by late 2012, both our boys joined in too. Lander was almost eight, in third grade, and Badge was almost five. Both boys were bright, and they were curious and engaged even at their young ages. Lander often asked questions about the people we talked about, and he liked Tester because they shared the same buzzed haircut.

That December, on Friday the fourteenth, I made breakfast for the family as usual; then Sara took both boys to school. I went to work at Kimber, and before I could even sit down, Sara called, frantic.

"Are you watching this?" she asked, shaken and starting to cry. "This is horrible. Little kids, Ryan, like our boys. Little kids!" I tried to calm her, but the weight of the unfolding news from Newtown, Connecticut, was too much for her to take.

"Calm down—"

"*I don't want you to calm me down, Ryan!* I want someone to fucking do something! These are little kids!"

Along with the rest of America, I learned about Adam Lanza, who first murdered his mother and then entered Sandy Hook Elementary School armed with an AR-15 and ten thirty-round high-capacity magazines. Lanza massacred twenty-six people in the school, most of them innocent first graders.

The horror was overwhelming. Even Leslie took notice as he sent a cryptic text informing me that there had been a mass shooting north of our Yonkers factories. As I sat there in our Kimber sales office, like so many others that day, I tried to imagine what the parents must be going through. Several times during the news updates, tears came to my eyes. Our office stayed quiet that day. Most of us had young kids, and everyone pored over the updates.

"Sick, huh?" Allen said after popping into my office. "And holy shit, things are going to change now. If this doesn't move gun control, I don't know what will." Allen's opinion seemed spot-on. Soon, gun consumers across the country came to the same realization, and they purchased guns in record numbers to beat the inevitable gun-control legislation we all anticipated. Lanza had used the same Bushmaster rifle I had seen in the popular advertisement in St. Louis: *Consider your man card reissued.*

Lanza's Bushmaster XM-15 E2S Shorty AK was specifically designed for professional military combat in close-quarter situations. The rifle incorporated a shortened stock and a hand guard, features developed to provide soldiers with maximum maneuverability in confined spaces. When combined with the short, eighteen-inch carbine barrel, the modifications made the rifle ideal for wartime fighting in vehicles, terrorist-filled caves, and buildings with numerous hallways and doors—buildings like grade schools.

Lanza's rifle was a result of years of competitive and continuous weaponry refinement within the industry. It incorporated dozens of small advancements made by all gunmakers that improved the design and manufacturing process of all AR-15-style guns. Each advancement had a singular purpose: to increase the lethality of the platform. Bushmaster also claimed competitive advantages that ensured flawless function of its guns through meticulous modern machinery and such fine materials as aircraft-quality aluminum. This culminated in a rifle so lethal and efficient that Bushmaster provided the weapons for more than a dozen high-level US and foreign military deployments around the globe. And one of them ended up in the hands of a deranged twenty-year-old kid in Connecticut.

Lanza was a twisted young man whose motives have never been fully understood. His rifle, on the other hand, was perfectly honed for his sick massacre. It even incorporated another noted upgrade: the Bushmaster factory added an AK-style muzzle brake to reduce what the industry calls "muzzle rise." This meant that the operator could more easily keep the rifle on targets as he fired multiple quick shots. The design, precision, and upgrades meant that no one could argue that Lanza was not equipped with the most lethal military weaponry ever made.

It had only been eight years since the days on the Kansas prairie when the wise men of our industry stepped in to enforce polite norms when J. Guthrie brought his assault weapon to my parents' ranch. And of course those wise men had well-founded concerns about the impacts of these guns, but no one could have imagined the actual horror unleashed on America by the unchecked proliferation of weapons like that Bushmaster XM-15.

The fear of being Zumboed had erased those old-fashioned objections and replaced them with *worship*. With the old-school barriers out of the way, the gun industry had filled the demand with ever-more-lethal versions of a gun designed to win wars through efficient mass killing. Social media accounts boomed. New companies were built. Fortunes were made. Lanza and his rifle were the products of it all, and when he arrived at Sandy Hook and pulled out his own black rifle, there were no norms left to break.

Lanza's massacre even brought President Obama to tears. At Kimber, we listened to the president speak and watched as he wiped his eyes at the White House:

> The majority of those who died today were children—beautiful little kids between the ages of five and ten years old. They had their entire lives ahead of them—birthdays, graduations, weddings, kids of their own. Among the fallen were also teachers—men and women who devoted their lives to helping our children fulfill their dreams. . . . And we're going to have to come together and take meaningful action to prevent more tragedies like this, regardless of the politics.[1]

As Obama finished his remarks, everyone in the shooting industry assumed that this was the final straw. Allen was right: this time there would be legislative action. Within a day, an already robust sales environment broke wide open.

"Just tell dealers we have no idea when they can get their order," I said during our sales meeting on the Monday following Sandy Hook.

"It's completely crazy out there," my staff reported. "People are literally buying any damn gun they can get their hands on. It's a panic."

In meetings with large retailers like Cabela's and Bass Pro, merchants reported daily gun-sales rates that were thirty to forty times greater than normal. "It was unbelievable," one of them told me later. "We would put some inventory on the web, and we sold like forty to fifty thousand high-cap magazines in just an hour." The official data from the government proved what we had all experienced. During the week after Sandy Hook and Obama's White House address, gun dealers in the United States registered nearly one million sales, by far the highest weekly total ever recorded. Monthly sales for that December topped 2.3 million units, or nearly eighty thousand guns *per day*, another staggering record.

If our country had still been operating in the same old political system once navigated by Bill Clinton, Americans would have seen relief in the form of political action on the horizon. But just like Guthrie's black rifle at Southwind, our national politics were a lifetime away from the older, more reasoned time of the 1990s.

Even with dead children, grieving parents, a nation on edge, and a tearful president, the NRA sensed that it could strike another massive blow to that old system. In his national address one week after the shootings, Wayne LaPierre pointed his bony finger and once again called the fear play: "How many more copycats are waiting in the wings for their moment of fame—from a national media machine that rewards them with the wall-to-wall attention and sense of identity that they crave—while provoking others to try to make their mark? A dozen more killers? A hundred? More? How can we possibly even guess how many, given our nation's refusal to create an active national database of the mentally ill?"

As it turned out, LaPierre had been consulting with the NRA's longtime advertising agency, Ackerman McQueen. The marketing professionals explained that the tragedy could be another huge opportunity for the NRA and that they had developed a memorable slogan to capitalize on the painful moment. LaPierre took their expensive advice, looked into the cameras, and offered an effective new rallying cry for the NRA's resistance: "The only thing that stops a bad guy with a gun *is a good guy with a gun.*"[2]

LaPierre went on to propose gathering up the gun owners of America into a vast protective militia—the same sort of armed "good guys" who would one day take it upon themselves to "guard businesses" during Black Lives Matter protests, to disrupt polling places, to try to kidnap liberal governors, and even to attempt an armed coup inside the US Capitol. They were the same amateurs who screamed and jammed their fingers into the chests of twelve-year-old boys like my son Badge.

"Now, the National Rifle Association knows that there are millions of qualified active and retired police; active, reserve and retired military; security professionals; certified firefighters and rescue personnel; and an extraordinary corps of patriotic, trained qualified citizens to join with local school officials and police in devising a protection plan for every school," LaPierre added. "We can deploy them to protect our kids now."[3]

The reaction from the Obama administration mirrored the mood of the general public. Something had to be done, and that something did not include armed amateurs inside schools. Vice President Joe Biden, a Senate veteran with a history of navigating complicated legislative deals, was entrusted with the effort to improve gun-safety laws. The future president, who believed in the same old system once driven by people like Jim Baker, sought consensus and even brought the NRA to the White House to discuss options. "There has got to be some common ground, to not solve every problem but diminish the probability" of mass shootings, Biden said. "That's what this is all about."[4]

In a foreboding sign, the meetings between Biden and the NRA broke down, and LaPierre issued an angry statement which made it clear that his organization was not interested in negotiations with Democrats, even with seasoned deal makers such as Biden. "We will not allow law-abiding gun owners to be blamed for the acts of criminals and madmen," LaPierre said, just minutes after he left the contentious meeting at the White House.[5]

As the vice president searched for possible legislative solutions, the NRA's withdrawal from negotiations meant that the path for bold action narrowed, leaving only one small area of agreement. In a last-ditch effort to do *something*, Democratic senator Joe Manchin of West Virginia and Republican senator Pat Toomey of Pennsylvania crafted an amendment to strengthen background checks on private gun purchases. Their modest proposal was essentially an attempt to close the gun-show loophole, which was still open even fourteen years after Columbine.

Initially, we anticipated bipartisan agreement, and it looked like the amendment might just pass. The NSSF, which represented all industry companies, first signaled that it would be for the legislation. Notably, despite sending signals of support, the organization left its options open while it waited for approval from the NRA, also rumored to be considering support. But within days, Chris Cox realized there was political opportunity in the wind, and he announced to all US senators that the NRA had decided to score the vote, even with a Republican as a cosponsor. In other words, any senators who cared about their NRA rating and relied on the organization's support had better damn well vote *no*. Scoring was a maneuver to ensure that any Democrat who voted for the amendment would bear the permanent record and the political repercussions. It also meant that virtually no Republicans (except Pat Toomey) could vote for the bill, especially if they needed their A+ ratings to win their next elections.

The NRA had succeeded yet again in converting an opportunity to make policy improvements into just another temperature increase for the national pressure cooker. Behind the scenes, most of us in the industry had no problem with the proposal. In fact, many executives strongly supported the initial NSSF openness, believing that expanding background checks was a good idea, if for no other reason than it reduced public relations risks and funneled all sales through established retailers.

I took this opportunity to try and hold support for the amendment, often reminding other executives that the policy would have nothing but good impacts on the industry. I knew that we could not go on just saying no to everything, and I kept thinking about the horror of those Newtown parents. I kept thinking about my own boys.

Initially, many gun-business leaders I spoke with shook their heads in agreement. Of course, they all knew how bad it looked to allow mentally deranged people like Lanza to legally buy guns without a check, and many industry insiders feared a subsequent high-profile mass shooting might result in far stricter policy solutions that would actually hurt sales. They also all understood that only a tiny percentage of sales would have been affected by the background-check bill, meaning that the Manchin-Toomey amendment would have almost no impact on the day-to-day business of any gun company. But the NRA's decision to ratchet up the political heat resulted in quick evaporation of the NSSF's initial support. Any thought that the NRA was not completely in charge disappeared too. Within days, the entire industry got in line behind Cox and LaPierre. Like a loyal lieutenant trying to stay in the good graces of a powerful general, the NSSF even issued emails and press releases cheering the NRA's efforts to kill the amendment. I could see that when the vote actually happened, Manchin-Toomey would be doomed.[6]

A few days before the vote, I found the political leader I had befriended in the back of the room at a Montana Democratic Party fundraiser. Senator Jon Tester, still new to his second term, handed me a drink and asked how I thought he should vote. "I think the policy is good, Senator," I told him. "Even the NRA has a history of being in favor of better background checks. So from a policy standpoint, you ought to vote for it." Tester cocked his head, as he often did when listening carefully, and I continued. "But it's not going to pass. You and I both know that."

"They're scoring it."

"So I guess I'm advising you to vote against it," I said, with hesitation. "They're just going to use it to attack you when you run again."

This set him off. I knew he wasn't angry with me, but he gritted his teeth and raised his voice. "You telling me those NRA bastards will kill this bill? It's a *pro-gun* bill, for God's sake. Who wants the 'bad guys' to have guns?"

"This ain't about good policy for them," I replied, after telling him he was right. "It's about laying a political trap for—"

"People like me."

"People like you."

Tester took a drink and held the whiskey in his mouth for a long time. He swallowed and then leaned close to me as he spoke. "Well, this ain't about me, goddamnit. I met with those parents. It was as hard as anything I have ever done." Clearly, Tester was no longer considering my political coaching; this was personal for him. "I'm a parent and a granddad, and no one should have to endure what those people in Connecticut are going through." He was animated now, his emotions taking over, and he poked me on the shoulder. "You can tell those NRA bastards that it's the right thing to do, and by God, it's about time *someone* in this country did the right thing."

Despite knowing the amendment would fail, Tester carried through with his promise to do the right thing. This was not the first time I had seen him cast a vote on principle, but given that the NRA was sure to use this against him, I was even more impressed. Tester voted yes because of his basic decency and because he made a commitment to those grieving parents. I knew then that our country needed a lot more of *that*.

The Manchin–Toomey amendment failed on April 17, 2013, by a margin of 46–54: six votes shy of the sixty votes needed to pass. Senators John McCain of Arizona, Susan Collins of Maine, and Ron Kirk of Illinois joined Toomey as the only Republicans who voted in support. And five Democrats—including Montana's other senator, Max Baucus—voted against it.[7]

As Cox and pro-NRA senators ensured the defeat of the legislation, gun companies like Kimber were in the middle of figuring out how to handle all the growth. During the first four months of 2013, gun sales continued to skyrocket, increasing nearly two million units over the same period a year before. AR-15 rifles and "Tupperware" guns made up most of the sales, but everything that went *bang* sold too, including every gun model that Kimber made.

In the middle of the post–Sandy Hook boom, the Kimber leadership team held a meeting to discuss my increasing sales forecasts and the resulting production plan. I had prepared a presentation laying out demand graphs which predicted that a robust sales environment would continue throughout much of the year. As we all sat down to get the meeting started, Leslie walked into the conference room. I would never know exactly what set him off, but I could see in his body language that he was furious. "Ryan, you're up first," one of the guys in the meeting said after bringing business to order. "You're making it rain, right?"

But just as I started my presentation, I recall Leslie jumping in with a sharp commentary aimed at me. "Ryan, what the fuck is wrong with the Democrats?" he barked. This got the attention of the entire room, and everyone went silent. I remember him ratcheting up another notch. "The fucking Democrats, they use this Sandy Hook crap to act like they care about kids. That's such a bunch of bullshit. They are fine with aborting kids, but *now* they care? What the fuck is that about, Ryan? Gun control. That's why the assholes say they care!"

No one moved or spoke for what seemed like minutes. Something in Leslie seemed to have snapped, and I knew that his words were just echoes of the NRA's paranoia. Maybe he had been on an NRA fundraising call, or maybe he had read one of the conspiratorial emails he sometimes forwarded me just before meetings like this. Whatever caused the outburst, I believed the result was that Leslie had now directly attacked Democratic policy makers with a vile lie, and because I was the one Kimber employee who was close to any Democrats, he spoke directly to me. After all, I had supported Tester a few months earlier and had just convinced the NRA to stay out of his race.

Not sure what to make of it, a few of the others started to break the uncomfortable silence with nervous small talk. I didn't respond to Leslie. Instead, I caught my breath and continued on with my presentation that day, but the damage was done. As far as I was concerned, Leslie had openly attacked a key member of his own leadership team. This made my professional life increasingly difficult, but there was also something larger and predictive about Leslie's outburst.

Of course, the politics meant only more sales and more power for the NRA, which never forgave Tester for his vote. They did not meet with grieving parents or make commitments to improving policy. No, they employed multimillion-dollar marketing firms that got paid to convert tragedies like Sandy Hook into slogans: opportunities to score points and build power. They wore tailored suits and were already preparing for the next NRA convention in Houston. But this time they weren't just after Tester. They were after me too.

TWENTY-TWO

WEARING A TARGET

IT WAS ABOUT AN HOUR BEFORE THE OPENING OF THE 2013 NRA convention, and just like the year before, I made my way through a large crowd and passed into the convention space to direct the final touches on the Kimber booth. One of my salesmen had excitedly told me I had a couple of important visitors before the show even started.

"How are you sharply dressed fellas doing today?" I said with a smile, extending my hand to Chris Cox and Jim Baker. They were both nervously waiting for me in similar blue suits. Neither man was used to waiting for anyone, and they were annoyed. I tried to break the ice as I approached, something I learned how to do at cattle sales with my dad as a kid. I hadn't expected to speak with Cox again after our argument before Election Day, and now he was pissed off and wanted to settle the score. He shook my hand, but it was more of a rushed formality. "Your boy Tester—he really fucked us with that vote!" Cox growled. "I trusted you on this, Busse. And he really fucked us!"

Before I could even respond, Baker, the old deal maker, put his hand on Cox's shoulder and stepped in. He played the part of good cop perfectly. "Look, Ryan," he started, polished and calm. "We made certain promises when we stayed out of the race. Those promises, well, they were predicated on things you told us were true. You said Tester was a good guy, that he was with us. And then this vote? I hope you can see why we might be a bit . . . unhappy."

"You said this guy was a champion!" Cox interjected. "You told us he would—"

"You have the fucking nerve to come to my booth to read me the riot act like I'm some goddamn third grader?" I shot back, cutting off Cox. "That is some world-class bullshit."

"Ryan—" Baker said quietly, raising his hand in an effort to cool both of us down. But I wasn't finished.

"First you lie to me, Chris. You tell me you'll stay out of Montana. Then you advertise his opponent to a few million people with the most valuable space in the industry? As if I wouldn't notice? You'll have to try that shit on someone else."

Cox just rocked back on his feet, surprised and clearly not used to being lectured by an out-of-line industry member. I went on: "And as far as the senator's vote goes, you know what? I told Tester not to support it. I told him you sons of bitches would do this and worse. I told him his vote didn't matter because you would make sure nothing would pass anyway. I told him he should just duck like everyone else in DC does. And you know what? I'm glad he didn't take my advice."

"Well, what does that leave us, Ryan?" Baker said.

"Well, fellas. It leaves you with a message Tester asked me to pass along: *You can tell those NRA bastards that it's the right thing to do, and by God, it's about time someone in this country did the right thing.* End-fucking-quote."

The three of us just stood there, no one sure what to say next. Cox was used to groveling apologies, and clearly this wasn't the tail-between-the-legs meeting he expected. Instead, I threw one more punch. "I don't know what the hell is wrong with all of you. Who thinks background checks are a bad idea? What industry wants bad things to happen with their products? Little kids died, Chris. And you decide to play politics? You guys are fucking sick."

"Ryan—" the old dealmaker tried again.

"And you are infecting everyone else in this place."

Cox looked at me for a moment, then glanced at Baker before he turned and marched away from me and the Kimber booth. Baker stayed back. "Hey, listen. Chris is wound a little tight, you know, but I want you to hear his point."

"Give it a fucking break, Jim. I know you don't believe that. You know this was a good bill. It would've had almost no impact on any lawful gun sales. This is about you trying to scare me. What scares me is all of you agreeing that crazy people should have guns and punishing the good guys, who should be on your side."

Baker finally dropped the pretense. He sighed, his shoulders sagged, and then he looked around as if to make sure no one else was listening. I could tell that he knew killing the background-check amendment was a bad move. He spoke quietly through tight lips: "We just had to score it. That's just how things are now." Baker's admission was political code for *Look, we saw another way to screw Democrats, and we didn't give a shit about the actual policy, no matter how important or minimal it was.* In that moment of candor, the old Washington insider just admitted the true nature of the NRA: this was nothing more than a political play to ratchet up the nation's political pressure. In making the decision to score the vote, the NRA guaranteed itself a win. If it scared off Tester, its totalitarian power grew. If the principled senator refused to play that game and voted his conscience, the NRA had a weapon to use against him in the next election.

"Not sure I agree with how this whole thing happened either," Baker finally added quietly. "Look, I told Chris that if we ever become just a bought-and-paid-for wing of the Republican Party, we're fucked."

"Well, Jim," I replied, looking him square in the eye. "I think it's a little late for that. Let's face it: you *are* fucked."

With that, I left Baker standing in the aisle. I walked back into the booth because we were about to be swamped by thousands of people. Looking back now, I guess those few minutes in the aisle marked the time when I decided to remove part of my disguise. After that NRA convention, I took a more public role in my efforts back in Montana. By that time, I was the board chairman of Montana Conservation Voters, and although I knew I had to be careful to stay away from any comments on gun policy, I also suspected I could test the limit on other policies such as conservation. I began writing letters to the editors of local newspapers. Soon I was asked to write op-eds for publications across the state and comment on national stories. I became an outspoken advocate for policies and politicians that I cared about. I spoke at rallies and fundraisers in support of people I believed in. Most of them happened to be Democrats.

Although the industry was hardening and people like Cox were working against the same policies and elected leaders I supported, I still loved the company that I helped bootstrap and loved the products that we built. And I realized that I still had more to do in my activism as an industry insider. I had access. After all, I just went muzzle to muzzle with two of the most powerful people in Washington.

And there *would* be more ugliness. During that NRA convention in Houston and in chat rooms and across the growing social media world of tactical influencers, the constant undertone of conspiracy and racism only got worse. With ever-increasing hyperbolic language that proved to be a precursor to the QAnon conspiracies of the Trump years, the NRA continued to falsely claim that America's first Black president had secret plans to end gun ownership, confiscate firearms, and create international courts to unlawfully prosecute US citizens.

Eventually, the constant hum of insanity and conspiracy even got to the president himself, and the White House invited the NRA to address the growing list of its theories in a televised town hall. President

Obama went so far as to extend a personal invitation. "I'm happy to talk to them," he told CNN's Anderson Cooper during a town-hall meeting in early 2016. "But the conversation has to be based on facts and truth, and what we're actually proposing, not some imaginary fiction in which 'Obama's trying to take away your guns.'"[1]

The NRA never did show up to talk to the president of the United States. In fact, the organization empowered a growing army of social media enforcers to feed old junk theories and invent new ones. The result was a continuation of the fear-driven market, which meant that President Obama's impressive reign as the country's best gun salesman only got stronger.

By the time Obama's presidency came to an end, the industry had recorded more than 101 million gun sales, a 75 percent increase over the administration of George W. Bush. Every gun company in the industry benefited from the growth. But rather than relishing the increase, the increasingly partisan politics also made my situation inside Kimber worse.

I don't know if Cox or LaPierre tipped off Leslie about my spat in the Houston Convention Center, or if they told him about my plea for the NRA to stay neutral in the Montana Senate race. Maybe Leslie was just radicalizing like so many other industry members, but after Houston, no matter how well my team performed or how much Kimber grew, Leslie began attacking my personal politics.

I stayed sane by insisting on the high quality of our products. I also sought out opportunities to use that Kimber cachet to counter the politics of the NRA. One of the ways I did this was identifying organizations that were also generally on the right side of conservation issues but were in bounds for the industry police state. None were considered progressive—in fact, some were outright hostile to Democrats—but at least they cared about wild places, and that meant I had a rare opportunity to tie my professional success to my personal advocacy. I pioneered innovative Kimber programs and products that helped large organizations such as Pheasants Forever, the Rocky Mountain Elk Foundation, the National Wild Turkey Federation, and Ducks Unlimited. Kimber guns soon produced millions in revenues for these and a dozen more conservation organizations, and we received top partnership awards from several of them. Leslie always seemed to be suspicious of my aims, and he did not seem to have any affinity for conservation policy. In fact, I suspected he was hostile to the idea of helping any organization other than the NRA, but I also knew he could not turn down the sales, so even though I never felt supported, at least he allowed my programs to flourish. I had figured out how to navigate a dangerous minefield for the better, and I was proud of that achievement. *This is what doing good while doing well looks like*, I told myself.

As I directed those conservation programs, I became particularly intrigued by a new group that focused on sound policies more than politics. Backcountry Hunters and Anglers (BHA) began as a small organization, but its nonpartisan mission was simple: members were unabashed advocates for wild animals and wild places. I was recruited to join the board of directors, and within a couple of years the organization started to take off, eventually establishing chapters in all fifty states and several Canadian provinces.

BHA was never overtly political, and unlike other orgs that never criticized a Republican, it stayed away from the splash zone of right-wing politics and the culture wars fueled by the NRA. Trolls and couch commandos attacked Backcountry Hunters and Anglers because we did not blindly toe the Republican Party line. Of course, this just encouraged me to work harder. After I was elected as North American board chairman, I was continually impressed with the passion of the organization's staff and leaders. Soon they made BHA into a national conservation powerhouse with tens of thousands of members. I loved my work there because the organization's members cared deeply enough about hunting and fishing to dispense with all-or-nothing political warfare.

Between my work at Montana Conservation Voters and the growing national attention garnered by my work at BHA, I made a lot of new friends. One of them was Montana's governor, Steve Bullock. Other than the fact that he was a Democrat, Bullock was exactly the sort of gun owner the NRA claimed to admire.

Bullock grew up with a single mom in Helena, and he scratched for spending money with a paper route that included the governor's mansion. Even in a single-parent household and without much money, Bullock learned to shoot and hunt early on. He had kids who were about the same age as my sons, and we often talked about spending time exploring Montana's public land with our children. Once, not long after he and I had shared some of those stories over a beer, Bullock called to ask a favor. "I need to get a new rifle," he said. "I mean, I don't really know if I *need* one, but I *want* one before hunting season."

I suggested that the governor buy a Kimber Hunter chambered in .270 Winchester. "It'd be perfect for what you like to do," I told him. He trusted me enough to give me his personal credit card number then and there, and I saw to it that we shipped his rifle to a store near the governor's mansion. A few weeks later my phone dinged with a text: a picture of Governor Bullock posing with a mule deer he had taken with his new Kimber. *Now that's pretty damn cool!* I thought. *Not many companies get to boast of being the preferred hunting rifles of sitting governors!*

I assumed that any company would want to use a picture like that to show off, so I forwarded it to Leslie, Grogan, and our CFO. "Would not have signed off on a Kimber rifle for a Democrat," Grogan replied to the group text a few minutes later. "How could Montana elect a Democrat?" The text didn't cut it, apparently, and a few minutes later Grogan angrily lit up my phone. "Why did you sell one of our rifles to a fucking Democrat?"

I knew Grogan to be bombastic and uninformed, but this was really something, even for him. "Are we not trying to sell our products?" I replied. "Because last I checked, that's still my job. Even to Democrats. Is their money any different than Republican money? We're just saying no to half the population of this country?"

"Well, I'm not sure that guy *deserves* a Kimber," he retorted.

"Well, that guy bought a Kimber rifle, and he loves it," I pushed back. "He's a goddamn sitting governor, and he's a friend of mine. And he just took a deer with his son. That is something this company should celebrate. What the hell is wrong with this picture?"

I hung up the phone and sat in my office with my face in my palm for a few minutes. Allen soon walked by and noticed my distress. "What's up, Busse? You look outta gas."

"I just got questioned for selling a gun. To the governor."

"Holy shit! That's cool!"

"Well, that's what I thought too. But apparently we don't sell guns to Democrats."

"I mean, should we tell the sales guys to stop selling guns to Democrats?" Allen replied, earnestly. He paused for a moment before adding, "Because that sounds pretty stupid."

That night Sara and I shared a bottle of wine. "I think Lander and I are gonna go hunting this weekend," I told her. "He wants to shoot his .243." Before either of the boys had been old enough to walk, I had purchased rifles for them in anticipation for the day we could hunt together. Lander's was a classic-model Kimber, chambered in the light-recoiling .243 Winchester.

"Dad, are we going to get up early?" Lander asked on Friday evening before our planned hunt.

"Yeah, buddy, I'll get you up at 4:30." He was excited, and we spent the rest of the evening making sure that our backpacks were ready. The next morning as we drove to our hunting spot, we talked about the day ahead. Lander knew that our hunt would involve a strenuous hike, maybe some shivering, and—more than likely—disappointment too. As with me, there was something visceral inside that excited him.

Part of that drive came from sharing our enjoyment of supplying food. Despite the fact that I grew up on a cattle ranch, my family almost never bought meat at a store. We ate wild game, and Lander enjoyed cooking it with me. We also enjoyed the time outside and the challenge of finding prey in wild places. Even at his young age, Lander was the sort of boy who was already connected to nature. On our hunts he noticed small details about birds or trees that other people did not see. He marveled at the habits of deer and had a deep respect for the animals.

"I just want to make a clean shot if we see one, Dad," he said as we bounced down the dirt road. "I don't want any animal to suffer." This was another important component of fair-chase hunting. He and I often talked about the moment when a responsible hunter pulls the trigger. He knew about the rush of emotion that would overcome him in that instant, and he knew that at least half that emotion would be composed of a unique mix of respect and sorrow.

As we arrived at our hunting spot, Lander swung his backpack over his shoulders, and I handed him his rifle. Not long into our hike up a mountain, the sun began peeking over the ridge, and the first rays struck him as if it were a spotlight in a theater. I turned to take a photograph. He stood, rifle over his shoulder, beaming with unbridled joy, a young boy hunting with his father. It's a picture I still look at today whenever I need a moment to recenter myself or remind me what is important.

Later that day, I took another picture as Lander knelt beside a nice mule deer buck. After the predicted rush of complex emotions passed, his joyful smile reemerged. A similar smile stretched across my face, and I paused for a moment to relish a dream come true: sharing the outdoors with my son and with a rifle I had helped design. Although forces were working against us, trying to turn my industry into a place that could never be pro-gun enough, I got a satisfying reminder of what our industry once was and I hoped could still be.

I relied on that picture of Lander often in the months after our hunt. As we approached the 2016 election, Leslie seemed to relish calling me out in front of others with regularity, as if it would somehow weaken my resolve. In another of our leadership meetings near the end of the Obama administration, we all agreed to discuss a challenging reality. A competitor threatened to overtake the sales of one of our small concealed-carry models. Sales for that particular model had been OK, but we all accepted the fact that there might be a problem.

"What do you think the issue is?" someone asked.

As I started to answer, I remember Leslie jumping in with another stab at me: "I can tell you what the fucking problem is. The problem is that we have Democrats. Let's solve our problems, Ryan. How about we just kill all the Democrats?" Leslie's words hung in the air. Realizing the cold tension around the table, he tried to soften his statement. "Well, all of them except you, Ryan," he chuckled. "Let's kill all the Democrats except Ryan."

Nervous courtesy laughs and uncomfortable sideways glances bubbled up from around the table. We all tried to go on as if nothing had happened, but I was pretty sure everyone had noticed the target sewn onto my back.

TWENTY-THREE

THE TRUMP SLUMP

A COUPLE OF WEEKS BEFORE OUR TRIP TO THE NRA CONVEN-tion in Louisville, in May 2016, Tom Daybrik called to ask me to attend an exclusive executive leadership lunch. "Wanna have lunch with Don Junior and the top hundred execs in the country?" Tom asked.

"Not sure I need to go, Tom. I already know everyone there, and as far as Trump, I'd vote for the first guy out of a Quickie Lube before I'd vote for his dad."

"Then you can just go and watch people throw their money away! There's no way Trump will *win*. Think of it as an excuse to start drink-ing at noon!"

Tom convinced me to accompany him to the swanky event for the industry's top leaders. I reasoned, reluctantly, that I could observe the politics from the inside to at least share with Sara. Maybe I could pick up some intel that might help a campaign I supported. So in Louis-ville, we crammed into a historic building for lunch the day before the main event.

I made my way around the room and chatted with a few old friends as white-coated servers poured champagne and offered hors d'oeuvres of caviar and smoked salmon. After lunch, I sat in the back and watched Donald Trump Jr. in what would prove to be a deft political approach to campaigning on behalf of his father. Don Junior had been making the industry rounds for months. The future president's son had tapped into a fearful and fragile reality. His outreach would help the campaign draw a cultural through-line to many of the gun-company CEOs at the event. Those industry leaders would, in turn, help his father connect with millions of their fearful and fragile customers. The younger Trump knew how to make his own connections; he had become a lifetime member of Backcountry Hunters and Anglers, the organization to which I devoted the majority of my volunteer time. Don Junior's membership both troubled me and provided a possible point of leverage. Within a year, it would be clear that he shared almost none of the foundational values of BHA—his membership was kind of like going to church once in a while just so people see you there. But it was smart politics for him. He even got a free Kimber pistol or Mountain Ascent rifle for purchasing his lifetime membership, one of the generous perks of supporting our growing organization. A lifetime membership and a Kimber were too good a deal for hundreds of supporters, who jumped at the opportunity.

"See? He's one of us," Tom quickly reminded me as we compared notes. "How bad can the guy be? He knows how to shoot a gun, and he's *important* to us." Tom's statement highlighted the fact that more than a decade of work by the NRA had made gun owners susceptible to the slightest affirmation from someone "important." Don Junior and his father both had strong political instincts, and they knew exactly what motivated NRA members and millions of other fed-up, scared voters across the country.

National Democrats had opened this door. Their party was great on conservation policy, but it had largely ignored the culture of hunters and gun owners, and some leaders even demeaned it. For many gun owners, Hillary and Bill Clinton were the worst offenders: Bill because he presided over the assault weapons ban and Hillary because she promised to reenact it. Hillary made everything much worse when she dismissed many Trump supporters as "deplorables." No matter what her true intent was, the comment was precisely the sort of blatant disrespect that the NRA trained its army to be on the lookout for. Trump and his son knew how to use the resulting anger to their advantage.

The Trumps rightly sensed that gun owners and hunters would play a leading role in the 2016 election, which focused on "making America great again" by protecting old cultural touchstones. Just a couple of months before that NRA convention in Kentucky, Donald Trump and his son sat for an interview with Mike Schoby, the editor of *Petersen's Hunting*, at the SHOT Show in Las Vegas. Schoby and I were friends, and we had hunted together many times. I even recruited him to join the board of BHA.

Mike was a commonsense conservationist, and I hoped he would use his upcoming interview with both Trumps to hold them to the fire. But the headline of the resulting story said otherwise:

WHY SPORTSMEN SHOULD VOTE FOR DONALD TRUMP

I called Mike to register my disapproval before I even finished his story.

"Look, man," Mike sighed. He sounded resigned, but he was firm. "Trump is pro–Second Amendment, and Don Junior is a hunter. He's one of us."

"Really? Our people are so fragile that they will rush to a candidate just because his *son* hunts? That makes him one of us? That's all it takes?"

"He gets it, Busse. *She* does not."

Schoby had just put the brewing anger and aggrievement of gun owners to words, but I pushed back. "You are using *hunting* to sell the worst candidate in the history of our country?" To me, this was just another chapter in the long story of how something as basic as hunting could become a political issue. Mike's acceptance that the Trumps were like us was even worse than renaming the AR-15 as a "modern sporting rifle."

Mike stood by his article. But years later, as we discussed the plain-as-day conservation failures of the Trump administration, he admitted to me that he was shocked at how the Trump campaign used Don Junior as an effective decoy to bring hunters into their camp.

Normally, political pundits don't pay much attention to hunters. True, millions of them vote regularly, but well-funded national campaigns rarely discussed the demographic's cultural significance. The Trump play in 2016, though probably devoid of actual policy, was a brilliant strategy. Like drinking beer or eating apple pie, hunting represents a traditional American value that signals a deep connection with aggrieved voters, never mind that the elder Trump had no clue about actual hunting. It symbolizes freedom, ruggedness, and independence, but somehow millions of Americans bought that symbol from a man who used a golden toilet. The strategy, combined with the fact that national Democrats didn't bother to talk to hunters, was one of the many reasons that Trump had such an enormous impact in rural America.

In the spring of 2016, the only solace I found was the hope that I was witnessing the failure of Trump's campaign. Because I was around so many future Trump voters, I was less dubious than most Americans, but like most everyone else I just did not believe that Trump had a real shot of winning the presidency. After the champagne and caviar that preceded our lunch, Trump Junior took the small stage and addressed our group. He spoke with sharp, excited vigor. And that's when I started to understand how the campaign strategy might work. It all snapped into place for me. The Trump campaign had decided to use the firearms industry as a cultural bridge to aggrieved voters across the nation.

"My dad is going to be the greatest president in the history of the country for the Second Amendment and the gun business," he declared. The crowd applauded, and even a few whistles emanated from the normally buttoned-down executives.

After Trump Junior finished retelling some of the hunting stories that Schoby had included in his article, he handed the microphone to Chris Cox. The invitations to this exclusive event stipulated "business attire," and Cox's impeccable but unbuttoned suit with no tie hit the mark. After heaping praise on both Trumps, Cox began his act: part auctioneer, part televangelist. "Let's raise some money to make Donald Trump the next president of the United States!" he exclaimed. "C'mon, everybody. No one in this room wants to wake up after Election Day with another Clinton as president."

"Five hundred thousand!" one of the executives said, as if bidding in an auction.

"Let's raise a *million* to defeat Hillary!" another added. "I'll match the next half million."

Hands shot up as their owners barked more dollar figures into the air. Within a couple of minutes, top gun executives had raised almost $5 million for Cox's NRA Institute for Legislative Action.

After the final commitment was made, Don Junior jumped back onstage, grabbed Cox's hand, and raised it with his in a sign of victory. The executives roared approval. I felt a chill.

"That's enough for me," I whispered to Tom. I had never seen $5 million raised in a matter of minutes, especially for someone who had no business being president of the United States.

"Let's stay and have a drink with all of these guys," he replied. "It'll be fun!"

"The only thing dumber than supporting Donald Trump is throwing away millions to do it."

"Oh, c'mon, Busse."

"The whole thing is just fucking crazy." And with that, I ducked out.

Much of the rest of America believed what the NRA was doing was crazy too. In what many political pundits saw as a risky gambit, Cox and the NRA issued a full-throated endorsement of Donald Trump the very next day. They did so in a political environment where most Republican power players were still reluctant to hitch their wagons to an unpredictable candidate with only a long-shot chance. But the NRA reasoned that an early and full commitment would position the organization well if Trump pulled off a win.

The timing of that 2016 approach was notable. In 2012 the NRA waited until October to endorse Mitt Romney, then followed with a paltry $12.5 million in spending to support him. For Trump in 2016, the NRA pushed all in during May, beginning a $30 million campaign. And that was just the official number. After the election, credible reports circulated about much higher totals obscured in the shadows of dark money.

During my week in Louisville I watched as other industry executives jumped on the Trump train, along with the NRA leadership. After Trump himself delivered a keynote speech in which he wandered in and out of the same angry and incoherent rambles that would define his presidency, I ran into one of the NRA's large funders, who was also a firearms company executive. He had just emerged from the ballroom. "You think he's ready for the biggest job in the world?" I asked.

"Damn right I do," he said, adding a refrain I heard countless times after that day: "He speaks our language. No BS."

As Cox announced the NRA's official endorsement, he defended the decision to back Trump by reminding everyone of the stakes. Former secretary of state Hillary Clinton, Cox warned, would "destroy individual freedom and the America that we love."[1]

Back in the Kimber booth, I watched people walk by, noting the T-shirts many of them wore. One of the more popular shirts in 2016 depicted Donald Trump on a Harley and Hillary Clinton falling off the back. Trump's shirt read: "If you can read this, the bitch fell off." A few were more blunt: "Trump the Bitch" in large block letters. In the same booths I also saw many families who had traveled to the convention as a sort of vacation. Many had small children who were reading those same shirts. The parents all seemed unfazed by or supportive of the blatant misogyny.

"It's going to be the worst two hours of my life," I texted Sara when she asked whether I had to attend the evening fundraiser. "But I gotta go. I just can't get out of it."

Tom Daybrik had spent so much of Kimber's advertising budget on the NRA that the organization made our company the headlining sponsor of the multimillion-dollar gun auction. Like our lunch auction, proceeds benefited the NRA's Institute for Legislative Action. This would be a follow-up to the $5 million raised after the champagne-and-caviar lunch. In addition to money spent on our advertising budget, Kimber also donated a custom-made 1911 pistol for the auction.

Grogan insisted on attending the fundraiser too. He was the sort of man who didn't fit in at fancy cocktail parties, but he was also a Donald Trump devotee who was giddy about Kimber's attention and smitten with the idea of rubbing shoulders with national political figures. "God, hope he doesn't make a scene," Tom muttered after hearing Grogan's plans.

That night in the ballroom, I grabbed a drink and started to weave my way to our seats. On the side of the stage, and in front of all auction items, a huge sign read: "NRA-ILA Auction—Presented by Kimber." *That's what $1.5 million will get you in this room.*

"Hey, Ryan," someone behind me said, grabbing my shoulder. The air in the room froze. "Good to see you here." Donald Trump Junior had made his way to me, and he reached out his hand with a smile. I imagined that Cox told him to find me with advice along the lines of "Keep your enemies closer." Don Junior gestured toward the Kimber sign: "Do we have you to thank for tonight's sponsorship?"

I wanted to tell him that I did not condone it and that Kimber didn't really sponsor this event. The truth was that our advertising budget with the NRA was so large that the sponsorship had just been invented as a way to justify the spend. "Damn, this place is full," I replied instead. I had never been good at small talk. "Must be a thousand people here! At $500 a pop?"

"We are going to need every penny," Trump Junior said, keeping his eyes on me like a detective who had sniffed out a suspect. The awkwardness continued, and he switched to the icebreaker that seemed to work on everyone else. "What're you hunting this fall?" he asked, trying to make his own small talk. I gave him a couple of quick answers and withdrew from the conversation as fast as I could.

As I parted ways with Trump, I found the Kimber team at the front table. Grogan was there, impressed. "Don't think we didn't see you yukking it up with Don Junior," he beamed. "And wow. Dana Loesch?" Loesch, the firebrand spokeswoman for the NRA, wore a tight black dress and took a seat at the table just behind ours.

Before dinner, we were all asked to stand for the invocation. Everyone but me bowed their heads and prayed for a Trump victory. *Amen.* With the request to God out of the way, an energetic auctioneer took the stage, arms stretched wide to celebrate the breadth of the night's options. "Are we ready to buy some guns?" he asked in a deep, gravelly voice.

Each gun, including our donated Kimber pistol, brought in thousands, and some matched pairs brought in tens of thousands of dollars. Once the event was over, I roughly calculated that the auction had netted another $3 million for NRA-ILA's political activities.

The organization spent most of this money—more than $30 million in all—on securing a November 8 win for Donald J. Trump. The NRA's messaging of Trump was not difficult; in fact, the NRA and the reality TV star could not have been more aligned. The NRA and its Political Victory Fund spent heavily in the key battleground states of Pennsylvania, North Carolina, and Ohio, targeting fearful White voters with ads like one that depicted a woman who was alone, unarmed, and terrified in her bedroom as she reacted to an intruder in her home. The foreboding narrator reminded voters: "Don't let Hillary leave you protected with nothing but your phone."[2]

The heavy spending was a risky move for Cox and the NRA, but they still largely had the field to themselves. For months after the embrace of Trump at the convention in Louisville, other conservative forces shied away from granting the kind of support normally extended to a presidential candidate.

The NRA pushed all in because in this rogue, unconventional candidate the organization immediately saw something others did not: Donald Trump had adopted so many of the NRA's own messaging and operational tactics that the NRA was, in essence, supporting *itself* for president. The self-absorbed real estate tycoon embraced the same hatred of the media, the same criticism of cultural elites, the same overriding belief that only power mattered, and the same innate sense that promulgating fear was the most efficient way to reinforce all of it.

That long-shot political bet paid off as if God answered the prayer from that evening in Kentucky, and the timing seemed divine too: Trump's inauguration, January 20, coincided with the last day of the 2017 SHOT Show in Las Vegas. That day, as I walked the long aisles toward our Kimber booth, I noticed something I had never seen at the huge convention: giant televisions tuned to network coverage in almost every booth. It may have been a Friday, but it felt like a Sunday worship service. Just half an hour after the SHOT Show opened for the day, the entire convention center came to a stop. Tens of thousands of people who normally moved with frenetic trade-show speed froze to watch Trump's inauguration as the audio piped in through the convention's entire sound system. All of them were glued to a foreboding address that history will remember as Trump's "American Carnage" speech.

"This is crazy," Allen whispered to me. At first I thought he was echoing George W. Bush, who famously called Trump's speech "some weird shit." But Allen was referring to the fact that he had never seen an entire convention pause in unison, as if listening to a sermon from Christ himself. I couldn't help but think that Trump's speech was actually an exact copy of Wayne LaPierre's 2012 NRA convention address. In fact, the similarities to Donald Trump's themes were too uncanny for anyone to ignore.

Starting with LaPierre's version of "American Carnage": "Something has gone terribly wrong in our country. Almost every aspect of American freedom is in some state of decline." LaPierre often asserted that only the NRA could defeat the media and tyranny imposed by the "global elitists and all their friends in the White House who were conspiring to hide the truth we all know in our gut." The NRA and LaPierre had also first succeeded in making the media into an effective scapegoat: "The truth is that the national news media in this country is a national disgrace." For years LaPierre had been setting the stage for Trump's attacks on "the elite" with statements like "They don't care about us or what we think or what we say. Because they are the elites. They are better than us and theirs are the only opinions that matter." And, just as Trump would do, LaPierre often made sure to position the NRA as above the entire system, as the sole arbiter of truth: "No politician in any party will tell you that."[3]

As if listening to a stern father, no one in the convention center moved. Only after the newly sworn-in president's final words did they break into rapturous applause. The fear that our industry had relied on for so long suddenly relaxed.

Of course, the attendees in Las Vegas were happy, but the immediate impacts on the business prospects of some of us exhibitors weren't going to be so joyous. "What do you think will happen to sales?" a fellow gun-company executive asked over breakfast one of those mornings. "You know, now that we don't have to worry about Hillary?"

"I think you'd better get ready for a 20 percent decline," I told him. "The air is going to fizzle out of the gun market."

"No," he replied, apparently blind to the impacts of a Trump Slump and wanting to believe that the industry was not beholden to fear. "It won't drop off very much. There are too many new customers now. It's different than it used to be."

That executive was wrong. My spreadsheets proved to be correct when, just weeks after Trump took office, the same people who contributed millions to the NRA and stood at rapt attention in the SHOT

Show began to experience a precipitous drop in gun sales. Suddenly an industry that had geared itself for continuous years of growth had to deal with a nearly 17 percent drop in sales. Public companies such as Smith & Wesson and Ruger experienced sharp drops in their stock values, and eventually even my friend James Debney lost his job.

When one of my buddies at Smith & Wesson called to inform me of Debney's departure, I asked how business was holding up. "It's tough, man," he replied. "The industry wanted Trump, but we got the Trump Slump." Over the coming months, numerous national political and business articles highlighted the same ironic outcomes with headlines like the *Wall Street Journal*'s "The 'Trump Slump': With a Friend in the White House, Gun Sales Sag."[4]

For millions of Trump voters, the president's victory released steam from the pressure cooker. But why didn't they see that they actually lost on the issues that affected them? Over Trump's turbulent four years in office, most of his voters experienced no improvement in income or living conditions, and the Trump administration continuously sought to overturn health-care legislation that provided support for tens of millions of them.

And when it came to hunters, the new administration immediately embraced an energy-dominance policy that made George W. Bush seem moderate, wrecking multistate bipartisan wildlife-conservation projects that had been decades in the making. The administration rolled back clean-water protections that had benefited wildlife across the nation, and it attacked bedrock laws such as the Antiquities Act.

All these rollbacks saddened and enraged me; they were an aggressive extension of the same thoughtless industrialization that had first spurred me to confront Bush's administration. The very industry that claimed to be for hunters—the same one that needed the cultural acceptance of hunting to rebrand new products—had just elected a president who gleefully enacted demonstrably anti-hunting policies.

Like a lot of other people in America, I hoped this would all soon wear thin on Trump's voters. Hunters, and the other groups that had supported Trump, would surely awaken to the disastrous realities of his actual policies: *Voters will abandon this bozo in droves. They'll wake up.*

What I did not anticipate was a whole new round of fearmongering from the industry that had perfected it. Now that Trump pulled the levers, the cultural street brawl started by the firearms industry was not going anywhere. In fact, the NRA was just winding up to deliver a new and even uglier sucker punch to a divided country already struggling to catch its breath. And Kimber would be cheering the cheap shots from the front row.

TWENTY-FOUR

CLENCHED FIST

"YOU AIN'T GOING TO LIKE THIS, BUSSE," TOM WARNED when he called me with some news. "We're going to get a screaming deal on NRATV."

"You're right," I responded. "I don't like it."

"I know, man, but they're gonna make Kimber the title sponsor," he added. "And Leslie really wants to do it. He's bought the pitch about reaching new customers."

Following the election in 2016, the NRA had launched its massive NRATV digital platform, complete with thirty-five original shows and dozens of original ads. The network was the brainchild of seventy-one-year-old Angus McQueen, the founder and CEO of the ad agency Ackerman McQueen. Angus had a fierce partisan reputation as the driving force behind many of the emerging conspiracy theories fermenting in the Republican Party. Kimber got in on the ground floor of NRATV.

"They're going to stream this everywhere," Tom said, trying to convince me that the whole idea was supposed to reach a new marketing demographic. "Even Amazon."

"Who will watch this shit? It's embarrassing, Tom!" My reaction was a last-ditch plea, but I already knew I would lose this argument, so I added: "If you're taking votes, my vote is *no*."

In fact, I had already lost the battle. Leslie was so excited about NRATV that he agreed to make Kimber one of its first and largest title sponsors, which meant that our ads were splashed all over it. I realized that for Leslie, this was all about cranking up the culture war. After all, propaganda was the NRA's specialty, and gun companies like ours got to plunder the riches. Trump's chief strategist, Steve Bannon, may have coined the dictum "Flood the zone with shit," but this strategy had already been perfected by the NRA.[1] For Wayne LaPierre, the new digital venture must have felt like an innovative new opportunity to widen the shit floodgates. The marketing slogan for the NRA's new propaganda network highlighted the real mission, which was to further degrade the country's shared facts: "America's Most Patriotic Team on a Mission to Take Back the Truth."

With a budget of more than $30 million, the NRA crammed its new network onto the nation's most popular streaming platforms. Those massive financial resources allowed for impressive quantities of content. Within months, the platform hosted dozens of original shows, including daily "news" updates from a Texas talk-radio firebrand named Grant Stinchfield, who gained notoriety outside the platform by equating US deaths in Benghazi with the school shooting in Parkland, Florida, then blaming both on Hillary Clinton.[2]

But the new network's most visible and bombastic star was the same woman who had sat at the table just behind ours at the NRA-ILA dinner. Striking, with straight black hair and piercing eyes, Dana Loesch was also quick-witted and articulate. She was a college-dropout-turned-internet-sensation, named by CNN as one of the top fifty most powerful "mom bloggers." She also hosted her own syndicated talk-radio show. But her real breakout came with her new gig as a headliner on NRATV.

Soon after being named as host of *The DL with Dana Loesch*, she went to work creating headlines with incendiary and racist rants. In one episode she attacked the media as "the rat bastards of the earth" and "the boil on the backside of American politics." When an attacker killed five people and wounded two others in a mass shooting at the Capital Gazette in Annapolis, Maryland, many blamed Loesch's hateful, anti-journalist vitriol for the violence.[3] "I am happy, frankly, to see them curb-stomped," she said of journalists, just months before the Annapolis murders. "These people are the worst thing that could ever happen to the American political system."[4]

Loesch became a top-tier celebrity in the gun business, and I never heard anyone else inside the industry express concern about NRATV (if they did, they never had the courage to do it publicly). But critics of the NRA certainly picked up on the issues. As people such as Moms Demand Action founder Shannon Watts declared, "There's no boogey-man in the White House now to make people afraid of, so they have to make us afraid of one another, and that is how they will market guns in an age when they have a president beholden to them."[5]

Despite the new network and the millions spent to give it momentum, gun sales during the first years of the Trump presidency continued to slide, creating tremendous internal pressures for almost every gun company. Leadership teams at all large manufacturers had spent the eight Obama years modernizing factories and expanding. They invested huge sums of money in facilities, new machines, and vast expansions in workforces. This meant that for the first time in the history of the gun business, firearms companies were now large, modern corporations. And they were not moving into old coffin factories. The new facilities were all sleek and efficient. That sort of investment and growth meant that the pressure to maintain volume was immense.

Up until the Obama years, gun companies never invested enough to get in front of volatile and uncertain spikes in demand. The risks were just too large; booms were always followed by quick busts. But that changed during the presidency of America's best gun salesman. The sustained eight-year growth in sales yielded sufficient confidence and investment to bring the industry into the realm of modern manufacturing. This meant that companies like Kimber had invested tens of millions of dollars on new machines, new facilities, and new people. It also meant I had to confront Leslie about the new reality we couldn't ignore. "For the first time ever, all of these companies have lots of capacity and not enough demand," I told him during a leadership meeting. "They aren't just going to give up all this infrastructure. Every company has to get creative. Just watch: prices will drop; promotions will start." My warning for Leslie was that gun companies were about ready to do whatever it took to push more guns into the market even if they had to almost *give* them away. It seemed that our industry had to figure out how to make guns—always considered durable goods—seem *disposable* to consumers; a quality gun should last forever. So how do we keep consumers buying new ones?

This, of course, was a problem for Kimber. We had enjoyed tremendous growth just like the others, but our products were still old-school, meticulously machined, and finished by hand. Everyone knew that Glocks and other "Tupperware" guns cost only about $100 to produce, but their $450 retail prices meant that there was a lot of profit to wring out. In other words, those companies had a lot of room to maneuver around the shifting market. Kimber's products were many times more expensive to produce. This meant that we just did not have the pricing space to move, and if the bottom fell out of the market, we'd be screwed.

"Well, that is a problem," Leslie admitted. "We don't have big, fat profit margins like the plastic-gun guys." And then he said something that he had often considered aloud, but this time I could tell he was serious: "I think we better get into the polymer business, Ryan."

As I had for more than two decades, I began to push back against Leslie. But my effort now was half-hearted. I already expected I would lose this time. I knew I was losing in other places too. There were just too many battles on too many fronts. If I was still a frog in that pot,

I now grasped just how hot the water really was. I was tired. By 2017, I thought more about the risks and payoffs of staying inside to fight principled, internal fights. I felt the desperation in Kimber and in the rest of the industry. If there were any vestiges of those old days, where wise men knew better than to start down the slippery path of money, fear, propaganda, and twisted facts, then they were now completely gone.

And then in June of that year I received more reinforcement about the hopelessness of the situation. "Busse, you ain't gonna like this," Tom warned again. "But you probably better watch it. I'll send the link."

The link he sent was to the latest ad for NRATV. The video began with Loesch in a maroon sweater—the type that any suburban mom would wear. She sneered and angrily spoke directly to the camera as if rallying a mob, between dystopian, black-and-white clips of riots and beatings on the streets:

> They use their media to assassinate real news. They use their schools to teach children that our president is another Hitler. They use their movie stars and singers and comedy shows and award shows to repeat their narrative over and over again. And then they use their ex-president to endorse the resistance—all to make them march, make them protest, make them scream "racism and sexism and xenophobia and homophobia," to smash windows, burn cars, shut down interstates and airports, bully the law-abiding. Until the only option left is for police to do their jobs and stop the madness. And when that happens, they'll use it as an excuse for their outrage.[6]

My jaw hung open. I could not believe what I was seeing. Hard-hitting TV ads had always been a specialty of the NRA and its marketing prowess, but this was downright horrifying. Loesch finished the ad by raising her voice and giving a jab that would be felt by an increasingly radicalized NRA nation: "The only way we save our country and our freedom is to fight this violence of lies with a clenched fist of truth. I'm the National Rifle Association of America, and I'm freedom's safest place."

As the ad trailed off, the Kimber logo flashed on my screen. I called Tom back immediately. *"What the fuck is that?"* I screamed into the phone. "I thought we were trying to be a respectable company? Something we could be proud of?"

"Come on, Busse. It's not so—"

"When you run out of Black presidents to hate, if you can't find anything to gin up the crazy-ass couch commandos, when there is not enough anger in the world to sell NRA memberships." I became angrier and louder with each word. "Well, you better just hate your neighbor, hate a celebrity, rally every son of a bitch you can find to shoot an immigrant or a random protesting kid—even better if she is a Black kid, and if that won't work, shoot your neighbor. *Kill your fucking neighbor?*"

"Ryan, that's not what it says—"

"That's what the fucking ad *means*, Tom, and you know it! It's embarrassing as shit and is just fearmongering to sell guns, plain and simple. We should just call that the 'Hate Your Neighbor' ad, and we should run from that as fast as we can. The whole country should run from this shit."

"Well," Tom said after a moment as I caught my breath. "That's a problem because I think Leslie really likes it."

"Then I am fucking done. No American should be OK with this kind of shit. It's going to blow up, and the mess is going to spray all over the industry." I hung up.

My assessment of what NRATV officially called its "Violence of Lies" ad proved correct, at least initially. The ad, which launched in late June 2017, created incredible controversy, enough that it even offended many NRA members. News stories around the country commented on the firestorm and blowback. Thousands of social media comments piled up on the NRA's pages. Many echoed my reaction, and several went so far as to call the NRA a "terrorist organization" or to accuse Loesch of fomenting hate with "pure, unpatriotic trash."[7]

If the goal of the "Hate Your Neighbor" advertisement was to spur gun sales, it did not immediately work. The gun-selling system had become desensitized to even this level of vitriol. Despite the weeks of controversy that the NRA video created, gun sales remained stagnant. Just like Leslie's expensive bet on Rick Santorum, the money Kimber spent on our NRATV sponsorship was not proving to be a good investment, but many people inside the industry knew it would be just a matter of time before something did spur sales.

Four months after the release of Loesch's "Hate Your Neighbor" video, a sixty-one-year-old named Stephen Paddock spent several quiet days transporting his personal arsenal of guns into his suite in the Mandalay Bay hotel in Las Vegas. Among Paddock's luggage: twenty-two AR-15 rifles, some equipped with bump stocks, the legal add-on feature that overrode physics to essentially make semiautomatic rifles fully automatic.

For reasons that may never be known, on the night of October 1, 2017, Paddock unleashed hell on a nearby outdoor concert, shooting randomly from his high-rise window into a huge concert crowd below, killing sixty innocent people and injuring more than four hundred in under ten minutes. The number of dead and injured roughly equaled the population of my small hometown in Kansas.

As if I needed any proof that the NRA had completely upended our nation's political system, the worst mass shooting in the nation's history did not result in a new push for gun legislation. It did not produce a series of press events, nor did it prompt a series of congressional hearings. Not even the many likely presidential candidates promised action.

In Las Vegas there were many times more victims than *all* the shootings that prompted the passages of the Brady Bill and the assault weapons ban. Yet America seemed to accept the tragedy as another unsolvable truth about life and death in a changed nation. The NRA had successfully shut down every single pressure relief valve. Now our country had to keep the hate and fear bottled up. There was no place for it to go.

I knew that this lack of reaction sounded the final death knell for the old political system. There was not so much as a hint of a sales spike, no panic, no discussion of meaningful legislation. Nothing. Just five hundred people who had been shot by America's Rifle.

To the gun business, October 1 was just another Sunday. By Monday, things were back to normal. A few days later, a dispassionate *Bloomberg News* headline noted the remarkable shift in public reaction: "Gun Sales in America Have Stopped Spiking After Mass Shootings."[8] For the NRA, the dog had finally caught the car. Without a fearful base of consumers, the gun industry could go into a tailspin. The NRA knew this damn well. It was, after all, the organization's system.

I wished that the wise men in our industry had stood their ground all those years ago. That our industry had not decided to glorify couch commandos. That our industry had not bent to the will of the NRA. But none of those things could be turned back now.

Not only did guns sales not spike in late 2017, but even after hundreds of casualties in Las Vegas, they continued to slump.

"Smith & Wesson: buy five get one free. Ruger is running big promotions too. The deals are crazy right now," I reported in a leadership meeting weeks after the Las Vegas tragedy with a PowerPoint presentation. Hundreds of unsuspecting concertgoers had been shot, but big companies that had spent millions to modernize were still doing everything possible to prop up firearms sales volumes. That meant the bottom was falling out from underneath gun pricing: "Retail prices are dropping fast, as much as 20 or 30 percent lower than last year."

"That's it," Leslie finally said after my report. He looked around the room and put his hands on the table. "We are launching the polymer project. The decision is final." Then he looked at me, knowing how I felt about the move. "Better get ready, Ryan. Kimber is going to have a plastic gun. You'll have to compete with Smith and Glock."

That was it. Leslie had clearly made up his mind. Kimber sales reps would soon have to give up our "Don't settle; buy metal" sales slogan, and I would have to figure out how to come to terms with it all. Or not.

TWENTY-FIVE

SPEAKING TRUTH TO BULLSHIT

K IMBER'S ASSOCIATION WITH NRATV WORSENED MY OWN
personal burden, but our country neared a boiling point too:
the increasing pressure brought on by more than a decade of cultural radicalization. On Valentine's Day of 2018, the radicalization
stormed its way into a suburban Miami high school. Just after 2:00
p.m., nineteen-year-old Nikolas Cruz told his Uber driver to drop him
off in front of Marjory Stoneman Douglas High School in Parkland,
Florida. He then pulled his backpack and rifle case from the back
seat and simply walked through the front door. Cruz used his Smith
& Wesson M&P15 rifle to kill seventeen people and wound seventeen more. Most victims were students, and some were heroic teachers
who died trying to protect kids from Cruz's rampage.

Florida law prohibited Cruz from purchasing a handgun because
he was under the age of twenty-one. But as proof that the old legal system had not kept up with the advancement of guns, Cruz was legally
allowed to purchase an assault rifle and as many high-capacity magazines as he wanted. This loophole was a holdover from a time when the

rifle market was mostly limited to sales of hunting and target guns. But now this market included assault rifles used by the military and police forces, hence the letters "M&P" on Cruz's own rifle. The country had changed, but laws had not. In fact, the national restrictions on such guns had only become more lax.

In a sickening replay of Columbine, Sandy Hook, and at least a dozen other massacres, people inside the gun industry watched the unfolding horror through the lens of what it would mean for business. Even despite the lack of action after Las Vegas, the industry immediately feared a legislative response because everyone knew that a shooting in a school was as bad as it could get.

Most others anticipated a threat to business. I saw the possibility that common sense might finally prevail, especially given the flabbergasting response by right-wing conspiracy theorists that the whole attack was somehow an elaborate hoax involving "crisis actors" pretending to be victims. The rest of America saw right through the bullshit. "It just feels like something is different about this one," I told Allen. "I think kids have finally had it."

Brave high school students who had survived the shooting included Cameron Kasky, David Hogg, and Emma González. They were part of a group of teens who seemed to have an intuitive sense about creating movements, and they knew how to use social media. Within weeks, they organized "March for Our Lives" to demand that lawmakers in Congress and across the country finally do something. The main event was a march planned for Washington, DC, but the young Parkland activists also helped organize a school walkout on March 14, one month after the shooting. Their call to action resulted in one of the largest protests in the history of the United States, with nearly two million participants nationwide. And it certainly got the attention of my younger son, Badge, who was ten that winter.

"Dad, you OK if I protest with the Parkland kids?" he asked at dinner.

"I'm more than OK with it, buddy. I would be proud of you."

"We *are* proud of you, honey," Sara added. "Stick up for your future."

"Just because we have guns and I work for a gun company doesn't mean you shouldn't be safe or that we don't want your friends to be safe."

"Or that we don't want laws that are good for the country," Sara said.

"I just wanted to make sure," Badge responded confidently. "I am scared, Dad. I just want my friends at school to be safe." I looked up at Sara, who looked up at me with watery eyes. I teared up too.

The next day ten-year-old Badge informed his fifth-grade teacher that it was his right to protest, and at the appointed time he left his classroom and stood on the sidewalk outside Kalispell's Peterson Elementary School in solidarity with the Parkland victims and the millions of protesters across the country that day. But at his school, he stood alone.

"I stood out there for seventeen minutes by myself, but it felt like an hour," he reported to us that night. Badge's protest involved standing in silence, one minute for each victim of the Parkland shooting. Our older son, Lander, did the same thing with a small group of kids at his middle school a few blocks away.

The political pressure exerted by young people like Cameron, David, Emma, Badge, and Lander that day struck a chord in America. The impressive national movement seemed like it might even persuade President Trump. In the weeks after the tragedy, the president made initial moves indicating he was ready to consider change. Trump welcomed Parkland survivors to the White House for a listening session, and he made comments suggesting he was open to new laws restricting sales of America's Rifle.

The movement even created cracks in the NRA, and in a reminder that America's young people ultimately have more power than any powerful pro-gun organization, the NRA even lost control of some Republicans. Nine days after the shooting, Florida Republican congressman Brian Mast penned a *New York Times* op-ed that might as well have been a restatement of the words expressed by Jim Zumbo or a rehash of the wise men's warning from our Kansas Southwind events:

Most nights in Afghanistan, I wielded an M4 carbine. . . . My rifle was very similar to the AR-15-style semi-automatic weapon used to kill students, teachers and a coach I knew at Marjory Stoneman Douglas High School in Parkland, Fla., where I once lived. . . . I cannot support the primary weapon I used to defend our people being used to kill children I swore to defend. . . . The AR-15 is an excellent platform for recreational shooters to learn to be outstanding marksmen. Unfortunately, it is also an excellent platform for those who wish to kill the innocent.[1]

Mast's piece received significant attention, and for a few days, at least, it felt like a rare moment of hope.

When I read Mast's words and found myself rooting for his courage, I realized that I had been ignoring an obvious truth. I was fooling myself, pretending I could make a change. I was both working within and cheering against an industry, and that dual existence was taking a toll on me and my family.

The truth was that as the industry slid further toward extremism, I became more influenced by the industry's critics. Sara brought many of them to my attention. For years she had been inspired by activists such as Brené Brown, Jen Hatmaker, and Glennon Doyle, all of whom advocated compassion and activism. And all of them made impassioned pleas for legislative action to protect young people following the Parkland massacre.

Doyle, a *New York Times* best-selling author, a gifted speaker, and an inspirational leader for millions, was particularly poignant. In one of many speeches posted to her massive social media audience, she summed up the frustration of millions:

To those who reject common sense gun reform in the name of "American freedom": Tell me, what country is free whose school-children are not free to learn without fear of massacre? American children will not be free unless we become the home of the brave by making association with the gun lobby toxic. Congresspeople: If the NRA has bought you, we will return you.[2]

Another of Sara's inspirations in the aftermath of the shooting was Brené Brown, whom she had told me about for years. "Whatever you're doing, stop and read this," she said, shoving her phone into my hand.

Brown, the author of five *New York Times* best-sellers and host of one of the most popular TED Talks of all time, was receiving renewed attention for her well-known blog post on gun issues. "Gun Reform: Speaking Truth to Bullshit, Practicing Civility, and Effecting Change," adapted from her 2017 book, *Braving the Wilderness*, echoed much of my own experience:

> I loved and was proud of this part of my family story. And, like most kids, I assumed that everyone who was raised in a hunting and gun culture was raised with the same rules. But as I got a little older, I realized that wasn't true. As laws governing gun ownership became more and more political and polarized, I became more skeptical of the gun lobby. I watched the NRA go from being an organization that I associated with safety programs, merit badges, and charity skeet tournaments to something I didn't recognize. Why were they positioning themselves as the people who represented families like ours while not putting any limits or parameters around responsible gun ownership?[3]

Brown concluded her post with words that hit me hard:

> I know that I'm not alone. I know that there are millions of us who believe in common sense gun laws and have no interest in vilifying respectful, responsible gun owners. I also know that there are millions of us who find the NRA and the politicians who take millions of dollars from them and, in turn, support laws that endanger all of us morally reprehensible.

Her writing convinced me that my doubts and activism were well founded, that I was not alone, and that my fight was important.

Despite the renewed attention to Brown's post and the impassioned pleas from people such as Doyle, the new US political system had been rigged by the NRA so effectively that it soon regained its footing. Within weeks, Chris Cox and Wayne LaPierre held several closed-door meetings and private phone calls with President Trump. What exactly they said will remain a mystery, but internal sources reported that Cox and LaPierre convinced Trump that his political base would not stand for even the most modest legislation. Almost immediately after those meetings, NRA-funded political gridlock drowned out the energy and enthusiasm built up by marching kids and gun-safety activists. This meant that national activists erupted with even more frustration. So did parents, who began mocking Republican politicians who offered only "thoughts and prayers" in response. Sara was no exception.

"I hope you follow up your 'Prayers for Florida' with ACTION," she wrote on Facebook a few days after Parkland. "The ONLY way this will EVER change is if the NRA goes up in FLAMES. Period. Remember that when you cast your next vote. If you are voting 'biblical values' just know that your vote is bought and paid for by the most powerful lobby in America, and it ain't Jesus."

Sara wanted the NRA to burn down, and I couldn't blame her. Not only was she worried about our boys; she was also driven by the anger created by an authoritarian organization that had been tormenting me and our family for nearly fifteen years. But the simple fact that Sara was married to me meant that her ire came at a price. Within an hour of her Facebook post, the volunteer army of NRA trolls watching our family sprang into action. Her words were almost immediately copied and reposted on numerous sites, including a popular "Kimber Talk" message board.

The reaction from consumers was swift, and as the angry calls and emails started to pour in to our office, I considered my next move. Sara was a mom of two boys, and she was worried about their safety. *Fuck these people! Why should she be precluded from being a citizen of this country?* Like Brown, I knew this was all part of the NRA's bullshit. How could anyone call *me* and my family anti-gun? But the grip of the NRA, just like the MAGA devotion it spawned, had no shades of gray. No one could *ever* be pro-gun enough, not even me. It may have been bullshit, but it was also reality. Then Kimber's social media coordinator called me from New York. "This stuff about you and your wife is really blowing up," he warned.

"Yeah, I saw it. My sales guys are already taking calls."

"Lots of calls here too. And you know the NRA is already on it, right?"

"Why do these people think they have the right to bully my family?"

"All I know is it's catching fire. I respect you, Ryan. And—"

"And?"

"We probably need to get it taken down. I'll send you some screenshots of stuff they are saying, just so you can see."

Sure enough, in a post titled "The Enemy Within," a forum member who went by *KimberSolo* made no apologies for this direct attack:

> Fellow Kimber owners, it never hurts to know the type of people in charge of the company that you give your money to. Ryan Busse, Vice President of Sales at Kimber is someone you should get to know. A simple google search will reveal that Ryan has long supported democrats. Ryan's wife gives you a look at how the Busse house feels about the National Rifle Association.

The post concluded with a screenshot of Sara's admonition of "Prayers for Florida." I had seen this game before, and I regretted that it had roots in the inside attacks I had encouraged on Ed Shultz so many years ago. I also knew that the growing power of these people meant they would stop at nothing.

"Look, man," one of my sales guys said as he stood in my doorway. "Some of us have been talking. We're worried about you, Busse. You and Sara. And the boys."

"Appreciate that."

"And you know these people are crazy."

"An understatement."

"And, well, we wouldn't put it past them to confront you or Sara. I mean, they might show up at your house or something. We know they all have guns."

He was right. The possibility of physical attacks on us was not off the table. I also knew that if it went on too long, the public pressure for me to be fired would be too great to tamp down. With that in mind I swallowed hard and called Sara.

"I'm not telling you to take it down," I said. "Not telling you that you don't have the right to say it. And I know you want me out of here. But I'm telling you that if your post stays up, it's going to keep attracting attention from the crazies."

"So you're not *telling* me to take it down," she said. "But you're asking me to?"

"I'm asking you to consider the fact that if you don't, Sara, there's a high likelihood that I'll be leaving here on their terms instead of ours. And their terms don't guarantee any safety. For any of us."

"I'll take it down. But these bastards are evil, Ryan. You have to get out. These fucking people do not care about kids like our boys. They do not care about our country. They are part of a sick cult. You don't belong with them. I certainly don't. And neither do the boys."

That was the day I accepted that I'd need to make an exit from Kimber. For years I had justified staying inside the industry. I used my position to win battles that others could not fight. For more than twenty years I worked to keep Kimber above the ugliness, but it was all slipping away now. I yielded to the fact that a multifront war was just too large for one person to win from the inside.

That did not mean the decision was easy. The election of Trump and the resulting conversion of the industry into a single-mission political action committee was the real catalyst, I suppose. The launch of NRATV and the need to produce cheaper guns to feed the hungry beast that the NRA had created were simply the final straws. The company that I helped build with a crazy Australian who begged me never to allow Kimber to build guns that would end up in crime scenes was about ready to embark on a project to build high-capacity polymer pistols that would be more likely to end up in crime scenes. I was losing on all my battlefronts. It was a failure, and it was not easy for me to admit.

Sara knew that all of this was incredibly difficult and sad for me, and she gave me time before she brought it back up.

"I've finally had it," I said. We had opened a bottle of wine, and I took another sip. Sara was curled up next to me with her own glass. "I gotta find a way out."

Sara gave me a big hug. "This fight is killing you. It's time."

But quitting was not in my nature. Sara and I both knew that converting my decision to action would take time, and she understood.

"I want to go out on my own terms."

"I know. That's fair. Look, this is hard, but it's too big now. Promise me you will do this, Ryan. Even if it takes a while, *promise* me this is going to happen."

Finding a way to go out on my terms was going to be very difficult. We had forged a great life in our favorite place on Earth, and I had an entire team of people who depended on me. Perhaps most importantly for me, I believed I had established a platform, as perilous as it may have been, to effect change from the inside. Letting go of the business was easy enough, but letting go of my fight was another thing altogether.

TWENTY-SIX

POSITION OF POWER

M Y COMMITMENT TO LEAVE THE INDUSTRY WAS MORE than just a promise to Sara; it was also an important milestone for me. I had already been picking more-visible fights and taking bigger risks. I had twisted a lot of identity into my career and the platform of resistance I had built, which means that it was all extremely complicated to unwind, and I was not so sure how fast I could do so.

My family held no such reservations about an impending career shift. Throughout the remainder of 2018, a week didn't go by without Sara or the boys encouraging me to make the change. Lander suggested I could just "find another job." Toss my keys on the desk and walk away.

I had spent more than twenty years in the business. At first, the industry and my thoughtless devotion to it owned me, and the experience of fighting through that personal conversion played a big role in my reticence about just walking away.

Clearly, the industry leaders wanted me out, and that weighed on me too. I had a very hard time letting them win, and simply quitting certainly felt like a loss. I was a constant target, yes, but I was also in a position where I could define my battles. Giving up my career would mean giving up that hard-won turf.

As I look back at it now, I know that even before my 2018 decision to leave Kimber, my increasingly outspoken stances were indicators that I knew the eventual outcome. Like a good poker player, I had kept just enough people guessing, but Donald Trump's victory changed that strategy. I became a lot less concerned about anyone seeing my cards, and I felt that I had no choice other than to push all in on any new opportunity to limit the power of the NRA and the nation's new president.

This included taking any opportunity to exert influence, especially on the things I cared about most: wild places within the interior of our country. The Trump administration, through Secretary of Interior Ryan Zinke, kept attacking those wild places and our bedrock environmental laws, and it was preparing to enact massive rollbacks of key national-monument designations.

Zinke was from northwestern Montana just like me, and I had a long, complicated relationship with the former congressman. At my request we held an off-the-record meeting in a school library before one of his scheduled speeches back in Montana. During our private talk I let him know I was going to stand up for hunters and was planning to publicly criticize the environmental rollback of the administration. During the meeting I got the feeling he did not believe me. Some texts that he had sent me a few days earlier let me know that the NRA had already got to him: "Who is the largest hunter organization on the planet?" his first text on the subject said. I shot back a note that guessed at the answer, but he responded with another note that might as well have been written by Chris Cox himself: "NRA, Brother. Others combined not even close. Just sayin."

Later that afternoon, as Zinke spoke to a group of western governors, I took part in an angry press conference attacking the monument rollbacks. The video of my attack quickly racked up tens of thousands of views, and like my first press event in Washington, DC, the news hook was that I represented a conservative industry and was criticizing a conservative Republican administration.

My opposition to Zinke was notable, but it was in keeping with my other efforts on behalf of conservation and wild places, and even as I was speaking to the cameras, my blood was boiling over Zinke's NRA texts. That's when I decided to take my first real bold action directly against the industry.

After my press conference I called my friend Elliott Woods, a talented investigative journalist who was working on a hard-hitting article about Secretary Zinke for *Outside* magazine. Elliott was in town to cover Zinke's speech and then to interview him in nearby Glacier National Park. "I have another story idea you might want to consider," I told Elliott. "Inside the NRA, the organization that brainwashed an entire industry. Hell, it's bigger than that. This is the organization that brainwashed an entire country."

"You willing to go on record?" he asked, as good journalists do.

I demurred, wondering aloud whether my going on the record would blow any cover I had left. If I was going to help with things like this, I had to stay and keep my head lowered. "The whole industry relies on fear, and the NRA is the authoritarian puppet master that yanks the strings of that fear. I can point you in the right directions."

"If I do it, I'll need access," Elliott said. "Think you can get me on the inside so I can sniff around? Maybe get me into a trade show?"

"I'll make you a Kimber employee for a day. Come to SHOT, and you'll have all the access that any industry executive would have. I know you'll be able to smell what's happening. Come to Vegas. Walk around and see for yourself."

Elliott, an Iraq War veteran and a dedicated hunter, had a keen nose for a good story, and he latched on to the idea. "I'd need industry sales data and maybe a pass for Range Day at SHOT too," he said.

"I'll get you whatever you need," I told him. "But some of the shit you see out there might shock you."

By then, Industry Day at the Range at SHOT had become a huge, live-fire production held every year at a massive outdoor shooting facility in the desert east of Las Vegas. The four-day SHOT Show was held indoors with deactivated guns on display, but "Range Day" was a chance for hundreds of exhibitors to show off the actual firepower of their guns, and it was open to throngs of supportive gun bloggers, writers, dealers, and fans. Attendees arrived in gigantic charter buses, which left the big Vegas hotels on the hour.

If you attended Range Day, your senses would be overwhelmed the minute that you stepped off the bus. You'd hear constant staccato punches of gunfire, much of it fully automatic. You'd see thousands of people, food vendors, puffs of dust and smoke, and gun writers armed with huge cameras. And you wouldn't be able to avoid the acrid smell of burning gunpowder. The event had the feel of a chaotic market crossed with a war zone in a third-world country.

Of course, companies that took part in Range Day used well-known "operators" to attract people to shooting locations, as if these men were famous celebrities or professional athletes. I knew this would catch Elliott's attention, and he immediately began texting me with the same disturbing observations I had experienced for years.

"Wannabes," he said. "There are all sorts of wannabes out here running around acting like they are military badasses. It's like a big cosplay convention where war is cool. I'd bet not one in a dozen of these tattooed fools have any idea what combat is about."

Elliott had experienced the real ugliness of combat in Iraq, where he earned the right to be judgmental about the appropriation of military valor to sell anything and everything in the Nevada desert. The massive industry-sanctioned scene disturbed him. In an event littered with red Make America Great Again hats, another particular ball cap caught his attention. "I just saw an asshole wearing a 'Make Zimbabwe Rhodesia Again' hat," he said in disbelief.

That hat referenced the bloody racial uprising in Africa that ended apartheid rule in the British colony of Rhodesia. At the demand of native Africans, the so-called Bush War also resulted in the country being renamed Zimbabwe in 1980. That renaming had long been a source of consternation for White nationalists everywhere. That ugly history leaked into the mainstream after an unsettling photo of Dylann Roof made its way to the public. Roof, the young White man sentenced to death for shooting nine Black parishioners at Charleston's Emanuel African Methodist Episcopal Church in 2015, wore a Rhodesian national flag sewn onto his jacket.[1] Elliott could not get over the fact that a hat openly celebrated the same racial hatred proudly worn by a mass murderer. "That is quite possibly the worst, most racist thing I have ever seen," he told me later that evening. "That guy wore it proudly for all to see, and no one said a fucking word."

"Welcome to my world, Mr. Woods. Now just go write a good goddamn story."

Elliott did indeed write a good story. It was better than good; it was *important*. The *New Republic* published the bombshell article, "Fear: The American Terror Industry," in April 2018. In it, Elliott admitted to attending the SHOT Show. Although he did not name me as the source of the illicit manufacturer's badge that got him inside enemy territory, I knew I ran a high risk of being exposed as his accomplice.

Elliott's article masterfully detailed our industry's overt racism, militarization, the Trump Slump, and the manufactured fear driving it all. Even though the protests and violent counterprotests of 2020 were still two years away, Elliott also had a sharp, predictive sense for the sort of cultural division that our industry was fomenting:

I found a poster from a Florida-based custom AR-15 manufacturer called Spike's Tactical that showed a squad of thickly muscled dudes in the foreground, backs to the viewer, dressed in jeans, black T-shirts, and ratty ball caps. Each of them wore body armor and carried some iteration of an AR-15. They stood in front of a concrete Jersey barrier, facing down a mob of ruffians wearing ski masks and bandannas who appeared to be burning down a city. None of the rioters carried firearms. The text at the top of the poster said: BERKELEY—PORTLAND—CHARLOTTES-VILLE—BOSTON—>NOT TODAY ANTIFA.[2]

"That's a damn good piece of writing," I told Elliott about a week before his story went to print. We had spent days going back and forth about the article's release. He had called and texted me several times, concerned that I would be found out as the internal traitor who let a loathed member of the press onto the holy ground of the industry's largest trade show.

"I'm really worried I'm gonna cost you your job," he told me more than once. "It's going to blow back on you. I can still pull the plug." I thought it might, but I had decided to make bolder moves now that I'd decided to leave. This risk, I knew, was worth it.

And eventually I told Elliott to just let it fly. He was, after all, simply writing a true story. "Sooner or later this is all going to end, so let's just do the right thing. They're going to figure out that it's me. I got you a Kimber badge, for God's sake. They'll eventually check the records. I'm just gonna own it. Let's get it printed!"

The article, which went to press on April 16, got everyone's attention. The industry buzzed. Dealers even discussed it with our sales staff. And eventually some of my sales guys got curious. "Did *you* get him into the SHOT Show, Busse?" they asked. "This guy seems like one of your friends."

"What does it matter who got him in?" I said to one of them in a moment of defiance. "If the dealers are pissed, please have them call me to discuss what is untrue in his article." The poor sales guy nodded, shrugged, and went on his way.

Elliott's journalism caught the attention of the NRA too. "They want me to go on NRATV to debate Dana Loesch," he said, not long after the story hit the press. "Should I do it?"

"Hell, yes. You'll shred any argument she throws at you. She'll just try to attack you over the racism stuff. She won't know what to do with an actual hunter, a war veteran, and someone who is . . . actually smart."

In an odd situation where I found myself weakening the same network my company was underwriting, Elliott and I strategized right up until the minute he went on air with Loesch. As I suspected, he stuck to his points, kept his cool, and did not take any red-meat bait. "I hope a lot of people saw that, Mr. Woods," I told him as soon as the debate aired. "You made her look like a fool."

Knowing that the article made a difference, and working from the inside to exert outward pressure, helped sustain me as I searched for the right off-ramp. I knew that our nation was only becoming more divided, and I had a duty to make smart decisions about how to use the platform I had built to fight back.

TWENTY-SEVEN

TOTALITARIO

AFTER ARRIVING AT THE DECISION TO LEAVE KIMBER, I FELT free to be overt in efforts like helping Elliott Woods expose the truth. It also allowed me to take a more public role on important political races. With Jon Tester facing another reelection campaign in 2018, I jumped in to help again.

Tester drew Republican Matt Rosendale as a challenger. Rosendale had a long record of terrible positions on hunting and conservation issues. Chris Cox and the NRA issued a full-throated attack against Tester anyway. No discussions with Ryan Busse or sneaky magazine articles this time. Even pretending to be bipartisan, or on the side of hunters, was now a thing of the distant past. The NRA never forgave Tester's 2013 vote in favor of background checks to keep guns out of the hands of terrorists, criminals, and the mentally ill.

For me, the gloves were off. I wrote op-eds, gave statements to national news reporters, and even spoke at political rallies in support of Tester's reelection. Despite the fact that President Trump, Vice President Pence, Donald Trump Junior, and Cox made nearly a dozen visits to Montana targeting Tester and urging their army to vote for Rosendale, the Montana farmer once again prevailed in a tight race.

"You didn't just beat Matt Rosendale," I said to the senator over breakfast the morning after the election. "You just beat Trump and the NR-fuckin-A."

Tester leaned toward me just like he had that night when we discussed doing the right thing on the Manchin-Toomey background-check legislation. "Yeah, I did," he said with his famous grin. "And it feels pretty damn good."

A few months later, in early 2019, I was asked to speak at an energetic rally of more than two thousand pro-public-lands activists at the Montana State Capitol. This was the sort of speaking engagement that up until my decision to leave Kimber, I would have been forced to forgo. Since my speech at the National Press Club, I had learned that my fights should be less public. But given the circumstances, I happily took this risk too.

In my speech I directly attacked the Trump administration and other Republicans for advancing policies that weakened environmental protections and sought to sell off the nation's federally owned public lands. Several news articles followed the rally, some with a picture of me at the podium, fist in the air, as I yelled to the applauding crowd.

I was simply standing up for hunters, but my political activism garnered increasing attention, and that meant the attacks from the trolls also intensified. My name regularly appeared in long podcast rants and in threatening posts in places such as the popular website AR15.com.

Despite my decision to leave, the attacks were unsettling. I never knew for sure if they were just words or if they would spur some unhinged person into uncontrollable rage and action, and from the looks of the comments, there were plenty of unhinged people. I tried to put those thoughts out of my head and find ways to score some last wins against the same radicalization that frightened me. I capitalized on one of those opportunities in 2018 as I dealt with one of Kimber's largest customers, Dick's Sporting Goods.

As part of our normal annual planning process, I traveled to Pittsburgh, where I had a meeting scheduled with the massive retailer's merchandising staff. As I entered the company's impressive modern headquarters, I noticed multiple framed news stories about Ed Stack, the company's iconic CEO. Stack was a proud Republican and had even been mentioned as a potential US Senate or presidential candidate. The embodiment of an all-American success story, Stack had taken over a small two-store business from his father in the 1980s. Despite the national retail trends threatening brick-and-mortar retail stores, Stack had grown Dick's into a national powerhouse with more than 850 locations. As I sat down to discuss Kimber's relationship with the members of Dick's merchandising team, I saw that they were nervous. "Don't worry; we don't have any intention of getting out of the Kimber business," they said defensively. "Fact is that we love having Kimber in our stores. You guys really class up the joint."

It was odd for a large retailer to seem apologetic. Leadership teams for big chains like this were schooled in how to intimidate suppliers like me, but we laughed it off. I knew that the odd compliments were a result of an ongoing firearms industry crucifixion of Dick's and that the normally confident buying team had good reason to be jumpy. They did not have many friends left.

They were frayed because in the weeks following the Parkland shooting, their popular CEO had initiated a corporate review of his company's involvement in the gun business. That investigation turned up a shotgun purchased by Nikolas Cruz, the teenager responsible for the massacre at Marjory Stoneman Douglas High School.

Despite the fact that Cruz had not used that particular gun in his murders, Stack was clearly affected by the discovery. Within days, Dick's publicly announced that it would remove all AR-15s and any similar weapons from its stores, along with a gut-punch statement: "We at Dick's Sporting Goods are deeply disturbed and saddened by the tragic events in Parkland. Our thoughts and prayers are with the victims and their families. But thoughts and prayers are not enough."[1] The announcement went on to spell out the actions that Stack and his board of directors were mandating:

> We deeply believe that this country's most precious gift is our children. They are our future. We must keep them safe. Beginning today, Dick's Sporting Goods is committed to the following:
>
> - We will no longer sell assault-style rifles, also referred to as modern sporting rifles.
> - We will no longer sell firearms to anyone under 21 years of age.
> - We will no longer sell high capacity magazines.
> - We never have and never will sell bump stocks that allow semi-automatic weapons to fire more rapidly.[2]

Stack did not stop there. Dick's called for "common sense gun reform," including universal background checks and a ban on "assault-style firearms." Stack funded lobbying efforts and made impassioned speeches on the national stage, advocating for changes. In one of those appearances, during a *New York Times* forum on the subject, Stack candidly reflected on his reaction to the Parkland shooting: "I'm not embarrassed to say I'm viewed as a relatively tough guy. I wouldn't characterize myself as a crier. And that weekend, I watched those kids, and I watched those parents, and I hadn't cried as much since my mother passed away."[3]

True to his word, Stack ordered the removal of assault rifles from his stores, and rather than assume any liability for those guns reentering the market, he destroyed more than $5 million worth of America's Rifles.[4] For the industry and the NRA, making statements about sympathy for kids was bad, but destroying AR-15s was among the worst sins that a pro-gun stalwart could commit. The new policies and gun destruction created tremendous vitriolic blowback for the retailer, especially toward the people with whom I met in Pittsburgh.

Even though Dick's still carried most gun models, the gun-industry howls were loud and vicious. The National Shooting Sports Foundation expelled Dick's and Stack from its membership rolls, an action I had never seen before.[5] Many gun companies issued public press releases bragging about their decisions to ostracize Stack and his stores by refusing to do business with them.[6]

I received a half-dozen calls from other executives asking me what Kimber was going to do. They were pressuring me and Kimber to drop Dick's as a customer. Aside from those calls, thousands of blogs and social media posts asserted that Stack was something between a George Soros–funded communist and an outright traitorous enemy of the United States.

The NSSF sent a message to all industry members with a claim that Stack had engaged in "conduct detrimental to the best interests of the Foundation." Among the NRA's many claims was a head-scratching statement that Stack, who was still selling plenty of guns, was somehow "punishing law-abiding citizens."[7]

The authoritarian NRA playbook meant that everyone in the industry was supposed to line up to crucify Stack. After all, I had helped the NRA hone that devastating strategy and had used it on Ed Shultz two decades earlier. But a lot had happened in those twenty years, and unlike my actions after the Smith & Wesson settlement, I did not encourage an industry lynch mob. I decided to make a point. I had committed to leaving Kimber, and I told myself that this freed me to do the right thing and be very public about it.

"As long as I am here, we will sell Kimbers to Dick's Sporting Goods," I told the other executives who called me about Stack, and I made the same promise to the nervous team in Pittsburgh. Of course, I knew that my refusal to gang up on them would only worsen doubts about my industry allegiance. At least this was one small chance for me to make amends for what I had done all those years ago. I had learned the lessons from thoughtlessly rushing into war.

This was a small victory but an important one. I was proud of that win because, like Stack, I knew that improving our national crisis would require a whole lot more courage. Courageous decisions could cost millions, but making a sacrifice for the right cause fits the definition of courage. I knew deep down that no solution would be easy or perfect. But whatever the answer was, it would have to start with a repudiation of the charged, radicalized environment created by the NRA and our industry. Any solution had to involve leaders who could speak truth to bullshit, just as my friend Jon Tester had done. Just as the industry wise men had once done. Just as Stack had done.

For the next several months I sought out more ways to speak my own truth. I spoke up where I could. I won some more battles like the one with Stack, but I knew I was losing ground.

I KNOW IT MAY BE DIFFICULT TO UNDERSTAND WHY I DID NOT immediately turn and walk out the door of the gun industry for good. I wrestled with that decision every single day. Even though I knew I would eventually leave, the last step was a blind one; I couldn't see what came next. I tormented myself with questions and what-ifs. Other than a few months hawking long-distance-telephone plans, the gun industry was the only real professional career I had ever known.

People in the industry whom I considered friends, and who at one point would have opposed the radicalization of our country, would probably never speak to me again. Some were like family. Should I stay to try and talk sense into them? I had no other prospects for employment, and I worried about what was the equivalent of a bad tattoo across my face. *Going to be tough to convince a new employer that my role in this industry does not define me,* I thought. The question I asked myself the most often was *Who will fight the battles if I leave?*

As I considered my next steps, I remembered people like the Black security guard at the NRA convention who endured the racists' T-shirts. I regret doing nothing for him. I thought about the children at Sandy Hook, who should be my own kids' age now, and the high school kids murdered in Parkland, as well as those who formed the movement to make change. No one inside this industry had stood up for them either.

I often talked through it all with Sara, and on the night of our twentieth wedding anniversary, the subject of my exit came up again. We had been looking forward to a short trip and a quiet dinner together, but it wasn't easy for us to celebrate. It was just like most other nights at home, when one of us worried aloud about attacks in my professional life or a new federal policy from the Trump administration that affected something we cared about. If it wasn't that, we wondered what the hell I would do when I quit.

Sara had reached the end of her rope. She locked the door and then turned to me.

"We are not leaving this room until we decide on the plan," she said, tossing me a small notepad from our hotel room.

This was to be our final discussion in the long debate over my professional departure. And for Sara, nothing lasting happened without a written plan. She sat down beside me and shoved a pen in my hand. "Write it down, and then we're sticking to the plan," she said sternly. "No going back." After, she gave me one of her signature big hugs and unlocked the door.

Our plan involved me leaving at the end of the 2020 summer. I'd stay just long enough to take a few notes, get my staff settled, and maybe win a last battle or two. I did not yet know that in my last few months in the industry, everything I fought against would explode into a firestorm that would shock even me.

It began with the COVID-19 outbreak. As the pandemic ensued, Americans scrambled for food, toilet paper, sanitizers, and especially *guns*. On March 20 we saw the highest-ever daily total for national gun sales. And just a couple of months later, in May 2020, the video of George Floyd's brutal killing consumed a nation already strained by the pandemic.

Part of that nation, including our family, rose up in solidarity with people of color as we grappled with the reality of unresolved racism. As if acting out an NRATV video, a different part of the country responded by overdosing on even more racism and paranoia. I experienced it close up when that middle-aged stranger with an American flag on his shirt jabbed his finger into my twelve-year-old son's chest while screaming insults at him.

In another NRA-inspired move, President Trump heaped more fuel onto the fire with even more race-baiting. More protests erupted; some became violent. It all looked like the Dana Loesch video that Kimber sponsored, and it resulted in monthly gun-sales numbers that dwarfed even the high-water years under America's best gun salesman, Barack Obama. This, I knew, grew from the fertile soil of the NRA's fear and radicalization. Fruit overflowed from the orchard that the organization planted decades earlier, and now it lay in acrid, rotting piles scattered across our country.

The type of guns being sold, and the rate at which they were selling, showed that the modern iteration of the firearms industry was nearly completely detached from the job I started twenty-five years earlier. Back then, during those first days with Dwight and Greg, the entirety of national gun sales averaged only about 350,000 units per month, a small fraction of the new American reality. By the end of 2020, the NSSF would proudly report a sales total that averaged more than 1.8 million units per month and produced more than eight million new gun owners during the year.[8]

As I approached the day in July that would be my last, the increasing national ugliness showed no signs of abating. On my final morning working for Kimber, I gave Sara a hug and left for work. I walked into the company in which I spent a quarter century of my life. I sat down at my computer, wrote a simple resignation letter, and then sent it to Leslie. Then I took a deep breath. I was sad, but also very relieved.

"Sorry to hear about your decision," he said when he called. But I knew he was not really sorry. Now he and Kimber could be rid of the only voice of dissent in the firearms industry. I had become a liability for the company and for the industry as well. Performance, growth, profitability, awards, accomplishment—none of that mattered without ideological purity and 100 percent loyalty.

In the time after I left, I studied totalitarian systems to make some sense of my long struggle. I realized that the gravitational pull I felt was purposefully manufactured, designed to keep people like me from hurling out of orbit. Everyone knew that leaving and then speaking up would result in threats of violence, ceaseless persecution, and immediate ostracization. The Trump and NRA operations ran identically. They kept people inside, and they kept them quiet. My attempts to explain it all pointed me to Benito Mussolini's original totalitarian directive in support of fascism, the same one that had become the guiding light for the industry, and indeed for half the country: "All within the state, none outside the state, none against the state."[9] *Totalitario.*

A few months after I left, I decided to speak out publicly on a gun issue for the first time from outside the industry. The new Republican majority in the Montana House of Representatives was pushing a bill to allow permitless, concealed guns in bars and on college campuses. I weighed in with a short opinion column opposing the bill because it dispensed with those safety rules my dad had drilled into me, the same ones the industry had also once supported and still demanded in its own facilities.

Even though it was only personal opinion in a simple newspaper column from a *former* industry employee, the police state immediately kicked into gear. *Totalitario.* My opposition was front-page news on most industry blogs and news sites.

"Kimber Vice President Hates Guns," one popular website proclaimed, ignoring the fact that I no longer worked at Kimber and that my column clearly mentioned I owned and enjoyed plenty of guns.[10] Comments on the sites numbered in the thousands, many stating that I should be harmed or even killed. One called for my beheading. Through Kimber, Leslie himself wrote a response, and he sent thousands of emails distancing Kimber from me. He threatened legal action against me and demanded that I tell newspapers to retract my column.

The truth was the NRA and my industry had convinced Leslie and the people who attacked me that *they* were the only real Americans; everyone else was a traitorous anti-gun enemy. It did not matter if I had sold millions of guns. I was finally an outcast.

TWENTY-EIGHT

UN-AMERICAN CARNAGE

THE GUN INDUSTRY AND THE NRA HAVE SUCCESSFULLY transformed an entire country. America has become a radicalized nation of competing tribes. The old system, with its pressure valves and bipartisanship, simply boiled away in the cauldron of fear and hate. Only a handful of people profited from the heat, but they had rigged the system to just keep getting hotter. There were no more wise men who stepped in. We no longer shared agreement on facts. We no longer stuck to any norms. We forgot basic decency. Those things just slowed down the spiraling irrational fear.

The new world is one where a power-hungry organization can blow $30 million budgets on entire media networks with a singular purpose: to make Americans hate their neighbors. Our new world is one where a president of the United States and the NRA use identical, conspiratorial, unhinged threats to frighten an entire population of hundreds of millions. They successfully built a system that relies on a political police state to enforce 100 percent loyalty: no one can dare ask any questions without immediate repercussion. It is a culture that praises violence, one where "getting your man card back" means that it's acceptable to do whatever it takes to establish your superiority.

As I boxed up the last of my possessions from a gun-industry career where I had spent most of my adult life, I held the orange bell in my hand and thought about how its sound seemed so simple all those years ago. A little ding meant that we inched closer to the American Dream. I wonder what we are inching toward now.

The NRA's gamble on Trump paid off. The NRA beat the Trump Slump thanks to bombastic totalitarianism that operates with its own "alternative facts" and a worldwide pandemic that amplified basic human fear. It was no coincidence that the most divisive period in modern US history coincided with gun sales that shattered all previous records. Hoarding spurred by wild conspiracy theories made it nearly impossible to purchase ammunition, even for sporting guns.

It was also nearly impossible to find a black rifle on any shelf despite the more than five hundred companies that produce a version of the AR-15. The 2020 sales levels were nearly six million units higher than the highest mark of the Obama years, much higher even than the sales frenzy in the months after children were murdered at Sandy Hook Elementary.

The same industry that once chastised J. Guthrie for using an AR-15 on the Kansas prairie now observed from the sidelines as its army of paid tactical influencers *celebrated* seventeen-year-old Kyle Rittenhouse's use of an AR-15 to kill protesters in Kenosha, Wisconsin.

"Just some *pew pewing*," or maybe he wanted "a little taste of the drug," as Mat Best might have said. But to many in my former business, Rittenhouse was more than just another customer. *He was a hero*, a boy celebrated for doing exactly what the NRA's own Dana Loesch had encouraged him to do. Rittenhouse, who beamed while wearing his Black Rifle Coffee T-shirt as he awaited trial, was a poster child for the new youthful demographic the industry had been paying to develop. I could see that Rittenhouse had made himself into an operator like the cool guys with all the social media followers. Thousands of people were even cheering him for delivering a lethal clenched fist of "truth."[1]

Sadly, Rittenhouse's story is far from unique. Much of our country has charted its course by NRATV and the hundreds of other influencers who echo the same social media rants and post with the same hashtags. Their message? *We are prepared for a civil war—whatever it takes to keep our superiority to you from slipping away. We will overthrow our government and murder political leaders in the name of America's Rifle.* Many of the people that glorify the thought of that war have no idea about the horrors of such a battle. It's terrifying stuff.

As the industry rings up more sales of America's Rifle and sells crate after crate of high-capacity magazines to anyone, including White nationalists who dream of more murders and espouse more capitol attacks, the feedback loop seems unstoppable. Well-armed militias are called upon by Trump to "free states" from the tyranny of Democrats. Nearly half the country openly cheers or condones the actions with their silence. Gone are the wise political advisers who should step in to stop a president who encourages the armed kidnapping and murder of sitting governors because they dare to enforce policies based on knowledge and science. True to the NRA playbook, there can be no dissent, not even against violent insurrection or the heinous beating murder of a US Capitol police officer.

The core tenets of our new politics, first espoused by Wayne LaPierre and then adopted by Trump, have formed this frightening national political landscape. To tens of millions of Americans, the NRA and the president they elected are the only trusted sources of truth. Not even Republican leaders who simply certify ballot totals or who stand up to vote for impeachment can be trusted. Just like Ed Stack, engaging in any principled action means that they are no longer loyal. Their membership must be revoked. It's all or nothing, just as the totalitarian rules demand.

After Parkland, I began to understand that I could not have prevented any of this, no matter which battles I picked or won. I had to take a bigger risk, so I held true to my promise to Sara and my family. My days in the firearms industry are over; my story is in the words of this book. Even though I am no longer in the business, there will still be those who try to Zumbo me. Industry leaders will dismiss or dispute the account of my life. And that's fine. Perhaps they have decided to forget the times when leaders upheld norms of decency, but we cannot allow those memories to be lost.

Of course, many will choose to deny that the gun industry actually developed our modern political toxicity. They may continue to look away, or they may even celebrate their success in cultivating fear, conspiracy, and totalitarianism. Perhaps they cheer the unhinged couch commandos who threaten lawmakers. But I ask our nation this: What ideology worth holding must be propped up by ever-increasing persecution, hatred, and falsehood?

The spiral of manufactured fear is a trap from which we must escape. That's why, just days after I left my job, I announced that I would spend my time working to ensure that Joe Biden was elected president. I served on a Biden campaign committee with other national leaders who understood that the firearms industry had poisoned our politics. I held no illusions about the Biden campaign holding perfect positions on guns, and as I suspected, I quickly encountered broad misconceptions about gun owners. I could see that the relative silence of people like me had convinced too many Americans that all gun owners were part of the angry, conspiratorial monolith.

I knew that this was wrong, that there were millions like me, and that we had been subservient to the extreme too long. I learned that it was incumbent on me to speak up, to fight for an environment where people like me would be heard, where the truth of responsible gun owners could be weighed in reasonable gun legislation. Of course, this sort of gun treachery angered NRA leaders and their internet trolls, but their leverage on me and my family had dissipated. And I have to say, that freedom felt pretty damn good.

I may be free from that leverage, but our nation is not. The NRA, and by extension the entire firearms industry, is at the heart of our national divide. We must address our wounds at the source, and that is why I believe that healing will begin when our country can address gun issues with intelligence, reason, and compassion.

Let's start by admitting that current national gun policy is divorced from the best interests of all citizens, including gun owners. Stronger, more efficient, universal background checks benefit everyone. We should demand their enactment.

Let's also agree that a culture based on the glorification of war and the weapons of war should not be tolerated. There is no law that can or should be passed to address this problem. Rather, it is an issue of common sense and decency. Many of our country's most important advancements happened because we simply decided who we were as a nation. And we are not a nation of people who worship weapons and hope to kill one another in a bloody civil war. I once worked in an industry that upheld such decency, and if we really want to make America great again, this would be a good place to start.

We must confront any person or group that uses firearms as tools of intimidation. We should enact laws that prohibit open carry and any related intimidation. These things should not be tolerated, normalized, or ignored. Our country is based upon civil dialogue, honest debate, and majority rule. There is no civility when one party is standing over the other with a loaded gun. Let's agree to castigate the armed men who make these threats. Responsible gun owners must speak up. We should lead this charge.

We must understand that perfect solutions will never exist. No, gun violence and murders will never go away completely, but we can agree that commonsense regulations greatly reduce the worst outcomes. We are a country that has already accepted widespread regulation because for more than two centuries we have known that all freedoms must be balanced with corresponding responsibility.

Consider that it is currently legal to own fully automatic weapons. Even the tommy guns of Al Capone's era are legal. Your neighbor may own one, and you can probably purchase one yourself, yet they have not been used in a single mass shooting since the 1930s. Why? Because federal law mandates strict regulation, not through a ban but rather through the use of a super-background check before anyone can own a fully automatic weapon. The risk of mental instability or criminal activity is obviously reduced by such commonsense measures, yet rarely do we hear the Right complain about this as an infringement on the right to keep and bear arms. We should learn from this to apply more policies that actually work. Stronger background checks *work*.

Most importantly, we must learn to stand up for our self-interests. It may be in the NRA's best interest for you to look the other way at racists' shirts, for you to believe that Joe Biden will rewrite the Constitution (a power thankfully not afforded to even the most popular of presidents), for you to hate your neighbor, or for you to prepare to kill that neighbor. But none of those things are in your own best interest. Moreover, it is not in your interest to let your friends and family spread hatred and lies. Shared facts built America; "alternative facts" will surely destroy it.

I was lucky, I suppose, that the NRA and the firearms industry condoned attacks on something so sacred to me that it startled me into reality. It took something like that to push me into the battle. Even so, my path was imperfect. Like a lot of people, I allowed myself to accept things that incrementally strengthened totalitarianism even as I was engaged in the battle against it. We've all done things like looking the other way when crowds demean Black security guards. We sometimes say nothing when a relative or friend repeats an insane conspiracy theory based on a meme. We allow powerful forces to appropriate the best parts of our cultures so that profits and political power can be built. Most importantly, we allow these things to be twisted into fearful messages that push us into voting against the things we really care about. Every time we do even one of these small things, we empower the larger authoritarian system that gave us our modern politics.

Now free from the stigma of being Zumboed, I have decided to seek out and help organizations that want to make our country better and confront the dark forces that have broken our nation. We must dispense with the irrational slippery-slope arguments that lead us to demonize high school kids for trying to make the world better. We must honor the brave struggle of people like former Arizona congresswoman Gabby Giffords, whose organization is working to empower gun owners who also want to do the right thing. We must be brave enough to be a part of the solution. This is bigger than just guns. The future of our nation depends upon it.

If you take nothing else from this story, know that individuals and small groups can have immense effects. Understand that none of our current national ugliness was predestined. This was all created by a small group of people with expensive suits and limited political expertise. I lived it, within it, and I saw these people institute unbelievable changes in our country, many of them for the worse. These people succeeded because they were determined, not because they had some special skill. I'm simply asking you to understand how it happened, to study the tools and tactics they used. Set your mind to confronting them in order to undo them.

Commit yourself to making positive change. We must all be part of a new group of people who rise up and release our country from the grip of this un-American Carnage. It is time that we commit to changing our country for the better.

ACKNOWLEDGMENTS

THIS BOOK WOULD NOT HAVE HAPPENED WITHOUT THESE three incredible people:

Julie Stevenson is an agent extraordinaire. She has a keen eye for the diamond, even when it is still in the rough. She is a warrior for progress, a student of the craft, and a believer in the art.

Aaron Murphy is the kind of person that you want on your side. He is never afraid to dispense assistance and honesty, and his finely honed writing skills helped form this narrative in ways I could never have seen. His ample personal grace made our long creative process positively enjoyable.

Colleen Lawrie is the editor other authors wish they had. She's a no-nonsense visionary who seeks difference makers, recognizes possibilities, and understands how to push a book to its potential.

NOTES

CHAPTER 1: ONE NATION UNDER GUNS

1. National Shooting Sports Foundation, "NSSF Thanks Trump Administration for Industry's Critical Infrastructure Designation," press release, March 28, 2020, www.nssf.org/nssf-thanks-trump-administration-for-industrys-critical-infrastructure-designation.

2. Kimber America, "Kimber Owner and CEO Awarded the Golden Ring of Freedom," press release, May 8, 2019, www.kimberamerica.com/press/kimber-owner-and-ceo-awarded-the-golden-ring-of-freedom.

3. Michael Daly, "He Made the Gun That Slaughtered Parkland's Kids," *Daily Beast*, February 24, 2018, www.thedailybeast.com/he-made-the-gun-that-slaughtered-parklands-kids.

4. NRA Institute for Legislative Action, "Not Funny: Firearm Prohibitionists Finally Target Elmer Fudd's Gun," June 15, 2020, www.nraila.org/articles/20200615/not-funny-firearm-prohibitionists-finally-target-elmer-fudd-s-gun.

CHAPTER 2: HOLE IN THE WALL

1. "Two Die at End of Gun," *Manhattan (KS) Mercury*, July 15, 1962, www.newspapers.com/newspage/423909818.

CHAPTER 3: GROUND FLOOR

1. United States Bureau of Alcohol, Tobacco, Firearms and Explosives, "Firearms Commerce in the United States—Annual Statistics Update, 2018," www.atf.gov/file/130436/download.

CHAPTER 6: KILLERS, CLINGERS, AND CLINTONS

1. Quoted in Osha Gray Davidson, *Under Fire: The NRA and the Battle for Gun Control* (Iowa City: University of Iowa Press, 1998), 30.
2. "Slaughter in a School Yard," *Time*, January 30, 1989, http://content .time.com/time/subscriber/article/0,33009,956847,00.html.
3. Andrew Kaczynski, "The Assault Weapon Ban Would Have Never Passed if It Wasn't for Ronald Reagan," *Buzzfeed News*, December 19, 2012, www .buzzfeednews.com/article/andrewkaczynski/how-ronald-reagan-passed -the-assault-weapon-ban.
4. Quoted in Zaid Jilani, "Donald Trump in 2000: 'I Support the Ban on Assault Weapons,'" *Intercept*, January 27, 2016, https://theintercept.com/2016/01 /27/donald-trump-in-2000-i-support-the-ban-on-assault-weapons.

CHAPTER 7: BEATING A HANGOVER

1. United States Bureau of Alcohol, Tobacco, Firearms and Explosives, "Firearms Commerce in the United States—Annual Statistics Update, 2016," www.atf.gov/resource-center/docs/2016-firearms-commerce-united-states /download.

CHAPTER 8: COFFIN FACTORIES AND HORROR MOVIES

1. "Free-Spending Embezzler Gets 14 Years," *Fox News*, September 14, 2006, www.foxnews.com/printer_friendly_wires/2006Sep14/0,4675,Playboy Producer,00.html.

CHAPTER 9: WAS IT A KIMBER?

1. Quoted in "Teen Who Climbed Out of Columbine Window Recounts Being Saved in Shooting," *Inside Edition*, April 16, 2019, www.insideedition .com/teen-who-climbed-out-columbine-window-recounts-being-saved-shooting -52234.
2. Quoted in Rick Bragg, "Leader as Hard as Nails Is Taking Reins at N.R.A.," *New York Times*, April 14, 1996, www.nytimes.com/1996/04/14/us /leader-as-hard-as-nails-is-taking-reins-at-nra.html.
3. "2020 Florida Statutes," Chapter 776.013(A), State of Florida, www.leg .state.fl.us/statutes/index.cfm?App_mode=Display_Statute&URL=0700-0799 /0776/Sections/0776.013.html.
4. Quoted in Serge F. Kovaleski, "NRA Officials Take Aim at Ousting Clinton in Fall," *Washington Post*, April 21, 1996, www.washingtonpost.com /archive/politics/1996/04/21/nra-officials-take-aim-at-ousting-clinton-in-fall /6077b977-6717-43b0-80b9-7477bf09e772.
5. Quoted in Kovaleski, "NRA Officials Take Aim."

6. Quoted in John Hendren, "NRA and Protesters Face Off in Denver," *Washington Post*, May 1, 1999, www.washingtonpost.com/wp-srv/national/daily /may99/nra050199.htm.

7. Quoted in Hendren, "NRA and Protesters Face Off."

CHAPTER 10: TOBACCO AND FIREARMS

1. Quoted in Fred Musante, "After Tobacco, Handgun Lawsuits," *New York Times*, January 31, 1999, www.nytimes.com/1999/01/31/nyregion/after-tobacco -handgun-lawsuits.html.

2. Quoted in Gail Appleson, "Two More Cities Sue Gun Makers," *Washington Post*, January 28, 1999, www.washingtonpost.com/archive/politics/1999/01/28 /two-more-cities-sue-gun-makers/1346a9b6-8638-424a-86c4-55c224a35c56.

3. Quoted in Sharon Walsh, "Gunmakers up in Arms over HUD Plan to Sue Them," *Washington Post*, December 9, 1999, www.washingtonpost.com/wp -srv/WPcap/1999-12/09/056r-120999-idx.html.

4. Joe Mathews, "After Columbine, a Political Sea Change on Gun Control; Pro-gun Initiatives in Many States Are Staggered by Events," *Baltimore Sun*, April 23, 1999, www.baltimoresun.com/news/bs-xpm-1999-04-23-9904230045 -story.html.

5. Quoted in Avi Selk, "A Gunmaker Once Tried to Reform Itself. The NRA Nearly Destroyed It," *Washington Post*, February 27, 2018, www.washingtonpost .com/news/retropolis/wp/2018/02/27/a-gunmaker-once-tried-to-reform-itself -the-nra-nearly-destroyed-it.

6. Quoted in Rinker Buck, "In Gun Industry, He's an Outlaw," *Hartford Courant*, March 26, 2000, www.courant.com/news/connecticut/hc-xpm-2000 -03-26-0003260053-story.html.

7. Quoted in Jim Herron Zamora, "Gun Maker Under Fire for Safety Agreement," *San Francisco Examiner*, April 2, 2000, www.sfgate.com/news/article/Gun -maker-under-fire-for-safety-agreement-3066904.php.

CHAPTER 11: THE WAGES OF SIN

1. NRA Institute for Legislative Action, "The Smith & Wesson Sellout," March 20, 2000, www.nraila.org/articles/20000320/the-smith-wesson-sellout.

2. Quoted in Paul M. Barrett, Vanessa O'Connell, and Joe Mathews, "Glock May Accept Handgun Curbs, Following Lead of Smith & Wesson," *Wall Street Journal*, March 20, 2000, www.wsj.com/articles/SB953314289586902859.

3. Quoted in Fox Butterfield and Raymond Hernandez, "Gun Maker's Accord on Curbs Brings Pressure from Industry," *New York Times*, March 30, 2000, www .nytimes.com/2000/03/30/us/gun-maker-s-accord-on-curbs-brings-pressure -from-industry.html.

4. Quoted in Buck, "In Gun Industry, He's an Outlaw."

5. Quoted in Selk, "A Gunmaker Once Tried to Reform Itself."

CHAPTER 12: BUSTED

1. Quoted in Peter Slevin and Sharon Walsh, "Conn. Subpoenas Firms in Gun Antitrust Probe," *Washington Post*, March 31, 2000, www.washingtonpost .com/wp-srv/WPcap/2000-03/31/044r-033100-idx.html.

CHAPTER 13: CENTER OF MASS

1. James Dao, "The 2000 Campaign: The Gun Lobby; N.R.A. Tightens Its Embrace of Republicans with Donations," *New York Times*, April 26, 2000, www.nytimes.com/2000/04/26/us/2000-campaign-gun-lobby-nra-tightens -its-embrace-republicans-with-donations.html.

2. Quoted in Bob Dreyfuss, "The NRA Wants You," *Nation*, May 29, 2000, www.thenation.com/article/archive/nra-wants-you.

3. Quoted in Joel Achenbach, Scott Higham, and Sari Horwitz, "How NRA's True Believers Converted a Marksmanship Group into a Mighty Gun Lobby," *Washington Post*, January 12, 2013, www.washingtonpost.com/politics /how-nras-true-believers-converted-a-marksmanship-group-into-a-mighty -gun-lobby/2013/01/12/51c62288-59b9-11e2-88d0-c4cf65c3ad15_story. html.

4. Quoted in Dreyfuss, "The NRA Wants You."

5. Quoted in German Lopez, "Most Americans Support Stricter Gun Laws. Here's Why Nothing Happens," *Vox*, October 13, 2017, www.vox.com/policy-and -politics/2017/10/13/16468902/gun-control-politics-intensity.

6. Quoted in "Gun Lobby Targets Gore, Democrats," CNN, May 23, 2000, www.cnn.com/2000/US/05/23/nra.politics/index.html.

CHAPTER 14: RESCUED BY THE SKY PEOPLE

1. Joan Lowy, "Sportsmen Protest Bush's Outdoor Policies," Scripps Howard News Service/ESPN, March 12, 2004, accessed via *The High Road* (blog), www .thehighroad.org/index.php?threads/kimber-vp-will-vote-against-bush.70814.

2. NRA Institute for Legislative Action, "Hunting and Conservation," www .nraila.org/campaigns/huntingconservation/hunting-home-page.

CHAPTER 15: TUPPERWARE PARTY

1. Quoted in Melinda Henneberger, "The 2000 Campaign: The Gun Lobby; Rallying Voters and Relishing a Leading Role," *New York Times*, November 3, 2000, www.nytimes.com/2000/11/03/us/the-2000-campaign-the-gun-lobby-rallying -voters-and-relishing-a-leading-role.html.

2. Quoted in "NRA Takes Credit for Bush's Win," *Deseret News*, April 28, 2002, www.deseret.com/2002/4/28/19651973/nra-takes-credit-for-bush-s-win.

3. Quoted in "NRA Calls Open Carry Texas Activists Demonstrations 'Weird and Scary,'" *Guardian*, June 2, 2014.

CHAPTER 16: COUCH COMMANDOS

1. NRA Institute for Legislative Action, "2002 NRA Annual Meeting Speech by Wayne LaPierre," transcript, May 1, 2002, www.nraila.org/articles /20020501/2002-nra-annual-meeting-speech-by-wayne-lapierre.

2. Quoted in Geraldine Sealey, "Has 9/11 Led to Relaxed Gun Laws?," *ABC News*, January 7, 2006, https://abcnews.go.com/US/story?id=91807&page=1.

3. Quoted in Simon Van Zuylen-Wood, "The Heavily Armed Millennials of Instagram," *Washington Post*, March 4, 2019, www.washingtonpost.com/news /magazine/wp/2019/03/04/feature/the-heavily-armed-millennials-of-instagram.

4. Mat Best, "Bitch, I Operate," lyrics, https://genius.com/Mbest11x-bitch -i-operate-lyrics.

5. "Because America, That's Why," July 10, 2017, www.youtube.com /watch?v=JAgpNdbnHLw.

6. Nikki Junewicz, "Man at Capitol Riot Seen with Coffee Company Hat On," WZTV-TV, January 13, 2021, https://fox17.com/news/local/coffee -company-speaks-out-against-violence-after-capitol-rioter-seen-wearing -merchandise.

7. Kyle Lamb, "Why This Sportsman Supports President Trump in Reversing Obama's Bears Ears Land Grab," *Federalist*, January 9, 2018, https:// thefederalist.com/2018/01/09/sportsman-supports-president-trump-reversing -obamas-bears-ears-land-grab.

8. Quoted in Van Zuylen-Wood, "The Heavily Armed Millennials of Instagram."

CHAPTER 17: ZUMBOMANIA

1. Van Zuylen-Wood, "The Heavily Armed Millennials of Instagram."

2. Jim Zumbo, "Assault Rifles for Hunters?," *Hunting with Zumbo, Outdoor Life* blog, February 16, 2007, accessed via Razoreye, http://razoreye.net/mirror /zumbo/zumbo_assault_rifles.html.

3. David E. Petzal and Phil Bourjaily, "Zumbomania: David E. Petzal's Take on the Jim Zumbo Fiasco," *Field & Stream*, February 22, 2007, www .fieldandstream.com/pages/zumbomania-david-e-petzal%E2%80%99s-take -jim-zumbo-fiasco.

4. "Jim Zumbo Talks on Nugent Forum," *Long Range Hunting*, archived thread, February 22, 2007, www.longrangehunting.com/threads/jim-zumbo -talks-on-nugent-forum.20936.

5. National Shooting Sports Foundation, "Modern Sporting Rifle: Introduction," www.nssf.org/msr.

6. Van Zuylen-Wood, "The Heavily Armed Millennials of Instagram."

7. National Shooting Sports Foundation, "Modern Sporting Rifle."

8. National Rifle Association, "America's Rifle Challenge," https://arc .nra.org.

9. "San Pedro Entrepreneur Gregory Warne Loved Costa Rican Hardwood," *A.M. Costa Rica*, June 16, 2006, www.amcostarica.com/061606.htm.

CHAPTER 18: THE BEST GUN SALESMAN IN AMERICA

1. Quoted in "Obama Election Prompts Surge in US Gun Sales," McClatchy Newspapers, November 7, 2008, accessed via the *Guardian*, www.theguardian .com/world/2008/nov/07/uselections2008-barackobama.

2. Quoted in "Obama Election Prompts Surge in US Gun Sales."

3. Quoted in D'Angelo Gore, "NRA Targets Obama," FactCheck.org, September 22, 2008, www.factcheck.org/2008/09/nra-targets-obama.

4. Quoted in Michael Dobbs, "The Fact Checker: NRA Misfires Against Obama," *Washington Post*, September 23, 2008, http://voices.washingtonpost .com/fact-checker/2008/09/nra_misfires_against_obama.html.

5. Quoted in Alan Berlow, "NRA's Doomsaying Sham," *Salon*, July 24, 2012, www.salon.com/2012/07/24/nras_doomsaying_sham.

6. Quoted in Gore, "NRA Targets Obama."

CHAPTER 20: DEAD OR IN JAIL

1. National Rifle Association, "2012 St. Louis Annual Meetings," www .nraam.org/past-meetings/2012-st-louis-annual-meetings.aspx.

2. Quoted in Ed Pilkington, "NRA Fired Up to Campaign Against Obama as Annual Meeting Kicks Off," *Guardian*, April 13, 2012, www.theguardian .com/world/2012/apr/13/national-rifle-association-annual-meeting-obama.

3. Phil Hirschkorn and Laura Strickler, "Inside the Super PACs Money Deluge," *CBS News*, February 22, 2012, https://web.archive.org/web/2013 1220035045/http://www.cbsnews.com/news/inside-the-super-pacs-money -deluge.

4. Quoted in Emil Shultheis, "Santorum: Bella Is Now an NRA Life Member," *Politico*, April 13, 2012, www.politico.com/blogs/burns-haberman/2012 /04/santorum-bella-is-now-an-nra-life-member-120479.

5. Quoted in Eli Watkins, "Santorum: Instead of Calling for Gun Laws, Kids Should Take CPR Classes," CNN, March 26, 2018, www.cnn.com/2018/03/25 /politics/rick-santorum-guns-cnntv/index.html.

CHAPTER 21: KEEPING SCORE

1. "President Obama Speaks on the Shooting in Connecticut," White House Press Office, December, 14, 2012, https://obamawhitehouse.archives.gov/blog /2012/12/14/president-obama-speaks-shooting-connecticut.

2. "NRA: Full Statement by Wayne LaPierre in Response to Newtown Shootings," *Guardian*, December 21, 2012, www.theguardian.com/world/2012 /dec/21/nra-full-statement-lapierre-newtown.

3. "NRA: Full Statement by Wayne LaPierre."

4. Quoted in Aamer Madhani, "NRA Blasts Biden's Gun Task Force After Meeting," *USA Today*, January 10, 2013, www.usatoday.com/story/news /politics/2013/01/10/biden-nra-wildlife-gun-control/1823511.

5. Quoted in Elspeth Reeve, "That Didn't Go Well: NRA Leaves Biden Meeting Vowing to Fight Gun Reform," *Atlantic*, January 10, 2013, www .theatlantic.com/politics/archive/2013/01/bidens-meeting-nra-results-pledge -more-lobbying/319636.

6. National Shooting Sports Foundation, "Tell Your Senators to Vote NO on Manchin-Toomey Amendment, Yes on Grassley Proposal," press release, April 16, 2013, www.nssf.org/tell-your-senators-to-vote-no-on-manchin-toomey -amendment-yes-on-grassley-proposal.

7. US Senate Roll Call Vote No. 97, April 17, 2013, www.senate.gov /legislative/LIS/roll_call_lists/roll_call_vote_cfm.cfm?congress=113&session =1&vote=00097.

CHAPTER 22: WEARING A TARGET

1. Quoted in Nicky Woolf and Scott Bixby, "Barack Obama Slams Gun Lobby 'Fiction' and Conspiracy Theories," *Guardian*, January 8, 2016, www.theguardian. com/us-news/2016/jan/08/obama-slams-gun-lobby-fiction-conspiracy-theories -controls-nra; "Obama: I'm Happy to Talk to the NRA About Guns," CNN, January 7, 2016, www.youtube.com/watch?v=sP4jDti85DY.

CHAPTER 23: THE TRUMP SLUMP

1. Quoted in Lois Beckett and Ben Jacobs, "Donald Trump Endorsed by NRA Despite History of Gun Control Support," *Guardian*, May 21, 2016, www. theguardian.com/us-news/2016/may/20/nra-endorses-donald-trump-convention.

2. Mike Spies and Ashley Balcerzak, "The NRA Placed Big Bets on the 2016 Election, and Won Almost All of Them," *Trace*, November 9, 2016, www.thetrace.org/2016/11/nra-big-bets-election-2016-results.

3. Quoted in Alex Yablon, Brian Freskos, and Nora Biette-Timmons, "How the NRA Stoked the Populist Rage That Gave America President Trump," *Trace*, November 11, 2016, www.thetrace.org/2016/11/nra-endorsements-donald-trump -populist-rage.

4. Zusha Elinson and Cameron McWhirter, "The 'Trump Slump': With a Friend in the White House, Gun Sales Sag," *Wall Street Journal*, April 30, 2018, www.wsj.com/articles/the-trump-slump-with-a-friend-in-the-white-house -gun-sales-sag-1535640346.

CHAPTER 24: CLENCHED FIST

1. Sean Illing, "'Flood the Zone with Shit': How Misinformation Overwhelmed Our Democracy," *Vox*, February 6, 2020, www.vox.com/policy-and -politics/2020/1/16/20991816/impeachment-trial-trump-bannon-misinformation.

2. Cydney Hargis, "A Guide to NRATV: NRA's News Outlet Is a Hybrid of Breitbart and Infowars," *Media Matters*, March 2, 2018, www.mediamatters

.org/breitbart-news/guide-nratv-nras-news-outlet-hybrid-breitbart-and
-infowars#anchor%203.

3. Timothy Johnson, "NRATV Urges President-Elect Trump to Continue Attacking the Press," *Media Matters*, November 28, 2016, www.mediamatters.org /donald-trump/nratv-urges-president-elect-trump-continue-attacking-press.

4. Quoted in Hargis, "A Guide to NRATV."

5. Quoted in Jeremy W. Peters and Katie Benner, "Where the N.R.A. Speaks First and Loudest," *New York Times*, February 21, 2018, www.nytimes .com/2018/02/21/us/politics/nratv-nra-news-media-operation.html.

6. "The Violence of Lies," December 12, 2018, www.youtube.com/watch ?v=169zQ1g-Ul0.

7. Kate Samuelson, "A Lot of Gun Owners Really Dislike This NRA Ad," *Time*, June 30, 2017, https://time.com/4841051/gun-owners-nra-advertisement.

8. Mira Rojanasakul, "Gun Sales in America Have Stopped Spiking After Mass Shootings," *Bloomberg*, November 7, 2017, www.bloomberg.com /graphics/2017-gun-sales-in-america-stopped-spiking-after-mass-shootings.

CHAPTER 25: SPEAKING TRUTH TO BULLSHIT

1. Brian Mast, "Opinion: I'm Republican. I Appreciate Assault Weapons. And I Support a Ban," *New York Times*, February 23, 2018, www.nytimes .com/2018/02/23/opinion/brian-mast-assault-weapons-ban.html.

2. Glennon Doyle, Facebook, May 21, 2018, 6:09 p.m., www.facebook.com /watch/?v=10156391160899710.

3. Brené Brown, "Gun Reform: Speaking Truth to Bullshit, Practicing Civility, and Effecting Change," *Brené Brown* (blog), November 8, 2017, https://brenebrown.com/blog/2017/11/08/gun-reform-speaking-truth-bullshit -practicing-civility-effecting-change-2.

CHAPTER 26: POSITION OF POWER

1. John Ismay, "Rhodesia's Dead—But White Supremacists Have Given It New Life Online," *New York Times*, April 10, 2018, www.nytimes .com/2018/04/10/magazine/rhodesia-zimbabwe-white-supremacists.html.

2. "Spike's Tactical," Instagram, January 25, 2018, www.instagram.com /p/BeYnUBXDISy/?taken-by=spikes_tactical; Elliott Woods, "Fear: How the NRA Sells Guns in America Today," *New Republic*, April 16, 2018, newrepublic .com/article/147804/fear-how-nra-sells-guns-america.

CHAPTER 27: *TOTALITARIO*

1. Dick's Sporting Goods, Facebook, February 28, 2018, 5:41 a.m., www .facebook.com/147285781446/posts/we-at-dicks-sporting-goods-are-deeply -disturbed-and-saddened-by-the-tragic-event/10155335308876447.

2. Dick's Sporting Goods, Twitter, February 28, 2018, 5:51 a.m., https://twitter.com/DICKS/status/968830988246765568.

3. Quoted in Alina Selyukh, "Soul-Searching After Parkland, Dick's CEO Embraces Tougher Stance on Guns," NPR, February 12, 2019, www.npr.org/2019/02/12/691999347/soul-searching-after-parkland-dicks-ceo-embraces-tougher-stance-on-guns.

4. Laura M. Holson, "Dick's Sporting Goods Destroyed $5 Million Worth of Guns," *New York Times*, October 8, 2019, www.nytimes.com/2019/10/08/business/dicks-sporting-goods-destroying-guns-rifles.html.

5. National Shooting Sports Foundation, "NSSF Expels Dick's Sporting Goods," press release, May 4, 2018, www.nssf.org/nssf-expels-dicks-sporting-goods.

6. Sean Davis, "Springfield Armory Severs Ties with Dick's Sporting Goods over Gun Control Lobbying," *Federalist*, May 3, 2018, https://thefederalist.com/2018/05/03/springfield-armory-severs-ties-dicks-sporting-goods-gun-control-lobbying.

7. Quoted in Chavie Lieber, "Big Gun Companies Are Refusing to Do Business with Dick's Sporting Goods," *Racked*, May 10, 2018, www.racked.com/2018/5/10/17339690/dicks-sporting-goods-gun-control-debate.

8. "NICS Checks Climb 23 Percent in December 2020," SGB Media, January 4, 2021, https://sgbonline.com/nics-checks-climb-23-percent-in-december.

9. Quoted in "Totalitarianism," *Britannica*, www.britannica.com/topic/totalitarianism.

10. "Kimber Vice President Hates Guns," AR15.com, archived thread, January 25, 2021, www.ar15.com/forums/general/Kimber-Vice-President-hates-guns-/5-2419584.

CHAPTER 28: UN-AMERICAN CARNAGE

1. Cam Edwards, "Black Rifle Coffee Company Thrust into Rittenhouse Story," *Bearing Arms*, November 23, 2020, https://bearingarms.com/cam-e/2020/11/23/brcc-thrust-rittenhouse-story.

INDEX

Ryan Busse is a former firearms executive who helped build one of the world's most iconic gun companies. He was nominated multiple times by industry colleagues for the prestigious Shooting Industry Person of the Year Award. Busse is an environmental advocate who served in many leadership roles, including as an advisor for the United States Senate Sportsmen's Caucus and the Biden presidential campaign. These days, Ryan provides consulting services to progressive organizations with the aim to undo the country's dangerous radicalization. He remains a proud outdoorsman, gun owner, father, and resident of Montana.

PublicAffairs is a publishing house founded in 1997. It is a tribute to the standards, values, and flair of three persons who have served as mentors to countless reporters, writers, editors, and book people of all kinds, including me.

I. F. STONE, proprietor of *I. F. Stone's Weekly*, combined a commitment to the First Amendment with entrepreneurial zeal and reporting skill and became one of the great independent journalists in American history. At the age of eighty, Izzy published *The Trial of Socrates*, which was a national bestseller. He wrote the book after he taught himself ancient Greek.

BENJAMIN C. BRADLEE was for nearly thirty years the charismatic editorial leader of *The Washington Post*. It was Ben who gave the *Post* the range and courage to pursue such historic issues as Watergate. He supported his reporters with a tenacity that made them fearless and it is no accident that so many became authors of influential, best-selling books.

ROBERT L. BERNSTEIN, the chief executive of Random House for more than a quarter century, guided one of the nation's premier publishing houses. Bob was personally responsible for many books of political dissent and argument that challenged tyranny around the globe. He is also the founder and longtime chair of Human Rights Watch, one of the most respected human rights organizations in the world.

·   ·   ·

For fifty years, the banner of Public Affairs Press was carried by its owner Morris B. Schnapper, who published Gandhi, Nasser, Toynbee, Truman, and about 1,500 other authors. In 1983, Schnapper was described by *The Washington Post* as "a redoubtable gadfly." His legacy will endure in the books to come.

Peter Osnos, Founder